VITAL MISSIONS ISSUES

Examining Challenges and Changes in World Evangelism

ROY B. ZUCK
GENERAL EDITOR

Grand Rapids, MI 49501

Vital Missions Issues: Examining Challenges and Changes in World Evangelism by Roy B. Zuck, general editor

Published by Kregel Resources, an imprint of Kregel Publications, P.O. Box 2607, Grand Rapids, MI 49501. Kregel Resources provides timely and relevant resources for Christian life and service. Your comments and suggestions are valued.

For more information about Kregel Publications, visit our web site at http://www.kregel.com.

Cover design: Sarah Slattery
Book design: Alan G. Hartman

Printed in the United States of America

1 2 3 / 04 03 02 01 00 99 98

Contents

Contributors

J. Ronald Blue
President, CAM International, Dallas, Texas

Russell H. Bowers Jr.
Professor of Theology, East Asia School of Theology, Singapore

Patrick O. Cate
President, International Missions, Reading, Pennsylvania

David F. Detwiler
Worship Pastor, Community Baptist Church, Manhattan Beach, California

Millard J. Erickson
Distinguished Professor of Theology, Truett Seminary, Waco, Texas, and Distinguished Professor of Theology, Western Seminary, Portland, Oregon

Gordon L. Everett
Associate Pastor, Shohomish Community Church, Shohomish, Washington

George W. Murray
Executive Director, The Evangelical Alliance Mission, Wheaton, Illinois

George W. Peters
Late Chairman and Professor of World Missions, Dallas Theological Seminary, Dallas, Texas

Robert A. Peterson
Professor of Systematic Theology, Covenant Theological Seminary, St. Louis, Missouri

Michael Pocock
Chairman and Professor of World Missions and Intercultural Studies, Dallas Theological Seminary, Dallas, Texas

Ramesh P. Richard
Professor of Pastoral Ministries and World Missions and Intercultural Studies, Dallas Theological Seminary, Dallas, Texas

Ronald D. Runyon
Late Training Director, International University Resource Team, Campus Crusade for Christ, Boulder, Colorado

Wayne G. Strickland
Chairman, Bible and Theology Department, Multnomah Bible College, Portland, Oregon

Preface

What is 750,000 miles long, reaches around the world thirty times, and grows twenty times longer each day? Answer: The line of people who are without Christ.

How stunning to think that two-thirds of the world's six billion people are unsaved! What could be a more compelling reason for a strong commitment to missions? The mandate to share the good news of salvation through Christ permeates the Scriptures. Jesus Christ came "to seek and to save" the lost (Luke 19:10). And because "there is salvation in no one else" (Acts 4:12), believers are to urge others to "be reconciled to God" (2 Cor. 5:20).

Many voices, however, would dissipate the biblical compulsion. Universalism says everyone will eventually be in heaven. Annihilationism holds that the unsaved won't suffer eternal hell; they'll be extinct. Others contend there are many paths to heaven. Still others suggest that after death people will have opportunity to be saved. If any of these is true, the need for missions collapses.

In a religiously pluralistic world we need to understand the message of missions (salvation is through faith in Christ alone), the motive of missions (to win the lost to Christ and build them up in Him), and the means of missions (local churches sending forth emissaries to share the gospel).

The chapters in this volume, taken from articles in *Bibliotheca Sacra,* Dallas Seminary's theological journal, address these issues—the what, why, and how of the missionary enterprise.

One way to test the spiritual health of a local church is to check its heartbeat for missions, to measure its pulse for the world, to weigh its concern for the lost. As missionary statesman A. T. Pierson observed years ago, "The vitality of a local church may be measured by its interest in the evangelization of the world."

I pray this volume will deepen your love for the lost and strengthen your commitment to missions. Let's "go into all the world and preach the gospel to all creation" (Mark 16:15) because "the Lord's coming is near" (James 5:8, NIV).

Roy B. Zuck

About *Bibliotheca Sacra*

A flood is rampant—an engulfing deluge of literature far beyond any one person's ability to read it all. Presses continue to churn out thousands of journals and magazines like a roiling, raging river.

Among these numberless publications, one stands tall and singular—*Bibliotheca Sacra*—a strange name (meaning "Sacred Library") but a journal familiar to many pastors, teachers, and Bible students.

How is *Bibliotheca Sacra* unique in the world of publishing? By being the oldest continuously published journal in the Western Hemisphere—1993 marked its 150th anniversary—and by being published by one school for more than six decades—1994 marked its diamond anniversary of being released by Dallas Seminary.

Bib Sac, to use its shortened sobriquet, was founded in New York City in 1843 and was purchased by Dallas Theological Seminary in 1934, ten years after the school's founding. The quarterly's 155-year history boasts only nine editors. Through those years it has maintained a vibrant stance of biblical conservatism and a strong commitment to the Scriptures as God's infallible Word.

Each volume in the Kregel *Vital Issues Series* includes carefully selected articles from the 1930s to the present—articles of enduring quality, articles by leading evangelicals whose topics are as relevant today as when they were first produced. The chapters have been edited slightly to provide conformity of style. We trust these anthologies will enrich the spiritual lives and Christian ministries of many more readers.

ROY B. ZUCK, EDITOR
Bibliotheca Sacra

For *Bibliotheca Sacra* subscription information, call Dallas Seminary, 1-800-992-0998.

CHAPTER 1

Missions in Biblical Perspective

George W. Peters

The last command of Christ is not the deep and final ground of the Church's missionary duty," reasoned Robert E. Speer in his Duff Lectures of 1910.[1] He continued by saying:

> That duty is authoritatively stated in the words of the great commission, and it is of infinite consequence to have had it so stated by our Lord Himself. But if these particular words had never been spoken by Him, or if, having been spoken, they had not been preserved, the missionary duty of the Church would not be in the least affected. . . . The supreme argument for foreign missions is not any word of Christ's,—it is Christ Himself, and what He reveals and signifies. . . . It is in the very being and character of God that the deepest ground of the missionary enterprise is to be found. We cannot think of God except in terms which necessitate the missionary idea.[2]

Lesslie Newbigin speaks to the same point:

> The purpose of the chapters which follow is to show that there are resources for the meeting of these perplexities within the Christian understanding of God as Father, Son and Holy Spirit, to invite the missionary movement to bind to itself afresh the strong Name of the Trinity. We have stated that the present situation of the missionary movement has brought us to the point where the question of the uniqueness and finality of Christ is presented with a new sharpness. We have now to say that this question will not be rightly answered, nor will the question of the relation between what God is doing in the mission of the Church and what he is doing in the secular events of history be rightly answered, except within the framework of a fully and explicitly trinitarian doctrine of God.[3]

The renewal of this emphasis prompted Georg F. Vicedom to entitle his work on the theology of missions as *"Missio Dei"* or "The Mission of God," which is a "radically theological statement of the source, motive and end of missions."[4] It is an affirmation of the Willingen Conference statement that "the missionary movement . . . has its source in the Triune God Himself."[5] Somewhat later Davison asserted, "Mission begins in God. . . . Mission is a divine activity springing directly from God's own nature."[6]

Such theocentricity in missions is a rarity, and it sounds almost like a novelty in an anthropocentric society, ecclesiocentric Christendom, and world-revolutionary humanism. It should find a welcome echo in the mind and heart of the evangelical who is trained in the Scriptures and who loves the biblical order of priorities. Certainly it is in perfect harmony with Paul when he writes, "For from Him and through Him and to Him are all things. To Him be the glory forever. Amen" (Rom. 11:36).

Of all needs in missions, there is no need more pressing than to rediscover and hold to a truly biblical perspective in missions.

Such perspective is found in the most familiar verse in the New Testament. In fact this verse is foundational to the New Testament and forms the missionary foundation, content, and intent of the purpose, plan, and program of God. This verse is John 3:16. It is not only the heart of the gospel and a summary of the all-determining act of God in history, but it also presents the dynamic, dimension, purpose, and demands of evangelical missions.

A beautiful balance in the verse may be viewed in two triangles. The first is formed by relating *God,* the *world,* and the *Son*. This is the *objective* aspect. This is paralleled by a second triangle, with an emphasis on *believe, eternal life, perish*. This is the *subjective* aspect. Missions concerns itself with both aspects and must keep them in balance.

The divine, objective aspect precedes the human, subjective aspect. In the gospel people are not reaching up to God but God is reaching down to them—and making it possible for them to respond and evoking a response from them. It is not individuals discovering God but God unveiling Himself and making it possible for them to know God. It is not humanity reconciling God but God reconciling those who believe. There is a consistent order of priorities in the Scriptures which is always from God downward. It is God seeking and encountering mankind.

The Objective Aspect

THE THEOCENTRICITY OF MISSIONS

The Bible is a unique book. It is revelation. It is not discovery, whether that be intellectual, scientific, or religious; it is not insight, whether that be intuitive or mystical; it is not deductive conclusions of some keen observations or sensitive experiences. It is unveiling. It is God disclosing Himself in His person, purpose, plan (or strategy), work, ways, and relationships. Because of this the Bible begins with God. It informs man that "In the beginning God created. . . ." And from here every major epoch of history opens with a new unveiling of God. It was so after the fall of Adam and Eve and the announcement of the Protevangelium (Gen. 3:15), the forecasting of the Flood and the covenant which followed, the call of Abraham and the promises and covenants, the call of Moses, with the redemption of Israel out of Egypt and the Sinaitic Covenant, the giving of the Law and the institution of the divine patterns and order of worship and salvation. Theocentricity is evident throughout the Old Testament, and the Old Testament is not so much a retelling of the history of Israel as it is an unveiling of the God of Israel and of history. It is God in history rather than merely the history of Israel.

Theocentricity is the foundation of the New Testament. It alone accounts for the history underlying the New Testament and the events it recounts. As in the Old Testament God created, called, covenanted, so in the New Testament God loved, gave, and proclaimed. Without this fact there would be no Savior, no new covenant, no gospel, no church, no world mission. Nothing but a spiritual wilderness—wasted by religious uncertainties, perplexities, frustrations, exploitations, and bewilderment—would have been the portion of mankind. This tragedy would have multiplied by a fever of burning passions, intense hatred of unconquerable forces and the dread of disease, death, and anticipated eternity. Such a condition combined with an unquenched thirst for certainty, reality, meaning, purpose, and eternal verities and values would presently cover the face of the earth, burden the aching and bleeding hearts of mankind, and make life miserable and almost intolerable.

However, this is not the case, "for God so loved." His essential Being is love as well as righteous holiness. That changes the total course of history, transforms the religious prospects and quests of man, and brings light and hope to mankind. And this is so not because people deserved it or were worthy of it but because God is love.

In Christian missions God is foremost the *subject* of missions and not simply the object. He is the gracious Actor, merciful Initiator, and sustaining Presence. Missions is of Him, by Him, and unto Him. He is its source, dynamic, and end. Canon Douglas Webster opened his lecture series with these words, "We begin, then, where mission begins, with God."[7] Only such a stance does justice to the claim of Georg F. Vicedom that mission is *"Missio Dei."*[8] And Leslie Davison is biblically correct when he writes, "Mission begins in God. . . . Mission is divine activity springing directly from God's own nature."[9]

Let it be said with all human emphasis and divine authority that world missions has become a possibility and necessity, and it will remain a reality so long as God has a people in this world who partake of His nature, know His purpose, walk in His will, and obey His Holy Spirit. Missions is not a human invention, a human institution, a human enterprise made up of loving but simplistic individuals, or volunteers of compassionate or sanctimonious people who cannot minister effectively in their homeland. Missions is made up of people who partake of the nature of God, enter fullest into the purpose of God and become colaborers in the plan and Will of God. God is foremost the *subject* of Christian missions. Missions is *"Missio Dei."* Where God is most prominent, missions is most obvious and intense.

The *object* of the *Missio Dei* is the *world*. "For God so loved the world," John wrote. Biblical missions concerns the world. The world is the theater of God's activities because it is the expressed object of God's love and concern. "For God did not send His Son into the world to judge the world, but that the world should be saved through Him" (John 3:17). Years later the same John wrote, "And we have beheld and bear witness that the Father has sent the Son to be the Savior of the world" (1 John 4:14). The object of *Missio Dei* is the world, the total world of mankind. This is natural, logical, biblical. *It is natural* because if God is the Creator of mankind, He is also the Redeemer of mankind. Redemption must be potentially at least as comprehensive, as broad, and as deep as the trunk, roots, branches, and fruit of sin if it is redemption at all. *It is historically logical* because the promise in the Protevangelium passage (Gen. 3:15) was given to Eve, the mother of all mankind, and thus it is the rightful heritage of the total human race. *It is biblical* because Christ in His incarnation identified Himself with all mankind and not with a single people, nation, or race. He was the Son of man in the messianic sense but also in the truly human sense. He is the man Christ Jesus, the God-Man in whom dwells all the fullness of the Godhead (Col. 2:19) and in whom all mankind is represented. Therefore John could write, "Behold, the Lamb of God who takes away [bears] the *sin* [not only sins] of the world!" (John 1:29). The two nouns—*sin* and *world*—are both in the singular, that is, the Lamb of God was bearing the totality of sin in its trunk, roots, branches, and consequences for the entire human race. Consequently John wrote later, "And He Himself is the propitiation for our sins; and not for ours only, but also for those of the whole world" (1 John 2:2).

Paul is no less emphatic in his affirmation that Christ procured salvation for all mankind. This is seen in such passages as Romans 5:6, 12–21; 2 Corinthians 5:18–21; Colossians 1:20; and 1 Timothy 2:3–6.

Such emphasis is in keeping with the total tenor of the Scriptures. In Genesis 3:15 is the great and glorious *leitmotiv* or morningstar of the salvation of God. Its promise is as comprehensive as the Fall and its consequences. Certainly the grace of God cannot be outdone by sin. Where sin abounded, grace did much more abound. When the corruption of humanity reached a God-defying height and God "gave them up," God created a mediatorial people in the call of Abraham. A mediatorial nation, however, is not a people with a self-centered purpose. The *cause* of the call of Abraham will never be unraveled but the *purpose* of the call of Abraham is known. It is expressed in the familiar words, "In you all the families of the earth shall be blessed." Five times this promise is stated to the patriarchs—to Abraham (Gen. 12:3; 18:18; 22:18), to Isaac (26:4), and to Jacob (28:13). The nations of the earth were never forgotten by the Creator of the world.

Of instructive significance are the words in Exodus 19:3–6. Israel had arrived at Mount Sinai and was preparing for a message from God who delivered them out of Egypt and who graciously led them in a trackless desert, provided for them in a wasted wilderness, and rescued them from the hostile Amorites. At Sinai the Abrahamic Covenant was complemented by the temporary Mosaic covenant and the slave tribes were welded into a structured people and a sanctified priesthood of God. For this purpose God addressed them in a most remarkable way. He reminded them of His great redemptive act, His gracious, providential care, of their blessed position because of His sovereign will and His great and holy purpose. God's gracious operations are always purposive. While Israel was to be uniquely related to God, it was to be a kingdom of priests in this world. It was to be in this world and for this world but not of this world.

It is simple fact that no priesthood exists for itself. A priest is a mediating person. His function is to mediate between man and

God. At Sinai, Israel was constituted as a nation or kingdom of priests to mediate between God and the nations. What the tribe of Levi was to the people of Israel, Israel as a nation was to be to the nations of the world. The *Missio Dei* was to be mediated through the people of Israel to the world of mankind. Israel's calling was of world significance and for a world ministry. "Ye are my witnesses, saith the Lord, and my servant whom I have chosen"—this was the Lord's charge to Israel. Thrice He called Israel "witnesses" and twenty-one times in Isaiah 40–54 He spoke of "servants." Israel was not an end in itself; God had the world in mind. The *Missio Dei* through Israel is emphasized throughout the Old Testament and greatly amplified and described.

It is possible that this did not register deeply and decisively with the majority of the people. Nevertheless the fact is clear and emphatic. The Old Testament is not a book for the Jews only. It was given *to* Israel but not just *for* Israel. Though it is Israel-centered, it is world-focused. Israel was called to be a mediatorial people, a kingdom of priests.

Of course it is recognized that many types in the Old Testament have been fulfilled, that the Mosaic Law has ended with the work of Christ on Calvary, and that the predicted restoration of Israel is yet future. However, these radical differences in the operational economy of God have not changed the fundamental purpose of God which relates to all mankind. Therefore a church (or seminary or other Christian institution) that is not focused on the world has not fully entered into the counsel and purpose of God. And if believers today desire to know to what degree they are living in the purpose of God, they should honestly and sincerely ask themselves, "To what degree are we possessed by the burden to share the gospel with the world? To what degree is world evangelization the focus of our life and ministry?" Here is an infallible measure and proof. Here is a divine criterion. It remains an eternal fact—"God so loved the *world*." How deeply have Christians entered into the concern of God for the world of mankind?

Thus the *subject* of missions is God Himself, and the *object* of missions is the world. The mediating *Person* of missions is the eternal Son. God so loved the world that He gave His only begotten Son. He is the Sent One, the Mediator between God and men, the man Christ Jesus (1 Tim. 2:5), the Apostle, the "missionary" of God (Heb. 3:1).

This Christ-mediatorship leads into the third of contemporary missiological discussions and debates. It raises such crucial questions as these: Is Jesus Christ the Savior or the great Teacher, Model, and Founder of the Christian religion? Is Jesus Christ the potential Savior or the actual, factual, and historical Savior in whom the salvation of all mankind has not only been procured but also is secured and assured? Is Jesus Christ a Savior who stands in line with other saviors, such as Buddha, Vishnu, Krishna, and others, or is He the only and sole Savior in whom alone salvation is to be found? Heated debates around each one of these questions are increasing as the Christian cause advances. Series of books have been published, conferences conducted, theories spun out, and positions maintained. Men are sharply divided and philosophies have collided. Of course this is nothing new. The first three centuries after Christ are filled with the debris of theological and semi-mythological religious structures that were designed as rational and natural answers to the perplexing and enduring problem of the Christ whom Christians proclaimed and loved, in whose name they served and for whose name they died. The great christological creeds are the present evidence of the struggle within the Christian church to define and proclaim the Christ of her faith and tradition. Christ did not only bring peace into the world. He also brought fire, the sword, and division. He is both the Foundation Stone and also the Cornerstone. Neither one of them can be altered or shifted without seriously endangering the total structure and encountering the judgment of God in some form. He is the "Great Divide" not of continents but of Christianity from religions, of Truth from philosophies and theories, of Light from darkness and human luminaries. Present-day struggles are not new. They may be new in intensity and extent, but they are not new on the battlefield.

Books have appeared with impressive titles such as *The Finality of Christ* and *The Uniqueness of Christ*. These books present strong arguments for the greatness of Christ. Certainly a historian would be blind not to admit the world-shaking and world-shaping impact of the life and teaching of Jesus Christ. The question, however, is this: Is Jesus Christ the finality in a series of revelations which run through all religions of the world? Is there only a quantitative difference? Is Jesus Christ only the greatest and perhaps the noblest and most attractive Savior among other saviors (as Mahatma Ghandi seemingly admitted but then retorted that such does not give Christians the right to put Him on a "solitary throne")? Is it possible to interpret the Scriptures in such terms? Or must one in loyalty to the Bible dogmatically insist that Jesus Christ is qualitatively distinct, that He is qualitatively unique in person and work and *the sole Savior* of mankind? Is John 3:16 a repetitive experience in the history of mankind and particularly in the history of religions or is it a first and a once-for-all and a once-forever experience? Has one the right to read, "For God so loved the world that He gave Buddha, Mahavira, Zoroaster, Lao-tze, Confucius, and eventually His only begotten Son" that the world might be saved?

In loyalty to the Scriptures one is compelled to take a radical stand for the complete "otherness" of Christ, the total "finality" of Christ, and the absolute "soleness" of Christ as Savior and Lord. He alone is *the* God-Man. He alone is *the* Light of the world, *the* Bread of life, *the* Door into the fold, *the* Good Shepherd, *the* Way, *the* Truth, *the* Life, *the* Resurrection. There is no other Name in which salvation is given. He alone is the Mediator and the God-Man to span the gulf between God and the human race. None other is good enough, none other is adequate. All others stand in need of a savior.

This is not to deny to other human luminaries the light of nature, of history, of conscience, of mind. This is not to deny other ethicists deep moral insights into human depravity and misery, designing lofty ethical philosophies and defining principles and setting patterns. This is not to deny to noble-minded humanists and philanthropists great depths of compassion, great measures of sacrifice, great deeds of mercy, and gracious schemes for alleviating human misery and suffering. This is not to deny to noble and meditative minds deep and beautiful religious insights which have formulated instructive parables and proverbs and even designed plans and created institutions for the betterment of mankind. People are capable of many moral, social, and beautiful things. To confuse these, however, with biblical salvation and saviorhood is a deception of the deepest and most disastrous kind. He alone is "our Lord Jesus Christ," and "God our Savior." "Therefore also God highly exalted Him, and bestowed on Him the name which is above every name, that at the name of Jesus every knee should bow, of those who are in heaven, and on earth, and under the earth, and that every tongue should confess that Jesus Christ is Lord, to the glory of God the Father" (Phil. 2:9–11).

The Bible could not be more expressive of the uniqueness of Christ and the sole saviorhood of Jesus Christ. *His* name is above *every* name; *every* knee shall bow to *Him; every* tongue shall confess that Jesus Christ is *Lord* to the glory of God. This of course includes the saints of old—Adam, Enoch, Noah, Abraham, Moses, David, Isaiah, Jeremiah, Daniel, John the Baptist, Mary the mother of Jesus, Paul. This also includes Buddha, Mahavira, Lao-tze, Confucius, Mohammed, Mahatma Ghandi, and numerous others—*all* of whom will bow to Christ! Jesus Christ is Lord and as Lord He is Savior. By no means does this suggest universal salvation. Instead it is to state that all—saved and unsaved—will ultimately bow in recognition of Christ as *the* sovereign Lord.

Thus in the first triangle God is the source of all missions and the *subject* of missions. The world is the *object* of the *Missio Dei*. God in missions reaches out to the world of mankind. And Jesus Christ is the mediating *Person* of missions. He is not only the Message, He is also the Messenger. He is not only the Sacrifice, He is the High Priest and the Sacrificer. This indeed is *Missio Dei*—the mission of God.

The Subjective Aspect

The subjective aspect of missions is also presented in John 3:16. The goal of *Missio Dei* is nothing less than turning perishing people from their path of destruction and bringing them into the fullness of God's salvation expressed in the words *eternal life*.

The words that make up the second triangle are *believe, eternal life,* and *perish*. The word *perish* is a strange and unwelcome word. It raises some arresting questions: Is mankind actually perishing? Are people actually lost? Are they actually on the path away from the presence of God and headed for destruction? What does such a statement mean? What are the implications of perishing? Some book titles on this subject are in the form of questions: *Is Man Actually Lost and on His Way to Hell? How Lost Are the Heathen? Are All Heathen Lost?*

The Bible does not directly answer these questions. It does not call for such a distinction. It has a different dividing line. It knows of people who believe in Christ Jesus and who do not believe, and of people who are in Christ and who are not in Christ. It knows of people who are born of God and of people who are not born of God. It assures people who believe in Jesus Christ, who are in Christ, who are born of God, that they actually possess eternal life, that they have passed from death to life. All others remain in death.

The condition of being without Christ and remaining in spiritual death is a piercing biblical reality that causes sensitive hearts to bleed and to cry out to God. It is a thought too difficult to share, a burden too heavy to bear. Yet the Bible is clear and emphatic: "He that believeth not the Son shall not see life; but the wrath of God abideth on him" (John 3:36 KJV). "He who does not have the Son of God does not have the life" (1 John 5:12). What must one conclude from these revelational statements about those who neither know nor believe in the Son? The Bible describes them as *perishing*.

Missio Dei directs itself toward these perishing people. It is a divine-human rescue operation, not of the developed to the undeveloped, the enlightened to the unenlightened, the upper to the lower, the Greeks to the barbarians, or the Western to the non-Western. In the words of the late Bishop Niles, it is one beggar telling the other beggar where to find bread.

Missio Dei makes sense only if one believes that men are actually lost and perishing without Christ. And the objective of *Missio Dei* is to lead people to see and accept the greatest gift God offers to man, the opposite from perishing—eternal life. The words *eternal life* are some of the richest and greatest words in the New Testament. They express in a positive manner the sum total of the salvation of God—forgiveness of sins, redemption, justification, regeneration, conversion, union with Christ, wholeness and fullness of life and personality. It is both quality and quantity, fullness and duration or endlessness. It is life in the fullest sense of the word, yes, the life of the eternal God imparted to those who believe.

Missions concerns itself with making known that the salvation of God is available to the perishing to rescue them and restore them to fellowship with their heavenly Father, to make them all that God designed them to be and to give them meaning, purpose, power, and hope to live the life of Christ here and now and to enjoy Him for all eternity—in conscious and rapturous fellowship.

If the goal of *Missio Dei* is expressed in the words *eternal life,* the means is given in the word *believe,* a uniquely biblical word which is not found in the same sense in other literature.

The Bible emphasizes the importance of *believing*. Combining the words πιστεύω (occurring 248 times), πίστις (occurring 244 times), and πιστός (sixty-six times), there are 558 references in the New Testament to this fundamental attitude, practice, position, and relationship. This is most impressive and speaks for its divine significance. Every New Testament writer and every book except 2 John mentions the word and emphasizes the practice. People today denigrate "believism." But there is a *biblical* believism. In fact it is so prominent and fundamental that it marks the divine line between the children of light and the children of darkness, the citizens of the kingdom of God and the citizens of this world, of being in Christ and not being in Christ, of being in the church of God and in the body of Christ and not being in the church and body. From the subjective aspect it constitutes "the great Divide" and separates believers and unbelievers. Faith is the universal distinctive mark of all great Bible characters, and the Bible declares that without faith it is impossible to please God (Heb. 11:6).

Biblical saving faith seems to be the simplest exercise of the human soul, so simple that the Lord expects every person to be capable of performing it. Yet it is the profoundest practice of the individual and together with prayer holds the greatest promises the Bible is capable of expressing and defining. This life and death, eternal bliss and everlasting damnation, the immediate presence of God and outer darkness, present meaning and purpose of life and emptiness and meaninglessness of life, joy and peace and unhappiness and misery—all these drastic differences hang in the balances around the words *believe* and *believe not.* Clearly John 3:16 and a large number of other biblical texts express this fact, and testimonies abound to substantiate its truth.

However, it is not faith as faith that creates such values in human history and experience. It is faith of a unique *content* and quality that matters. John 3:16 states that it is *believing in Him* that is decisive. Jesus Christ, the only begotten Son, is the content and object of saving faith. The Gospel of John is very explicit in its proclamation, and its emphasis on believing in Jesus Christ is marked. The object of faith makes all the difference. It is not faith in a dogma, faith in a system, faith in an institution or an organization, faith in a philosophy and idealism, but faith in a *person* which characterizes biblical saving faith. In such emphasis and demand Christianity stands unique among the religions of the world. All religions are practice-centered, works-oriented, and system-bound. The central and founding person for each world religion is a great teacher or guru or a great prophet. In those religions faith therefore is anchored in a system, in a philosophy, in an idealism. Because of this, it results neither in life nor in fellowship.

Not so in Christianity. Here faith is person-related and person-anchored. And this person is of a unique kind and a unique accomplishment. Reducing the doctrines of Christ as recorded in the New Testament to a minimum, one stands before two mystery-miracles. On the one hand is the God-Man, the Incarnation-deity mystery; and on the other hand is the Cross-resurrection event. No further reduction is possible if one wishes to remain loyal to the New Testament and claim biblical saving faith. Here is Christ the Cornerstone on which the Christian stands and beyond which he dare not move. Here also is Christ the foundation stone, that tried stone, a precious cornerstone, a sure foundation (Isa. 28:16), that "chief corner stone, elect, precious: and he that believeth on him shall not be confounded [shall never be put to shame or disappointed]" (1 Peter 2:6 KJV). Thus in Christ one has the absoluteness of exclusiveness and the absoluteness of inclusiveness. On the one hand only faith in Him has true meaning and eternal value. All other pretenders and saviors are excluded. That is exclusiveness. On the other hand faith in Him, whoever it may be that believes, brings that indescribable eternal reward designated by one of the profoundest terms in the New Testament—*eternal life,* the opposite from *perishing,* with all that that word implies with its indescribable consequences of woe and horror.

John 3:16 in two great triangles leads into missions in biblical perspective. The church's mission has its *origin* and *source* in God, its *object* is the world, and its mediatorial *Person* is Jesus Christ, the only begotten Son of God. Missions has the *goal* of saving people from perishing by offering them the salvation of God expressed in the words of eternal life. This salvation, however, must be appropriated by faith in Jesus Christ.

CHAPTER 2

Missions in Historical Perspective

George W. Peters

The year 1792 has been pinpointed as the birth date of modern missions, and William Carey has been called the father of modern missions. Both facts are only relatively true. Nevertheless they are remarkable and of world significance. This is so because within half of a century after that date every Protestant country had been awakened to world evangelization, missionary societies had been formed, missionary training centers had been established, and scores of pioneers had been recruited, equipped, and sent out into Asia, Africa, and the islands of the South Pacific. In all of this the American churches did not lag behind. Within seven years (1810–1817) three major societies had been organized and by 1825 all major denominations were involved in missions abroad.

Once the breakthrough had come, the missions movement continued to gain momentum and soon became a world phenomenon. Though an ebb and flow is evident in the history of missions, the flow has continued to gain over the ebbing and only recently has it leveled off and in some areas somewhat receded.

What was the milieu that brought about missions or made it possible for missions to break through? What historical factors have aided missions in its motivation and expansion?

From history it is evident that three factors played a most decisive role in the creation of the missionary movement. These are Western expansionism of Protestant countries, Western enlightenment and philanthropy, and Western evangelical restoration. The first two factors will be bypassed, not because they are insignificant but because they are dealt with adequately in sources of secular history.

In Western evangelical restoration, two main currents—a theological restoration and a spiritual restoration—merged and became a stream of living water on parched Protestantism.

Western Evangelical Restoration

THEOLOGICAL RESTORATION

It may seem strange to speak of the need for liberating theology. But such was the case. Theology may become ensnared, in fact, imprisoned in scholastic shackles which make it impossible for certain truths to break forth. This is what had happened in the course of history following the Reformation. It made the breakthrough of a missionary theology practically impossible. These shackles were broken in the evangelical restoration.

The world owes much to the Protestant Reformation. It can be said with great delight that the Reformers discovered the *missionary message* without which missions would be purposeless.

However, it is evident that the immediate successors of the great Reformers did not advocate world evangelization. A new orthodox Protestant scholasticism soon captured Protestant theology, which was interested mainly in theological, rigid confessionalism. Theology became enshrined but not incarnated. Therefore it became a lifeless skeleton of speculative dogmatics and not the dynamic of God unto salvation and missions.

Yet theology in the proper sense of the word is the science of God and ought to lead to light, life, liberation, and power. To do so it must be liberated from the "sacred shrines" of rationalism, sentimentalism, traditionalism, and even creedalism. It must be free to set forth the word and mind of God in every age anew. Strangely enough this came in Europe mainly through laymen and theologians on the periphery, and in the English world from men of freedom, the Puritans, and mainly in America, the land of freedom. In Europe there were such men as Adrian Saravia (1531–1613), Baron Justinian von Weltz (1621–1668), Jakob Spener (1635–1705), August Herman Francke (1663–1727), and particularly Count Nicolaus Ludwig von Zinzendorf (1700–1760). In America there were such men as John Eliot (1606–1690), Cotton Mather (1663–1728), and Jonathan Edwards (1703–1758). The latter broke through every recognized system of theology in his theologizing, and became a liberated person to whom God could speak afresh. In consequence God not only made him the sharp and central instrument initiating the Great Awakening in Northampton and then throughout New England, but also used him in giving to the Anglo-Saxon world a dynamic missionary theology.

The first revival wave visited Northampton in 1734. It came as a result of a series of messages on the Book of Romans. In 1740 Edwards sensed that the revival in his church was ebbing. So he preached a series of messages on the history of redemption in which he charted the operations of God in history. His emphasis was on God's controlling history and His progressively expanding the realization of redemption. He pointed to the glorious triumph of the church in the course of history, which would bring about not only the destruction of Antichrist but also the Christianization of the world. At the conclusion Christ would appear, judge the world, and the church would be glorified in the millennial reign of the Lord. This would be the full realization of the kingdom of God.

As a result of the messages, a greater revival than before visited the church and the community. It was in these messages that the missionary theology of Edwards took shape.

In this history of redemption five elements are discernible—elements that became the framework of Anglo-Saxon missiology. First, Edwards had strong faith in God who controls all of history and who works out a glorious purpose in history. God can never be defeated. The kingdom of God will be realized in history. Second, the church, which he (erroneously) identified with the kingdom of God, is central in the purpose of God. It is assured of its triumph over Antichrist and all evil in this world. It will be composed of peoples from among all nations. At the coming of Christ it will manifest the mercy and glory of the Lord. Third, the church in history has a missionary purpose and is *called to be a colaborer with God in proclaiming the gospel among the nations and thus to actualize the purpose of God.* Fourth, man is a responsible, moral being and in hearing the gospel man is able to believe in the Lord Jesus Christ for salvation if he so wills. Fifth, God is operative *in history.* The church must be God's colaborer *in history* because God's cause will triumph *in history.*

Here was fresh air in stale, static, and stately Calvinism. It was evident that a new era in ecclesiology and world missions was dawning. The church, in order to function as the church of God, must move from the position of *a passive recipient* to the position of *an active participant* in the realization of God's purpose.

Edwards's emphasis was a tremendous advance over anything that had come from the pen of previous scholars and theologians in relating to missions. Optimism, assurance, responsibility, and possibility became great motivating impulses in Edwards's theology of missions.

Any historian of missiological theology realizes that with some modifications Edwardian theology of missions remained dominant in Anglo-Saxon missiology. British and American missionaries went forth to build the kingdom of God and bring back the King. Eventually this type of postmillennial theology led to a head-on collision with German missionary theology.

In Pietism, as expounded by Spener and Francke, the salvation of the individual and the gathered-out church of truly converted people were dominant concepts. This type of missionary theology was incarnated in the movement of the *"Herrnhuter Bruedergemeinde,"* or Moravian Brethren, under the guidance of Count Zinzendorf. Basic to this missiology was the concept that the world was evil, lost, and doomed, and therefore it was the mission of the missionary to proclaim the gospel in all the world and save as many souls as possible out of this world before the Lord would return to judge the world. Thus the saving of the individual and the gathering of the saved persons into *"Gemeinschaften,"* or fellowships, and building them into churches after the confession of Lutheranism became the dominant note in continental missions. Gustav Warneck later gave theological content to these pietistic concepts, considerably enlarged the scope of missions, enriched its content, and molded it into a solid and reputable theology. Thus it is clear that missiology had broken through in theology.

SPIRITUAL RESTORATION

As valuable as the contribution of theology was, theology alone does not move the church to missions. Theology can be trifling and stifling, it can be chilling and killing. However, it can also be thrilling, enlivening, and compelling. Biblical theology, infused with the fire of the Holy Spirit, is the greatest dynamic that can be released in this world. It overcomes all obstacles and sufferings; it inspires the deepest devotion, dedication, and commitment; it generates the greatest compassion and constraint; it sustains the most lasting motivation. It has sent men and women to the farthest corners of the earth and to the most savagelike people, into the most trying circumstances and the most painful experiences, and into martyrdom and death. It simply knows no limit in its outpourings for the benefit of others in sharing with them the greatness of God's salvation in Christ.

This fire of the Holy Spirit did come on the germinating

missionary theology in waves of "Great Awakenings," which God graciously sent to Protestantism.

Spiritual restoration within formal but lifeless Christendom came in three forms: German Pietism in Europe, evangelicalism in Great Britain, and the "Great Awakenings" in America.

Although these movements differed considerably, essentially they were one great movement of the Holy Spirit. They all helped to quicken the life of the church; to deepen the spiritual experience of the professing church memberships; to convert the church from traditional rationalism, orthodox scholasticism, and introversion to evangelicalism, evangelism, and extroversion; and to motivate God's people in the evangelization of the multitudes who knew experientially nothing of Christ. At the same time they ignited the fire that eventually sent its rays and beams around the world, lighting the fire of God in every country of the globe. As a result the church of Jesus Christ today is present in the whole of the inhabited world.

Continental beginnings. Early in the course of the evangelical restoration, the concern of the conversion of the heathen became a lively issue. World missions became a subject of serious discussions, prayer, and concern. Its firstfruits manifested themselves in Denmark in 1705 when King Frederick IV, under the guidance of Chaplain Luetkens, sent forth two German Pietists, Bartholomew Ziegenbalg and Neinrich Pluetschau, to India with royal endowments. This mission continued for many years as the pioneer mission to India's millions and is now incorporated in the Lutheran Church of India.

A breakthrough of greater historic significance came in Herrnhut among the Moravian Brethren because of a revival which began on February 10, 1728 and continued for many years. Four years later, in 1732, the first Moravian missionaries were sent out, with literally scores following in the next years.

Soon the voices of Jonathan Edwards and George Whitefield were heard, and the words of John Wesley began to echo through the church: "The world is my parish." It was evident to the spiritually discerning that God was moving in on His church in an extraordinary manner.

The breakthrough in Great Britain. Inspired by unique circumstances Edwards published in 1747 a missionary treatise entitled "An Humble Attempt to Promote Explicit Agreement and Visible Union among God's People, in Extraordinary Prayer for the Revival of Religion, and the Advancement of Christ's Kingdom on Earth." This book, to quote Charles L. Chaney, "had a fantastic influence in stimulating missionary interest, organization and support in the early National Period and throughout the nineteenth century."[1] This book came into the hands of Andrew Fuller, a prominent Baptist minister of Northampton, England, who already had been seriously stirred by reports of the Great Awakening in America and who was deeply involved in the evangelical movement in Great Britain. By Edwards's challenge to prayer Fuller became gravely concerned for world evangelization. As a result he conducted concerts of prayer. This was in 1784. It was these prayer meetings as much as any other influence that prepared the small group of Baptist ministers (thirteen in all) to form the Baptist Missionary Society.

William Carey, the father of modern missions, was himself a fruit of the evangelical movement in Great Britain. Captain Cook's reports about the plight of the people of the islands of the South Pacific stirred his heart to action. Though his suggestion to discuss world missions by the Baptist Association was coldly brushed aside as being the idea of an idle enthusiast, his publication of a tract could not be disregarded. Its title is significant: "An Inquiry into the Obligation of Christians to Use Means for the Conversion of Heathen, in Which the Religious State of the Different Nations of the World, the Success of Former Undertakings and the Practicability of Further Undertakings Are Considered."

The same year Carey preached his world-famous missionary message at Nottingham before the Baptist Association. It was on May 30, 1792 when he read his text from Isaiah 54:2–3 and preached on the subject, "Expect great things from God; attempt great things for God." The impact was profound. As a result, ministers in a meeting at Kettering on October 2, 1792 agreed to form a Baptist missionary society known as "The Particular Baptist Society for Propagating the Gospel among the Heathen." William Carey became its first missionary, leaving England on June 13, 1793 and arriving in Calcutta, India on November 10 of that same year. The triumph for the cause of God was incalculable. The dam was broken and the waters gushed forth. It was timed by the Lord. The Second Great Awakening was just around the corner to reinforce and propel the infant movement as well as to provide prayer partners, financial support, and the recruits needed to launch the world movement.

It is impossible to imagine the launching of the Protestant world missionary movement without the Great Awakenings. This truth is fully established by the historical fact that all the early organizers and leaders of the missionary societies were men deeply touched by and involved in the Great Awakenings and/or were its subsequent converts. Somehow the missionary movement has remained dependent for its scope, intensity, and effectiveness on awakenings within the church.

Reinforcements through awakenings. The modern missionary movement may be compared to the rhythmic movements of the waves of the ocean with new pulsations heightening the waves intermittently. This was so not merely in the birth of modern missions and its tremendous reinforcement by the revival wave in 1800–1802, but particularly so by the revivals of 1858 and 1905. *The First Great Awakening* in the eighteenth century gave rise to the great historic missionary societies which soon spanned the globe. *The Second Great Awakening* roused an even larger circle of Christians into activities. It brought about the British and Foreign Bible Society. The missionaries arising out of the awakenings were noted for their heroism and endurance amidst fiercest opposition, indescribable hardships and sufferings, abominable misjudgments by fellowmen and often churchmen, and cruel mistreatments by trade companies. And yet the missionaries' joyous sacrifices, persistence, and martyrdom equaled in every way the devotion and commitment of the Christians of the early centuries.

The Third Great Awakening was of peculiar importance. From it came men and movements of unique character and world significance. Such men were William Booth and the resultant Salvation Army, James Hudson Taylor and the China Inland Mission with the largest mission staff in the past century, and Andrew Murray and the South Africa General Mission. Also the roots of the Regions Beyond Mission reach back into this Awakening. And it was there that Dwight L. Moody and the Moody Bible Institute, C. T. Studd, and John R. Mott and the great Student Volunteer Movement had their springs. From the Third Awakening came also the world famous Keswick Convention of Great Britain with its worldwide impact in revival and missions.

The Great Awakening of Wales, or the Welsh Revival, at the beginning of this century (1904) was unique in many ways. It is evident that it transformed multitudes of people. The profoundest effect of the Welsh Revival, however, was experienced in a number of mission fields. Missionaries coming under the impact of the revival carried the fire into distant lands. Thus the great movements in Madagascar and South Africa, Assam and the Ramabai revival in India, Korea and the Goforth revivals of China, and subsequent great movements in this land in the first and second decades of this century—all these are traceable directly to the Welsh Revival. Its echoes were graciously transmitted to distant shores, and in Korea and Assam they are still reverberating.

From this spiritual restoration certain truths are evident: First, missionary motivation becomes most dynamic when it is derived from studies of the nature of God and the purpose of God in history as unveiled in the Scriptures. This became the strength of Jonathan Edwards's approach. He discovered the scriptural truth that the unchanging purpose of God demanded missions. The church must be a missionary church. Later Robert E. Speer went one step further and anchored world missions in the very nature of God. Many theologians have also emphasized this truth. In theology the sources of missionary motivation are either opened or clogged.

Second, in order to be lasting and dynamic, theology and revival must be interrelated and must be channeled into evangelism and world missions. It is a sobering fact of history that theology can grow stale and static. It needs the companionship of revival. On the other hand no revival has been able to sustain its glow unless it was built on a sound biblical basis and had built into it an energetic "go" of evangelism. Therefore biblical and theological studies must not be separated from revivalism and missions in the training of Christian leaders, and revival and evangelistic fervor are necessary in order to keep evangelicalism from growing stale and becoming a sort of lifeless "modern-day scholasticism."

The Advances of Missions

Because of these missionary endeavors the church of Jesus Christ around the world is a reality. All major countries have had the witness of the gospel of Jesus Christ. Its sounds have gone out into all lands. People have turned to Christ and churches adorn almost every major city of the world and countless villages. Millions have heard and responded to the call of the gospel of God. Total islands have turned toward Christianity and the Lord is being acknowledged widely. Today the gospel is heard more widely than ever before. Christian radio studios are producing and releasing scores upon scores of gospel programs. Literally the air is filled with the story of Jesus Christ as the gospel is being broadcast in song and spoken word.

The entire Bible, or the New Testament, or portions of the Scriptures are available today in more than 1,600 languages and in the tongues of about ninety-seven percent of the world's population. The ninety percent of the people speaking the world's fifty major languages have the entire Bible. This is an achievement of enormous proportions.

The total Protestant missionary force operating overseas is impressive. Approximately 55,000 Protestant men and women are serving in various parts of the world other than their home countries. More than 35,000 of these are from the United States and Canada. More and more the churches of the third world are shouldering responsibilities for the evangelization of their own countries, or at least people in their own communities. Also numerous missionary societies overseas are beginning impressive ministries outside of their own countries. Thus there are positive and encouraging signs in missions.

Cooperative efforts were urged early in the history of missions. Today American missions are sailing mainly under four flags: AAFM (the American Association of Foreign Missions), DOM (the Division of Overseas Ministries of the National Council of Churches), EFMA (the Evangelical Foreign Missions Association), IFMA (the Interdenominational Foreign Mission Association). In addition there are numerous other independent missions.

It is most encouraging that substantial forces for evangelism are beginning to operate in the third world and that the telling of the good news to every person may yet become a reality in this century. The fact remains, however, that if America is to continue to play a vital role in world evangelization, the fire in a great awakening will need to ignite evangelical theology once more.

The Prospects of Missions

In the words of Adoniram Judson, the future is as bright as the promises of God. And Paul wrote, "A wide door for effective service has opened to me, and there are many adversaries" (1 Cor. 16:9). It is easy to emphasize one side or the other—the open doors or the adversaries. Unquestionably Satan is actively opposing world missions. Christian missions is not a call to ease and comfort. Adversities arise and the going is rough. Missions is a call to engage in warfare, to invade the realm the Evil One claims, to storm the forts of the enemy, and to set the captives free. It is not impossible that Satan will operate more by infiltration and dissipation, by creating suspicion and disunity among the evangelicals than by direct confrontation. His strategy cannot be foretold. One thing is certain: he will not be sleeping while evangelization goes forward.

On the other hand there are unprecedented harvests for the Lord in many countries of the world. Nothing in the New Testament precludes believing that great movements can take place and multitudes can turn to the Lord in the next several decades, if the Lord tarries with His coming. It would not surprise this writer if in the last two decades of this century at least as many people would claim the name of Christ as have come to know Him in the last two centuries. Certainly a widespread revival seems to be coming to parts of Western Europe. Movements are evident which one dared not expect a few years ago. It may yet be that the dead bones of Protestantism as well as many Catholics will be revived by the gracious operation of the Holy Spirit and will live again. Europe could once more become a strong evangelical leader in the world.

In sub-Saharan Africa the masses have been loosened from their traditional moorings and are drifting toward a form of Christianity. Churches and missions simply cannot cope effectively with the situation. Therefore, syncretism and nativism are becoming the greatest danger. A new evangelical strategy is needed if Christianity in a pure form is to dominate. Some Latin American countries present a similar challenge and churches are multiplying rapidly.

In Asia the situation is more spotty. But there, too, a great and effectual door is awaiting evangelical entrance. Radio and literature, the uncertainty of the times, pressing circumstances, and the gracious cosmic operations of the Holy Spirit are setting before the church unprecedented harvest fields. But the laborers are few. "Pray ye therefore the Lord of the harvest, that he will send forth laborers into his harvest" (Matt. 9:38 AV). Only a depth-revival in the biblical training centers in all the world can change the situation and halt the dangers that are at the steps of the church.

CHAPTER 3

Missions in Cultural Perspective

George W. Peters

In the book *Christ and Culture*[1] H. Richard Niebuhr discusses several theories about the church's relationship to culture that have been emphasized in the history of the church. His chapter headings are indicative of the theories. After an introductory chapter he speaks of "Christ against Culture," "The Christ of Culture," "Christ above Culture," "Christ and Culture in Paradox," and "Christ the Transformer of Culture."

Each of these positions has had its proponents who have wrestled with this issue honestly and in the light of their understanding of the Scriptures. The Christ-culture relationship is neither new nor simple. Because of this, Niebuhr speaks in his introductory chapter of "the enduring problem." Unfortunately it has endured to the present day. Never before has the gospel and biblical Christianity interacted with more and widely differing cultures than it does today. At the same time never in history have cultures asserted their identity more emphatically than they do today in a time of heightened nationalism and messianism.

The Enduring Problem

Of necessity modern missions has been forced into the foreground in this issue and for three reasons. First, the Bible had to be translated into the languages of the people, many of whom had no written language while others had only a limited religious vocabulary. This has raised the question of literalness in translation or translation that in many cases would be better if given in dynamic equivalents. The second reason for lively interaction with culture was the serious intention of many missionaries and leading nationals to build truly indigenous churches, that is, churches that were so related to the native cultures that the people would feel at home in the churches and function freely in them.

A third reason for cultural interaction is the issue of revelational absolutism and cultural relativism. Questions such as these have been raised: Which doctrines and principles are absolute and which patterns and practices, forms and structures are culture-related and therefore relative? Are there ethical absolutes that are abiding and must be universalized, or is all behavior culture-related? What and who determines the standards of sin and wrong? Is sin defined by culture and custom or by revelation? Are moral standards set by science or the Bible, by social anthropology or biblical theology?

No doubt absolutism versus relativism is becoming one of the most serious struggles in Christianity today. Yet few evangelical scholars are wrestling with it in depth and fewer missionaries are prepared to be of real help to the struggling churches. Because the church has failed to a great extent to speak out as a conscience, much of society is becoming conscienceless. Evangelical and biblical guidelines are urgently needed in this matter.

The matter of the relationship of the gospel to non-Christian cultures is not as simple as it may seem and is not easily resolved. The West is not the East and the East is not the West. But history is merciless and a world-culture is in the making. The Western world thinks in terms of two realms, the religious and the secular. While these realms dynamically and functionally interrelate, a distinction can be made. In Western culture one's religion can be changed without his experiencing serious repercussions. But such dichotomy does not exist outside the Western world. There a basic organismic unity exists, and all of life is penetrated by religion and held together by the element of religion. Religion is the cement of the cultural structure and relationships. It is the soul that governs the body. The anthropologist Malinowski points out that religion is not a cultural epiphenomenon but is "a profound moral and social force which gives the ultimate integration to human culture."[2] It is thus a most sensitive area to approach, and a change in religion in the non-Western world has tremendous repercussions on the totality of culture. It threatens all of life.

Missions and Culture

Missions and the church have responded to world cultures in various ways.

1. *Separation from culture.* Some missionaries have insisted that believers separate from practices that definitely militate against Christ and the gospel as unfolded in the Scriptures—practices such as idolatry, destruction of life, and others.

2. *Bold condemnation.* Others have condemned in principle many practices that violate Christian ideals, although temporarily tolerating them in practice while awaiting a development of a more sensitive conscience on the part of the national church or at least the national leadership.
3. *Cultural conversion.* In this reaction missionaries have retained the patterns and practices native to the people, while giving them, however, a new content, meaning, and purpose or substituting functional equivalents for them in order not to create a void or vacuum in the lives of believers and the churches.
4. *Adoption.* Many cultural patterns and practices seemed to be neutral and inoffensive and therefore constituted no problem to the convert and the church. These were retained and fully incorporated in the new lifestyle of the church.
5. *Enrichment or new creations.* These came in the form of functional equivalents or new additions from the enriched Christian culture of the missionary. After all, Christendom does possess values that have grown out of the soil enriched by the gospel of Jesus Christ.

This fifth procedure presupposes a comprehensive understanding of the culture of the people. It also indicates that the gospel can never be completely indigenized. The gospel is a judge of every culture and leaves no culture undisturbed when it is applied in full scope and measure. This is nothing new. The apostles were accused of turning the world upside down (Acts 17:6). Paul was condemned for exceedingly troubling the city of Philippi and for teaching customs which were not lawful for Romans to receive and to observe (16:20–21). The gospel does cast down imaginations and every high thing that exalts itself against the knowledge of God and seeks to bring into captivity every thought to the obedience of God (2 Cor. 10:5). This chapter discusses the first two reactions—separation and condemnation—and then discusses the enrichment principle. Before doing so, however, a brief discussion of missions and prevailing theology and of missions and colonialism will cast some light on the attitudes and practices of missionaries.

Modern Missions and Prevailing Theology

Theology gives content to one's faith, direction to one's life, and motivation in one's work. It colors all of life. This holds true in missions also. The preceding chapter pointed out that Anglo-Saxon missiology was influenced by kingdom ideas and ideals. Missionaries went out to build the kingdom of God. Under the influence of Puritanism and later the impact of Albrecht Ritschl of Germany, Western culture was highly idealized and seen at least in part as the realization of the kingdom of God. Therefore building God's kingdom involved the transplanting of Western culture to other cultures. Missionaries expected that the kingdom of God was being ushered in and that Western culture was so linked to the kingdom of God that it would prevail around the globe. Thus many missionaries strategized not only to advance the gospel of Christ but also simultaneously to introduce and advance Western culture. They were confident that Christianity would soon supplant all other religions and Western culture would replace all other cultures or at least transform them considerably. Ritschl spoke boldly of *Kulturchristentum* ("culture-Christianity"). This was the ideal of the Edinburgh Conference of 1910, in which the coming of the kingdom of God was the keynote. It was believed that the kingdom of God was just around the corner.

The above idea was greatly aided by the conviction of denominational churchmen that church structures and practices (in addition to church doctrines and principles) were divinely ordained and biblically prescribed. Thus each denomination expected to export its own image as well as doctrine. Consequently many cared little about indigenization. They were reproducing their home churches because of the conviction that they were divinely modeled.[3]

While premillenarians repudiate the postmillennial theology of the early advances of missions and while many church and mission leaders would be critical of the lack of concern for indigenization, one cannot impugn the honesty, sincerity, devotion, and depth of motivation of those early missionaries.

Missions and Colonialism

While missionaries have always been children of their times and cultures, this is only relatively true of modern Protestant missions and does not hold true of all missionaries. Most of them went out to serve the Lord and to minister to the people of faraway lands. The atmosphere of the times blinded some missionaries to the evil of colonialism and at times they allied themselves with this system. In many ways they were molded in attitude and pattern by colonialism. A deep-seated paternalism determined many of them consciously or unconsciously. This is admitted today with humility and regret.

However, it still is a fact that missions in many ways ameliorated the sad plight of many subjugated and exploited people.

Courageously, Christian missions has functioned as the conscience of the colonial powers and as the benevolent representative of the nationals. Boldly missionaries protested against the misuse of power, publicly they denounced unjustly inflicted cruelties and oppression, forthrightly they spoke against unfair laws and the exploitation of the colonial subjects by their overlords and money-greedy companies. Stephen Charles Neill's book *Colonialism and Christian Missions*[4] should be read by any critic of missionaries before he thinks of this noble company of men and women as stooges of colonial powers or as collaborators in colonial exploitation. At the risk of life, work possibilities, reputation, and other sacrifices they stood firm in most cases and represented the people of the land, demanding reforms, justice, and benevolence. To the anger of the companies and governments, they exposed the injustices and cruelties of their compatriots and stood up for the rights of the people they had come to serve.

Missions and Religio-Cultural Abuses

Christian missions has been blamed for breaking up cultures of people and for disrupting the normal life of multitudes of tribes and clans. Such accusations have come mainly from anthropologists. It must be said, however, that such charges are based largely on non-Christian premises and spring from inadequate historical knowledge or from blind prejudice.

Christian missions can be credited with ridding the world of many cruelties and inhuman beliefs and practices. It is largely because of the impact of Christian missions that cannibalism, infanticide, the murder and burning of widows, and the destruction of the elderly and seriously ill have been abolished and that trial by the poison cup of the witch doctor has been outlawed. The sacredness of life simply is not a part of the natural religions of mankind. Life is cheap, greed is strong, anger is hot, self-preservation is dominant. Therefore the destruction of life was rife and warfare was a pleasure if not a sport. Christian missions has set itself energetically against such attitudes and inhuman practices. Even though it has not been able to move the nations away from the cruelties of warfare, many personal cruelties have been halted and changes have taken place.

Modern Missions and Religio-Cultural Enrichment

Western civilization and culture are certainly not to be identified with Christianity and even less so with the gospel. This was one of the faulty ideas of nineteenth-century Christianity. Western materialism, secularism, and two world wars have shattered this idea.

However, it still remains a fact that the gospel does bring enrichment as well as judgment. Modern missions has taken with it values into the world which have done much good—benefits which have enriched peoples, nations, and continents. These speak most favorably for missions to any unprejudiced person. Enrichments have come in such forms as education, modern medicine, industry, vocational training, and values wrapped up in the Christian community.

MISSIONS AND EDUCATION

Wherever missions went, education was carried. Great emphasis was placed on education not merely in order to train national Christian workers and leaders but also in order to serve the general advancement and development of the people. Many of Asia's most prominent institutions of higher learning today are of missionary origin. Similar is the situation in Africa where between eighty and ninety percent of all education has developed under missionary initiative and direction though the governments subsidized many institutions.

> Higher education in the Western tradition was first introduced to many parts of the world by Catholic and Protestant missions. Some of the earliest institutions became in time great sprawling universities whose present relationship to the founding churches, especially the Protestant churches, is quite tenuous. Many other colleges and not a few universities remain substantially church related, and new institutions of this kind continue to emerge. . . .
>
> The most recent directory lists 268 colleges and universities related to Protestant churches in Asia, Africa, the Pacific islands, and Latin America. These range in size and scope from small and poorly equipped schools to great universities, but they are all postsecondary schools which classify as institutions of higher education. Theological colleges are not counted in this number, except those which are departments within universities, but the list does include a few medical, vocational, and professional schools which grant the college degree.[5]

Added to this were scores upon scores of technical, professional, and agricultural schools established to train men and women in practical skills and to equip them to serve their community, country, and mankind in the advancement of culture and welfare.

The education of women in most of Asia and Africa has been pioneered by missionaries. Ewha University of Seoul (the world's largest women's university), Beirut College for Women, Kinnard College for Women (Pakistan), and Madras Woman's Christian College (India) are monuments to missionary courage and faith.

In recent years tremendous efforts have been put forth in the field of literacy. Through the worldwide ministry of Frank Laubach and his associates and trainees actually millions have learned to read.

MISSIONS AND MEDICINE

The missionary contribution in the field of medicine has been extensive. Hospitals, medical centers, clinics, dispensaries, and leprosaria in the third world are the silent but impressive witness to the loving ministry of missions. It is a simple fact of history that modern medicine was first introduced in Asia and Africa by missionaries. Large and prominent medical centers have grown up and are even today some of the best on those continents. This credit must be given to missionaries and missions.

THE CHRISTIAN COMMUNITY

The greatest contributions, however, have not come by way of schools and hospitals, as great as they may be. The most significant contribution is that Christian missions has been instrumental in bringing about a worldwide Christian community of spiritual, social, and moral significance. Christianity in and by the presence of the church adds a quality of love, benevolence, truth, righteousness, and justice to human existence which is not found in other social or religious movements. The spiritual nature of man and the greatness of human personality because man is created for fellowship with God; human rights because every man is equally accountable before God; human freedom because man is a moral agent reflecting the sovereignty of God; human equality because all mankind has a common source in Adam—such values are fruit not reaped from other sources. The worth of mankind is emphasized not only in relation to eternal salvation but also to life here and now. Christianity as light and salt expresses itself through the

Christian community for the benefit of all humanity. The church is not a holy huddle, a secluded club. It is a witness in and to the world. As a this-worldly phenomenon it exhibits "holy worldliness" (Warren) while at the same time it is a sign of other-worldly reality.

By calling, the church is to be an *apostolic church*. It is sent into the world. "As the Father has sent Me, I also send you" are the Lord's words to His apostles (John 20:21). It is sent into the world to be a witness. "You shall be My witnesses" is the Lord's commission (Acts 1:8). The church has no choice. A truly apostolic church is an evangelizing and a missionary church. The New Testament foresees no postmission era.

The church is also to be a *servant church*. It is to render loving, humble, unselfish service in this world. It does so in the name of Christ, after the pattern of its Master, for the glory of its Lord, out of a heart of compassion, and for the welfare of mankind.

Such service is not rendered out of selfish motives nor to seek any advantages or rewards. Christian service is a divine virtue and is practiced because it is a virtue. In humble and joyous submission to Him who is the "Ideal Servant" the church too becomes a servant to mankind.

As the *societal church* it is to be a community of God's people of a unique kind (1 Peter 2:9). It is to strive to manifest the "manifold wisdom of God" (Eph. 3:10) and to demonstrate the reality of a new society in the midst of a broken and disintegrating society (Eph. 2:11–3:7). It is to be a new race, a new humanity (2 Cor. 5:17) which seeks to incarnate the divine principles of "righteousness and peace and joy in the Holy Spirit" (Rom. 14:17), to administer the "ministry and word of reconciliation" (2 Cor. 5:18–21), and to advance the liberation of mankind from the oppression of sin and degrading, dehumanizing institutions and practices (Luke 4:18–19). As a model society, it demonstrates before the world the experiential reality of the saviorhood and lordship of Christ and His presence among His people. It shows that a life of repentance from sin and of faith in Jesus Christ is a possibility as it depends wholly on the Holy Spirit. The church is God's society in the midst of man's society.

The church of Jesus Christ is also to be a *pilgrim church*. It shares in the journey through the experiences of life, the difficulties and struggles, the hardships and afflictions, sacrifices and weariness of the journey. However, its journey within history is full of meaning because it knows that its Master is in command of history and that He is leading the church as well as history to a definite goal. This makes all the difference in the pilgrimage.

Therefore, the church must constantly and clearly define and pronounce boldly the meaning of history and the destiny and goal of life which are not found this side of the grave. Unhesitatingly and unmistakably it must point to the certainty of eternity and the reality of a "Father's home" for all those who know the Father through Christ, and it must emphatically declare that Jesus Christ is the *only way* to the Father and the eternal home (John 14:6). Christians are a pilgrim people. Their citizenship is in heaven from whence also they look for the Savior, the Lord Jesus Christ (Phil. 3:20). People are born with eternity in their hearts and for eternity. Nothing but eternity will satisfy people's cravings and do justice to their being. Yet they must constantly be reminded that they are here only for a very little while.

The church of Jesus Christ also must be a *prophetic church*. Although the church is not of this world, it lives and functions in this world. It shares in the total life milieu of mankind—its economic, intellectual, social, and political experiences, whatever they may be. While the church may have a distinct history, it must live such history in the midst of the history of the nations. It is this twofold relationship which creates also a twofold responsibility and a most serious tension in the life of believers and churches.

The church in its proclamation and in and through its membership is to be the moral and social conscience of society in example, precept, and prophetic utterance. It may well be that the church often falls under the judgment of Isaiah when he complained, "His watchmen are blind; they are all ignorant, they are all dumb dogs, they cannot bark; sleeping, lying down, loving to slumber" (Isa. 56:10). However, the church has the sacred responsibility to speak out in the name of a righteous and holy God against prevailing wickedness in society and culture and encroaching, prevailing, enslaving, and dehumanizing influences of religions, organizations, institutions, and establishments. The church dare not be silent when welfare, lives, and souls are being imperiled. The church must realize that it is *in* history and *for* history, although not *of* history. It has a sacred obligation to speak in and to history. History has meaning and is controlled either for good or for evil.

The church must also point individuals to divine ideals and principles that build a people and that elevate, free, and ennoble mankind and encourage and support what is good in culture, society, institutions, establishments, and programs. As salt of the earth and light of the world the church must continuously and energetically pursue the well-being of mankind.

An Important Distinction

Christendom has failed to a considerable degree to be the light of the world, the salt of the earth, the conscience of society, the prophetic voice among the nations, a model society, and in many ways to create an effective counterculture. Believers have often permitted themselves to be molded by the forces of this world and to be slaves rather than liberators.

It must also be admitted that many evangelical missions have created churches in their own image instead of laying foundations for the development of full-orbed New Testament churches. The churches, therefore, continue to function within the specialized and limited sphere of those missions and do not mature into properly and responsibly functioning churches to be the light and the salt of the community and nation they are divinely designed to be. This is a serious matter.

However, a careful distinction must be made between missions and the church. Missions is a specific and limited ministry within the total biblical assignment to the church. Operating in a foreign land as a guest in that land, it ought to behave as a guest. Missions is not the church, which is at home in that land. It must not usurp the authority nor accept the total assignment of the church.

Ideally missions is the agency to introduce the gospel of Jesus Christ into new frontiers and to plant churches and nurture them to a degree of maturity so that they may function independently and assume the full role of the broad church assignment. The confusion of these assignments or fusion of them usurps the church of its biblical rights and responsibilities and will bring missions into conflicts sooner or later. As Oldham has affirmed, "The aim, then, of foreign missionary work is to plant the Church of Christ in every part of the non-Christian world as a means to its evangelization. Both parts of the definition are necessary."[6] Oldham adds that "We cannot say that any area has been adequately evangelized until it has had the witness of a native Church, sprung from the soil, expressing its faith in its own characteristic ways, and as a distinct community representing a new type of life in the midst of a non-Christian environment."[7]

Missions and the church are closely related, yet they are distinct entities in function and purpose—the first with a specific and limited assignment, the latter with a comprehensive assignment. While the missionary may be of great help to the church in teaching and counseling, in the final end the national church must accept the responsibility and regulate its own relationship to its culture. Missionaries must therefore place their confidence in the Holy Spirit, the Word of God, and the brethren to do what they believe is right. They must be able to say, "It seemed good to the Holy Spirit and to us" (Acts 15:28).

CHAPTER 4

Missions in a Religiously Pluralistic World

George W. Peters

Religious pluralism is nothing new. Throughout the millennia of history various religions have functioned in the world. The Bible refers to numerous gods and systems of worship in various cultures of the ancient Near East. These religions—which are historic realities of tremendous significance—cause no little perplexity to the student of the Bible and to the missionary. The latter is confronted by this reality in its most vivid complexity, and he experiences it as a life-determining and community-governing force.

Of course religious pluralism is no longer something overseas and beyond the boundaries of this nation. Several million adherents of non-Christian religions are fellow citizens in the United States. They have become neighbors on the same streets where Christians live. Christians share with them the same post office and postman, the same bank, the same grocery store, the same playground. Yet they attend their temples and worship their god or gods in the very cities where Christians attend church and worship the only true God.

The New Image

Religious pluralism has become a universal phenomenon and is becoming an accepted pattern of life. This has raised some searching questions in the minds of many people. One question is this: Are "the heathen" actually as pagan as either mission reports or one's own imagination has projected them to appear and to which Christians have liberally and sympathetically responded in missions and charity? Since non-Christian religions are no longer isolated from North Americans and other parts of the "civilized world" by great distances, a new image arises. Newbigin mentions five change factors that are affecting the thinking of many people.

> Students from every part of the world and from every religious community jostle one another on the campuses of Western universities, share the same studies, the same books, the same discussions of world affairs. The great international and inter-governmental organizations, both the United Nations itself and also its many specialist agencies, provide a sphere in which some of the ablest men of all religions are constantly co-operating in seeking the solution of the pressing problems of mankind. In UNESCO there is an organization which deliberately seeks to create the means for a common spiritual basis for the life of mankind. In a multitude of international conferences, for all sorts of commercial, scientific, and cultural purposes, men and women from all over the world meet as equals in a milieu in which any suggestion that absolute truth belongs to one of the many strands of human religious life seems simply absurd. And finally, for those who do not share in any of these opportunities for inter-cultural meeting, there is the ceaselessly growing flood of tourists bringing ordinary men and women of every land into direct contact with each other, not to mention the movements of migrants, refugees, people forced by pressure of population to seek work in other lands.
>
> It is not surprising if, in the face of these new experiences, some of the traditional supports for the missionary enterprise began to shake. For it must be frankly admitted that—whatever might be said from the pulpit about the true basis of missions in the Gospel itself—the motives with which they have been supported have been mixed.[1]

The "poor heathen" out there made a tremendous appeal to the conscience and the sense of sympathy and responsibility in many people. The urge of compassion became a strong motivating power.

A second penetrating question is addressed to the church and missions: Are "the heathen" actually as destitute of spiritual light and truths as Christians have believed them to be? Evaluating the noblest elements of their religions and entering into the religious experiences of some of their poets, philosophers, "theologians," and "saints," can one deny or even question the presence of Christ and the reality of the ministry of the Holy Spirit in their midst? Has not God disclosed Himself to them? Are they not meeting Him in their experiences? Is not Christ the Lord of history who at no time and place has left Himself without a witness (John 1:9; Acts 14:17; Rom. 1:18–20; 2:7, 10, 14–15)? And does He not operate in historical processes in order that "in the dispensation of the fullness of times he might gather together in one all things in Christ, both which are in heaven, and which are on earth; even in him" (Eph. 1:10 KJV)? These questions cannot be dismissed lightly.

A number of years ago Arno C. Gaebelein published a book of considerable importance. The title—*Christianity or Religion?*—

was a message in itself.[2] Then Samuel G. Craig wrote a book entitled *Christianity Rightly So Called*.[3] W. H. Griffith Thomas narrowed the circle when he entitled his publication *Christianity Is Christ*.[4] Thus the tunnel narrowed. From the wide entrance of religion it narrowed to Christianity, then to Christianity "rightly so-called," and then from Christianity to Christ. This narrowing and focusing on the person of Jesus Christ is of utmost importance. The widest circle thus is that of religion.

The Significance of Religion

No one should think lightly of religion. It is not only a universal human phenomenon; it is also the most meaningful and most sacred possession of mankind. Humanity makes mockery of the thought that people have matured beyond religion and that humanity is advancing toward a postreligious world. The world is more religious today than ever before. Four observations can be made in relation to religion, including Christianity as a system of religion, beliefs, and practices.

ALL RELIGIONS HAVE PRACTICES WHICH APPEAR TO BE ALIKE

Bavinck has written about the similarities in religious practice between Christians and followers of non-Christian religions.

> A Christian who is accustomed to pray cannot help recognizing that the Moslem whom he sees praying is doing something similar. And seeing a Hindu bowing down before his god stirs the Christian, because he himself has learned to bow his head before the God who appears to us in Jesus Christ. Indeed, he cannot deny that our Christian faith and those other religions have something in common, that there are certain similarities between them.[5]

Similar things can be said about the vocabulary among religions. There seemingly is a religious vocabulary that is quite universal.

ALL RELIGIONS HAVE A UNIQUE FUNCTION TO PERFORM

Religions are purposive and meaningful. They are uniquely sacred and filled with awe, fear, reverence, and expectations. They are to serve life and to produce effects. While for people of the non-Western world all of life is sacred and all of culture is religion-permeated, it still remains a fact that religion is sacred and has a specific function to perform. Malinowski states that the African distinguishes well between folklore (and legend) on the one hand and myth on the other hand.[6] Modern man, however, thinks of the former as secular and entertaining and of the latter as sacred. In case of extremity he resorts to the mythology and practices of religion. His expectations from religion are real and demanding. He expects religion to perform and to produce results.

ALL RELIGIONS HAVE STRUCTURE

Just as there is no unstructured society, so there is no unstructured religion. The peculiar thing is that basically all religions are structured very similarly, including Judaism and Christianity.

First is the outer ring that includes the total ethos or religio-cultural atmosphere and worldview with its traditional presuppositions and philosophy, whether formulated or not, which determines or at least influences the lifestyle of the devotees or adherents and related societies. *Second* are the personnel or functionaries (such as priests, or other officiating personnel and people of religious influences); institutions such as sacrifices, holy days, holy places and pilgrimages, and special observances; and practices such as prayer, fasting, and almsgiving. Beneath this second level is a *third* layer consisting of the codes of behavior, the written and unwritten rules and regulations that constitute the ethic and general beliefs of the religions. The innermost heart of the *fourth* circle consists of a specific core of beliefs that forms the soul of the total religion. In some of the primitive religions, such as Shamanism of Siberia and the religions of many of China's tribespeople, this innermost core is difficult to discover because it is a mystery kept as a sacred trust and is known only to the initiated shaman. In some Australian tribespeople only men above a certain age level are allowed to know the inner core of teaching. But, however this may be, religion has a structure and the structures are surprisingly similar.

ALL RELIGIONS ARE EXPERIENCE-ORIENTED

A strong psychological aspect or "soulishness" exists in religion. This is universal. No religion could survive as a mere doctrinal system, ethical code, or practice-oriented system if it did not reach into man's inner being with deep and impressive psychological imprints. Carried to the extreme, this results in mysticism and/or ecstaticism which sweeps man along in prolonged experiences. Without some kind of experience, religion would soon die a natural death. This more than anything else makes man cling to religion. And it has accurately been said that man is incurably religious.

These are some of the things all religions have in common. Are all religions, therefore, also alike? Do they all represent truth? How is it then that Christians claim total uniqueness for the gospel of Jesus Christ, the heart and core of Christianity? Indeed, Christians make for Christianity "rightly so-called" the most astounding claims. These claims, however, are not always fully incarnated, utilized, or even recognized and expressed by the Christian church. And of course Christians do not claim to have discovered them nor has the genius of Christianity invented them. Followers of Christ humbly confess that these unique claims come to mankind as God's gracious disclosures or revelation. They come from Jewish men who were devoted followers of Jesus Christ—and who received the truth by revelation through the Holy Spirit. These are not Western ideas. Therefore no credit comes to believers today. They are merely passing on what they have received from others and what they have experienced as truth and reality.

Therefore Christians witness to the following truths.

1. Christianity claims to be the religion of absolute fulfillment, bringing wholeness and completion to the human personality in all sanctified aspirations, hopes, and potentials.
2. Christianity asserts absoluteness in religious authority, contending for total control over one's mind, conscience, conduct, and relationships in all spheres of life.
3. Christianity claims completeness and finality as a revelation of God's person, work, and purpose; it cannot be supplemented or complemented by other religions.
4. Christianity claims universality in scope and rule, and promises to supplant all other religions in the world. Christ is the sole Savior and sovereign Lord of all history.

Sincerely one may ask, Are not such claims devastating in one's relationship to non-Christian religions? Can a person be as categorical as all that? In a world that strives for unity, harmony, tolerance, and peace, such questions are legitimate. It seems evident, however, that the Bible leaves no choice. There is such a thing as "holy intolerance" which is more wholesome to mankind than "unholy tolerance." Yet Christians should be as open as truth permits them to be and as charitable as the Bible bids them to be.

Theories to Build Natural Bridges

Theories have abounded in man's search to build natural bridges from the gospel to non-Christian religions. Elsewhere the present writer has referred to eight such theories.[7] Gensichen, of Heidelberg University, analyzes four theories;[8] and Braaten, of the Lutheran School of Theology at Chicago, wrestles with three theories presented by John Hick, Karl Barth, and Karl Rahner.[9] If the vastness of the field is an indication of the depth of the issue, then there is little hope of finding a human solution.

To think, however, of all religions as alike, interrelated, and originating from the same source and leading to the same conclusions and destiny is a serious mistake. That approach betrays either intellectual distortion, if not dishonesty, or presuppositions which are neither biblical, historical, nor acceptable to the conscience attuned to truth and the eternal. *The revelational concept of God as the Father of Jesus Christ as revealed in the Trinity, the creation of the world with its history and purpose, and the biblical doctrine of humanity as created in the image of God, fallen into sin, and redemption in Christ, simply cannot be fitted into the ethnic religions of the world.* Revelational religion in its fundamental concepts remains unique, no matter how much of value, ethical precepts, social cohesiveness, beauty, and elements of truth may be discovered in or ascribed to non-Christian religions. The gulf cannot be spanned. There is a "total otherness" in revelational Christianity "rightly so-called" and in the gospel of the Lord Jesus Christ. It simply is incomparable.

Christianity is and remains the "nonmixer," as Hammer has called it.[10] Christianity possesses a "total uniqueness." There is a fundamental "discontinuity," to use Kraemer's term,[11] a "total uniqueness" in Christianity, which refuses to be acculturated. To the contrary, it *confronts* culture and demands a verdict.

The Present-Day Debate

In recent years an attractive theory has captured many minds and constitutes the heart of a far-reaching debate. It may be stated in two propositions: (a) Jesus Christ is Lord. As the Lord of all history, He is present in all history. There is no history beyond Him and outside of Him. (b) As Lord of history and in history, Jesus Christ can be met by men of faith in living experiences whatever their outward religious allegiance may be and whether they recognize Him as Savior and Lord or not.

Consequently there is "the Unknown Christ of Hinduism" (Raimundo Panikkar), the "anonymous Christian" (Karl Rahner), and the "latent church" (J. C. Hoekendijk and Paul Tillich) in the world of non-Christian religions. Though these men represent extreme views, it is a fact that they express widely held positions.

From the natural point of view these two propositions appeal to the human mind and natural sympathy. One could almost wish they were true and could be proven. Therefore they must be more closely evaluated.

The Bible and History

It is the clear doctrine of the Bible that God is the Creator of this universe and all that is in it. The New Testament adds the emphasis that such creation was in and by Christ Jesus (John 1:3; Col. 1:16–17; Heb. 1:2). It also affirms that Jesus is Lord of lords and King of kings, on whom all depends and who holds all authority in heaven and on earth (Matt. 28:18–20; Rom. 14:9; 1 Cor. 12:3; Phil. 2:9–11; Col. 1:16–18; Heb. 1:2–3; Rev. 19:11–16). The Bible leaves no room for doubting the creatorship of God, the saviorhood of Jesus Christ, and the lordship of Christ. As such, Christ is *the ultimate source* of all things, the *hope* of all things, the *purpose* of all things, the *meaning* of all things, and the *destiny* of all things. The material universe and human history are neither meaningless nor purposeless. They have a goal toward which they are being guided. This is confirmed by the Scriptures.

The Fateful Surrender

To give such an unconditional affirmation, however, would require a twofold surrender. First, one would need to surrender the teaching of *Heilsgeschichte* (sacred history) as a unique history within the history of all mankind and accept the position that all history is alike and sacred. Thus the qualitative distinctness of the history of Israel as it began in Abraham and continued throughout the times of the Old Testament must be yielded. The faith in the uniqueness of Old Testament revelation in the history of religions would need to be relinquished. What Christians have considered as a sacred and qualitatively unique stream of revelation in the midst of the religious streams of the world would cease to claim qualitative distinctiveness. While there still may be quantitative differences, the claims to qualitative distinctiveness would need to be surrendered, and all history acknowledged as one.

A second surrender would be the biblical truth that a second force is operative in this world and uniquely so in the history of mankind and not least in the realm of religion. Christians would need to yield the doctrine that this force is an outflow of a person known in the Bible as Satan, the devil, the dragon, that old serpent (Rev. 20:2). The Bible, however, does not present a unified sacred history. There are parallel lines of serious interactions and bitter conflicts between Christ and Satan, though of course Christ is and will be the Victor.

To ascribe present evil to the bestiality of man because of his supposed evolutionary background or to structures, institutions, establishments, and traditions is too superficial from the biblical point of view. The Bible sees as the ultimate source of evil in this world a person—Satan—who is also known as "the god of this world" (2 Cor. 4:4) and "the prince of the power of the air" (Eph. 2:2). The Bible concretizes evil by informing believers that "our struggle is not against flesh and blood, but against the rulers, against the powers, against the world-forces of this darkness, against spiritual forces of wickedness in the heavenly places" (Eph. 6:12). The Bible warns Christians against the strategies, the cunning devices, the clever schemes of the devil (Eph. 6:11). And the Bible states that he is deceiving the nations and leading them astray (Rev. 20:3). The world system (Col. 2:8, 20) binds and blinds the world of mankind and threatens to destroy it (Gal. 4:3).

These are not empty words. They speak of stark reality. And human history is the most convincing commentary on these truths. The last two world wars and all the horrifying bloodsheds that are continuing into the present are merely a prolongation and intensification of the "conflict of the ages." And they will not stop until finally the Prince of Peace comes and bids them cease.

The Invasion of Human History

An invasion of human history by evil forces has taken place and this invasion affects every aspect of life. Can one be assured that the religions of mankind are exempt from this invasion with its evil influences and effects? Is religion insulated against demonic influences? Are religions too sacred for satanic invasion? Paul seemingly did not think so (Rom. 1:18–25; 1 Cor. 10:14, 19–21) and history would not validate such a position. As one cannot claim such insulation for Christianity as a religious system, such insulation cannot be claimed for the other ethnic and living religions. Of course, reforms have occurred in some of these religions, and evil aspects and some inhuman practices have been eliminated in the course of the past centuries.

Two tendencies, however, are evident in non-Christian religions. The first is that their "perfecting" at the same time results in greater cohesiveness and they become an increasingly closed system. The second tendency is that they become increasingly immune and adverse to the gospel of Jesus Christ. They grow more self-contained and more resistant. If Christ were in all of history and all of history were of Christ, including the world's living religions, then these religions would be moving toward Christ. But such is not the case. Instead, there is a misleading, deceiving, opposing, immunizing, and resisting force at work which adopts and absorbs Christian elements while at the same time it resists and opposes Christ as the only Savior and sovereign Lord.

The Reality of Religious Experiences

The situation differs little when the second proposition is considered and one studies the religious experiences of "men of faith" in the world's religions. This is not to deny that people encounter deep religious experiences. They are realities and cannot be disregarded or explained away. They may even be ecstatic, mystic, rapturous, absorbing, ennobling, and personality-transforming. Their psychological phenomena and immediate after-effects may closely resemble types of "Christian conversions" in many respects. It is not unusual to find such experiences accompanied by rapturous glory, insensibility to the world, ecstaticism, tongues phenomena, utterances and visions, or lostness in meditation. They are real to the individual involved and may become life-determining for the devotee, as was the case with Gautama Buddha and numerous others. The many documented cases presented by William James cannot be dismissed lightly.[12] They deserve serious consideration. There are transreligious experiences of great similarity wherever religion is taken seriously and motivation is sufficient and sustained.

Christians who believe in the lordship of Christ, in the cosmic operations of the Holy Spirit, and in a certain commonness and unity of mankind, and who are interested in finding as much truth as possible, can earnestly inquire into the source, nature, and meaning of such experiences. Whence are they? Where do they lead? What is their meaning?

The *possibility* of such is in itself an indication of the grace of God. It may well be that this possibility could be ascribed to the religious nature of man. However, were it not for the grace of God, sin would no doubt soon destroy such possibilities and man would become a religionless creature, incapable of any religious experiences. It is difficult to fathom the depth and awfulness of sin in its destructive powers.

It may also well be that the *search* for such experiences finds its source in the cosmic operation of the Holy Spirit which seems to be touching every human life (John 1:9). A restlessness and yearning in the heart of man is the result. One certainly cannot overlook such scenes as were witnessed in India in January and February of 1977 near the city of Allahabad, India. In five weeks fifty million Hindu pilgrims from all over India converged on the place where the Yamuna River meets the Ganges River. The occasion was the Jar Festival (the *Kumbh Mela*). At tremendous expense and personal hardship, these pilgrims came to bathe in the waters of the Ganges hoping thus to be cleansed completely and forever from all their sins and to be assured of eternal bliss after death. Their goal is to be released from the wheel of transmigration or reincarnation. This underlying motivation, thirst, and yearning was not merely human or demonic. The cosmic operations of the Holy Spirit preserve men in a savable condition and it is possible that from time to time the slumbering yearning becomes an intense search for spiritual reality. However, as people so readily ignore or misuse God's natural gifts (Acts 14:17; Rom. 2:4–5), are they more prepared to accept God's gracious spiritual gifts and acknowledge them in humble gratitude? History seems to be pointing in a different direction.

It can hardly be established historically that the rapturous experiences of men and women in non-Christian religions have caused them to be more open to the message of the gospel of Christ. Instead, it is more accurate to state that such experiences have insulated them to the penetration of the message and immunized them against the gospel of Christ. Nor is it conceivable that so-called "men of faith" (i.e., religious people) met an unrecognized Savior and Lord in their depth experiences and then became more closed to Him when He was presented to them in the gospel. For people more often turn from Him or even against Him. Of course it is fully acknowledged that God works in mysterious ways, but does He work in self-contradictory ways?

Does He work in experiences that alienate people from Him and immunize them against the gospel of Christ and the gift of God in Christ Jesus? To say the least, this is rather peculiar and self-contradictory.

Regarding so-called "men of faith" in non-Christian religions, two facts need to be emphasized. First, there seems to be a mystic-realistic relationship between saving faith and hearing the Word of God. Faith is born out of hearing the Word. Paul wrote that "faith comes from *hearing,* and hearing by the word of Christ" (Rom. 10:17). Similarly he questioned the Galatians, "Did you receive the Spirit by the works of the Law, or by *hearing* with faith?" (Gal. 3:2). This is in keeping with the words of Christ: "No man can come to Me, unless the Father who sent Me draws him; . . . It is written in the prophets, 'And they shall all be taught of God.' Every one who has *heard* and *learned* from the Father, comes to Me" (John 6:44–45). These passages relate saving faith to hearing the Word of God similar to the way James and Peter relate the new birth to the Word of God (James 1:18; 1 Peter 1:23). Does one therefore have a right to speak of "men of faith" *apart* from the Word of God? Abraham "staggered not at the *promise* of God . . . being fully persuaded that, what [God] had *promised,* he was able also to perform" (Rom. 4:20–21 KJV). The Word of God was the source of Abraham's faith. While the psychological basis and processes may be similar, could there be a qualitative distinction between the religious experiences of people in non-Christian religions and the experiences of those who hear the Word of God?

Another point to keep in mind is the fact that the object of faith, not the man of faith, is significant. Abraham believed *God* and that was counted to him for righteousness (Rom. 4:3). Faith may be the channel but the nature of the inflow is not determined by the channel but by the source to which it relates. Therefore the Bible is insistent and totally consistent in affirming that life-bringing faith must be related to Jesus Christ who is Life, outside of whom there is no life (1 John 5:11–12). Salvation is possible only by receiving Him (John 1:12; Acts 4:12). And "whosoever believes in Him should not perish but have eternal life" (John 3:16). The object of faith becomes the decisive and determining factor.

Conclusion

Categorically one may affirm that all history is *not* of Christ, and Christ is *not* in all history. Nor is Christ in all religious experiences or necessarily encountered by "men of faith." Satan too is busy in history and present in religious systems and experiences (2 Thess. 2:7–12; 2 Tim. 3:5–8; 1 John 4:1–3; Rev. 13:1, 2, 8, 11–15). These words cannot be erased from the Bible or history. They are horrifyingly factual. One dare not go beyond biblical criteria.

Does this make Christ less than Lord? No! Instead, it proves Him to be Lord as much as He proved His lordship on the Cross (Col. 2:15). In the dispensation of the fullness of times God will "gather together in one all things in Christ, both which are in heaven, and which are on earth; even in Him" (Eph. 1:10 KJV). For some undisclosed or veiled reason, however, He permits history to take a course beyond human comprehension, assuring man only that His is the victory. In this the Christian rests with confidence!

CHAPTER 5

The Destiny of the World and the Work of Missions

Michael Pocock

While many people are almost agnostic in matters of eschatology, declaring that nothing can be known for sure, Marxists and neoorthodox thinkers[1] and liberation theologians[2] are hard at work on the subject, and it affects what they do as their mission in life.

A person's concept of eschatology has a definite effect on his life and service right now. To radical thinkers, eschatology is a study of where things are going, and as such it controls their lifestyle and concept of ministry and mission. Until relatively recent days, eschatology was a concern primarily of conservative evangelicals, but after the cresting concern for prophetic truth in the 1890s few people outside the dispensational premillennial camp have been doing much thinking about eschatology except to react to premillennial dispensationalists.

The somewhat divisive arguments about the timing or order of Second Coming events have led some to disregard the issues in favor of "getting the job done." But it must be remembered that the "job" to be done takes place in the context of eschatological truth.

In Acts 2:17 Peter indicated that the events of Pentecost were happening literally in "eschatological days." The writer of Hebrews indicated the same when he wrote in Hebrews 1:2 that the earthly ministry of Christ was taking place in the last days. The sense of living in a time sphere that could end at any moment permeated the ministry of the apostles. Their expectation of the return of Christ qualified their own work and they expected it to do the same for others. "Since all these things are to be destroyed in this way, what sort of people ought you to be in holy conduct and godliness, looking for and hastening the coming of the day of God, on account of which the heavens will be destroyed by burning, and the elements will melt with intense heat" (2 Peter 3:11–12).

Quite clearly, Peter and the other New Testament writers, under the inspiration of the Holy Spirit, were not dissuaded by the passage of time from their belief that Christ could come at any moment. They did not expect believers to become any less conscious of coming prophetic events simply because more time passed than what some expected would be the case (3:3–10).

Conscious awareness of the imminence of Christ's return has ebbed and flowed through the years. It was obviously high during New Testament days, likewise near the close of the first millennium of the Christian era, and again toward the close of the nineteenth century. A high level of missionary activity has usually accompanied these peaks of interest, but when the church has not been absorbed with thoughts of the Lord's return, its belief about the nature of this age and the direction of history has still conditioned what the church has done as its mission.

Eschatology also affects the *spirit* in which one's mission is executed. Hope or despair, expectancy or despondency, patience or impatience, perseverance or disillusionment all depend to a large degree on one's eschatology. This chapter examines the effect of eschatology on missions, giving particular emphasis to the premillennial position. It is the author's contention that eschatology defines the *context, nature,* and *motivation* for missions. As such, this sometimes-neglected area merits close attention.

Certain eschatological convictions are held commonly by all devout believers, whether of amillennial, premillennial, or postmillennial persuasion. These convictions exercise a controlling effect on evangelical ministry and missions, though their very commonality sometimes removes them from what is popularly considered "eschatology." The reality of a future judgment—of believers for their work done as believers (2 Cor. 5:6–10) and the final, or Great White Throne, judgment of unbelievers (Rev. 20:11–15)—is held commonly by all evangelicals. The reality of eternal lostness outside the presence of God in conscious suffering (Rev. 20:10; 21:27) is likewise a common evangelical conviction. So also is the concept that heaven, while unknown in many details, is as real or more so, and infinitely more wonderful than anything in this life (2 Cor. 5:1–10).

These great rock-bottom convictions that are shared by all true believers who take the Word of God seriously—the return of Christ, the judgments, the eternal state—transform this life into an age with *limits,* an age of *preparation,* a time that is *relatively transient* as compared to eternity. Sacrifices can be made and limitations accepted when it is realized that either in a millennium on earth or in the eternal state, much greater issues are at stake, and the difficulties that plague humanity now—growing out of man's fallen nature—will all be set straight. "Now the dwelling of God is with men, and he will live with them. They will be his people, and God himself will be with them and be their God. He will wipe every tear from their eyes. There will be no more death or mourning or crying or pain, for the old order of things has passed away" (Rev. 21:3–5 NIV).

These convictions about the future are receiving less emphasis today than they should. The possibility of Christ's return at any moment does not dominate the thinking of many Christians. They plan and project as if there were no limits. The reality and consequences of lostness are being passed over; evangelism emphasizes salvation as present forgiveness and as the key to a present life of meaning and abundance. The awful consequences of unbelief are often forgotten. "They will be punished with everlasting destruction and shut out from the presence of the Lord and from the majesty of his power" (2 Thess. 1:9 NIV).

But apart from the great areas of eschatological unity, what are the distinctives of a premillennial approach, and how do they affect the missionary endeavor of its adherents?

Premillennialism Compared with Other Viewpoints

Premillennialism embraces a certain diversity of particular beliefs—though not as many as its detractors claim. In essence, however, premillennialists believe in a definite period of a thousand years in which Christ will personally and bodily rule the world and its nations (Rev. 20:1–10). Israel will enjoy a special reconstituted existence in which it will exhibit the spiritual and territorial fullness promised to it through the covenant with Abraham (Gen. 12:1–3; 15:1–20; Rom. 11:25–32). The church will also reign with Christ during this time (2 Tim. 2:12; Rev. 5:9–10). Christ will return before this millennial period (Rev. 20:1–10), and His saints will be raised from the dead to enter into the millennium (1 Cor. 15:20–28; 1 Thess. 4:13–18). Premillennialists agree that before the millennium things on earth will get progressively worse and will culminate in a unique time of terrible tribulation (Matt. 24:1–25). They differ with each other about whether believers living near the close of this age will be spared from the tribulation by a "rapture," a catching up to be with Christ (1 Thess. 4:13–18), or whether they will instead suffer through the tribulation. They generally believe that both resurrected and then-living believers will give account to Christ for their stewardship as believers. This judgment has nothing to do with heaven or hell, but relates to Christ's evaluation of believers' works and the assignment of rewards accordingly (2 Cor. 5:10).

During the one-thousand-year reign of Christ, Satan will be bound, but he will be loosed near the end of the millennium (Rev. 20:1–10). He will apparently be capable of leading a final rebellion against the Lord, which will be put down in a fiery finale. After this will come the Great White Throne judgment (vv. 11–15) and the assignment of the wicked to the lake of fire, and the eternal state will then commence with new heavens and a new earth (21:1–8). During the millennium, peace, universal equity, and justice will prevail (Jer. 23:5–6).

Though premillenarians believe that Christ's kingdom will come to earth literally in the future, and thus has not yet come, there is nevertheless an aspect of that kingdom present today. This is called "the mystery aspect."[3] Christ was rejected as King of Israel, and so the earthly kingdom that could then have ensued did not. On the other hand a "mystery form" of the kingdom was described by Christ (especially in the parables of Matt. 13). Ryrie enumerates these aspects of the mystery form of the kingdom.

1. Religious profession, with relatively little reality, will be a mark.
2. There will be many counterfeits among true believers, but they will be left until the end of the age.
3. False religion will grow abnormally under the guise of true religion.
4. Evil doctrine will permeate the kingdom.
5. The reality of the kingdom is something of great price, worth whatever effort to discover.
6. The kingdom will contain a great mixture of peoples up to the very end.[4]

Ryrie, a leading exponent of dispensational premillennialism, feels that even the mystery aspect of the kingdom does not represent the church, but if it does not, it at least describes the situation in Christendom during the past 1,900 years. Many premillennialists believe that the kingdom of God does refer to God's rule in believers' hearts now, but that this sense of His rule does not exhaust the meaning of the kingdom today and in the future.[5]

Premillennialism, like the other two main eschatological positions, takes Scripture seriously and attempts to base its conclusions on a system of hermeneutics which has been well accepted by faithful scholars everywhere, namely, the "normal" or literary, grammatical, historical approach to interpretation. Advocates of amillennialism and postmillennialism would say the same in regard to the bases of their own systems, but premillennialists feel that they understand everything in the Bible literally or in its normal sense. A premillennial scholar knows a simile or a metaphor when he sees one, as well as other obviously figurative or symbolic material. Most amillennialists would grant that if the key Scriptures regarding the millennium are taken literally, premillennialism must be the conclusion.[6] Many opponents of premillennialism suspect that the whole system is based solely on Revelation 20:1–10. Such is not the case. But in regard to that clear passage, Alford says:

> I cannot consent to distort words from their plain sense and chronological place in the prophecy, on account of any risk of abuses which the doctrine of the millennium may bring with it. Those who lived next to the Apostles, and the whole Church for 300 years, understood them in the plain literal sense: and it is a strange sight in these days to see expositors who are among the first in reference of antiquity, complacently casting aside the most cogent instance of consensus which primitive antiquity presents. As regards the text itself, no legitimate treatment of it will extort what is known as the spiritual interpretation now in fashion.[7]

Space does not permit a further defense of premillennial hermeneutics except to say that while amillennial interpreters are known to be devout men—people for whom premillennialists have great respect because of the fine contributions they have made in many areas of biblical exposition, ministry, and missions—it is difficult to discern why they depart from a normal understanding of Scripture when interpreting prophetic material.

Historically, premillennialism has been advocated by key church figures through the ages. Granted, it may differ in a few modern particulars from what was held in the early church. Nevertheless chiliasm, or belief in a literal reign of Christ on earth, has a long and honored history. Ryrie notes that "in the first and purist centuries the Church was premillennial in her belief."[8] He points out that Clement of Rome, Ignatius of Antioch, Papias, Justin Martyr, Irenaeus, Tertullian, and Cyprian were all premillennialists.[9]

Unfortunately the general premillennial orientation came to have some gross hyperliteral overtones, and a reaction set in. Certain forces—particularly Origen, in the Alexandrian school; Constantine, in his establishment of a Christian empire; and Augustine, who repudiated gross literalism and embraced the allegorical method as his hermeneutic—managed to turn the tide to a more amillennial perspective. These men saw the kingdom of God both as the growing power of the church and as an inward rule of Christ. Early amillennialists were as grossly allegorical as the premillennialists had been literal. The pendulum had swung precisely at the point when the church was gaining a distinctly Roman character. As a result amillennialism has been the eschatological orientation of the Roman Catholic Church from that day to this. Even the Reformers did not correct the imbalance, as they dealt primarily with matters of soteriology.

Premillennialism stayed alive primarily among those who were persecuted by the Roman Catholic Church (like the Waldensians) and those persecuted by the Reformers (the Anabaptists).

In the relatively modern post-Reformation period, Mede, Bengel, Alford, Lange, Faucett, Bonar, Ryle, Seiss, Delitzsch, and Darby all were premillennialists.[10] So were James H. Brooks, Nathaniel West, and William Blackstone in the last century. Among these some were Reformed and others were Arminian. In view of premillennialists like these, it is difficult to see why amillennialists like to insist that premillennialism is unhistorical and a North American hobbyhorse.

The Application of Premillennialism to Missionary Endeavor

Comment has already been made on some common elements of eschatology shared by believers of all eschatological persuasions. These may now be linked with some premillennial distinctives to see what the implications are for missions today. Three main eschatological ideas will be examined for their impact on missions.

THE IMMINENT RETURN OF CHRIST AND THE TRIBULATION PERIOD

Premillennialists have regarded this item as a key point in their life and service for Christ. They are certain from Scripture that Christ will return bodily and in such a way and time as to surprise many (Acts 1:11). He will come "as a thief in the night" (1 Thess. 5:2). The implications of the coming of Christ are that time is limited and that what believers are expected to do has an aspect of urgency to it.

Beyerhaus once mentioned that a dominant impression he received from the Consultation on World Evangelism at Pattaya, 1980 was that the participants appeared to be dealing with a totally open future.[11] These were evangelicals, and yet in their planning they failed to think consciously of the limits placed on them by the possible return of Christ at any moment. In contrast, turn-of-the-century evangelist and founder of The Evangelical Alliance Mission, Fredrik Franson, lived in the daily expectation of Christ's return. Edvard Torjesen has chronicled the life of this great man of God.[12] Torjesen was so impressed with the controlling aspect of Christ's return on Franson that he chose the theme of Christ's coming for a paper read in honor of Franson to a gathering of fourteen missionary societies at Ewersbach, West Germany in 1983. The interesting point is that Franson had founded or inspired the founding of all fourteen of these societies from Europe and North America.[13] Like many others of his day, Franson was energized by his conviction that Christ could come at any time. This conviction both placed a limit (unknown to him) on the time he had to work and at the same time lent an urgency to fulfilling his mission. He evangelized across Europe and North America and channeled many hundreds of his own converts into missions through the China Inland Mission and the Scandinavian Alliance Mission (which later became TEAM) and thirteen other societies.

The almost uniform response to Franson's revivalism and evangelism and emphasis on the Second Coming was a concern for missions. Everywhere his hearers sought to start sending agencies where there were none and to get to the fields as they heard his challenge concerning the return of Christ. Franson and Moody frequently worked together and shared a similar concern for prophetic truth. Both were premillennialists; both were consumed by the Great Commission as the Christian responsibility par excellence during the time allotment given them *until Christ returns*. Christ Himself had set the commission as His primary concern until the "end of the age" (Matt. 28:19–20). As the evangelization of all nations, the task was integrally connected with the purpose of God in history expressed in the Abrahamic Covenant, "All peoples [plural] on earth will be blessed through you" (Gen. 12:3 NIV). To these men evangelism and missions were part of the purpose of history—the reason time goes on. In this they agreed with Peter when he said the only reason Christ had not returned in New Testament times was the patience of God toward the unconverted: "[He] is patient toward you, not wishing for any to perish but for all to come to repentance" (2 Peter 3:10). Moody, possessed by this same concern, was a major motivating force behind the formation of the Student Volunteer Movement that ultimately sent thousands of missionaries to the field.[14]

Although Howard does not connect Moody's conviction of the Second Coming to his evangelistic and missionary impact, it is no mistake that the Bible institute founded by Moody, which became the model for hundreds of similar schools, has been a major bulwark of both missions and premillennialism. Cox, a rather unsympathetic amillennialist, has said that American premillennialism can be reduced to the eschatology of the Bible college movement.[15] It is also an observable fact that as major denominational mission efforts began to wane in the first half of this century, most evangelical missionaries were being produced by the Bible college movement.[16]

Premillennialists differ as to whether the task of world evangelism will be accomplished before the millennium or before Christ returns prior to the Great Tribulation. Christ Himself said that the gospel of the kingdom will be preached among all nations, and then the end will come (Matt. 24:14). Many evangelicals take this to mean that Christ cannot come until the task is finished. In this sense only the need to spread the gospel to all nations or people groups hinders the Lord's return. They do not expect to be surprised by Christ's return; they hope to facilitate it by obeying the missionary mandate.

Premillennialists who believe that Christ will return before the Tribulation believe that they could very well be surprised by Christ's return. They notice that Revelation 7:4–8 says 144,000 Israelites will be "sealed" to prevent their destruction. These are considered by pretribulationists to be witnesses during the time of the Great Tribulation. It is *their* work that actually completes the task of world evangelism. Pretribulational thinkers believe that by the work of these witnesses, the "great multitude, which no one could count, from every nation and all tribes and peoples and tongues" (Rev. 7:9), are finally saved. These believers who represent a comprehensive mix of the world's people are "ones who come out of the great tribulation, and they have washed their robes and made them white in the blood of the Lamb" (v. 14). The conclusion seems to be that whether the 144,000 are the evangelists who reach the last unreached people groups, it *is* during the final Great Tribulation that the task is finished.

If there are any implications of this view for pretribulation advocates, it is this: Avoid being complacent about completing the Great Commission. Do not rely on a future group of witnesses to finish the job. Aside from whether world evangelization precedes the Lord's return, believers are admonished to "live holy and godly lives as [they] look forward to the day of God and speed its coming" (2 Peter 3:11–12 NIV). What is it that could hasten the Lord's coming? Apparently it is a combination of personal and corporate holiness in the church, an attitude of eagerness about the Lord's return, and involvement in that for which history now continues—the evangelization of the lost.

THE POSTPONED KINGDOM

Premillennialists, especially of dispensational persuasion, are convinced that the kingdom Christ offered Israel was both spiritual and material in nature. Since the kingdom was rejected on both counts by the nation, although accepted by some, it was withdrawn in its material aspect. This is the meaning of the parable of the tenants in Matthew 21:33–44. Israel did not produce the fruit of righteousness, and so the kingdom was taken from them and offered to "another people" which, of course, turned out to be the Gentiles. However, they did not, on belief, receive an earthly kingdom, but they did become the people of God (Rom. 9:25–26).

Premillennialists believe that the church is in a real sense the people of God, and that from the point of view of relationship to God, they have entered into the covenant with Abraham (Acts 3:24–26). Premillennialists differ from amillennialists on this point. Premillennialists believe that the material promises to Abraham will yet be fulfilled to Israel when it is finally brought to belief in Christ. Paul clearly stated that God is not finished with the nation of Israel (Rom. 11:1–11). In this age God unites believing Jews and Gentiles in the church, which is the present manifestation of the people of God and which in a *real* but *partial* sense represents the kingdom of God (Eph. 2:11–22). The church is the kingdom in its spiritual sense of *salvation* and *relationship to God*. This kingdom was preached by the apostles after the rejection of Christ by Israel and represents the content of Paul's preaching (Acts 28:31).

Amillennialists believe that there is no more kingdom of God than what is seen or experienced of the rule of God in the lives of believers and the church and in sovereign control of the world at large. They believe that the premillennial expectation of the literal kingdom in the millennium is, as Cox clearly says, no more than an extension of the materialistic mistake of the Pharisees and the bumbling, materialistic expectation of the pre-Spirit-filled apostles.[17] He ignores the fact of the disciples' last exchange of words with Christ when they asked, "Is it at this time You are restoring the kingdom to Israel?" Christ's response was not, "How long are you going to persist in your mistaken impression that I was offering a terrestrial kingdom?" It was simply, "It is not for you to know times or epochs which the Father has fixed by His own authority" (Acts 1:6–7).

Premillennialists believe, then, that believers today are in the Church Age and that this age is not a fulfillment of all the promises to Abraham. But, since God is true to His promises and since the calling (election) of God is without repentance (Rom. 11:29), all these promises will be fulfilled in a millennial, terrestrial reign of Christ.

The Church Age, as can be observed from the last two thousand years of history, has not been marked by the existence or growth (as postmillennialists believe) of universal justice, brotherhood, and equity. Premillennialists are not even expecting that these characteristics will ever mark the present age. Premillennialists are realists. They believe that equating the kingdom with the church brings disappointment as with the Roman Catholic expression of the kingdom. It is not because Catholics are inherently worse or more mistaken than anyone else, but because they, like other branches of the church, are a *mixture* of redeemed and unregenerate people, and all participate in the fallen nature.

Premillennialists do not believe any *system* set up in this age has a chance of realizing true kingdom of God characteristics. Calvin's Geneva was a fine effort, but it failed over *fallenness*. Marxism has, does, and will fail, not because it is the wrong theory of social arrangement, but because it fails to comprehend that its most radical adherents do not have the *capacity* to produce the society to which they aspire. The same is true of democratic capitalism. No efforts will make these systems perfect. None of these systems can be *saved* or *redeemed* as the liberationists believe. The radical reordering of the world will occur only when Christ returns and establishes His millennial reign.

Meanwhile the principal task of believers is to preach the gospel, teach new believers to obey all the commands of Christ (Matt. 28:19–20), and participate fully in the formation and life of the body of Christ, His church. As Christ was compassionate, so believers are to be compassionate. They are to "do good to all men, especially to those who are of the household of faith" (Gal. 6:10). They are to practice personal, family, and corporate integrity (Eph. 4:17–32). They are to obey and seek the good of governments and rulers (Rom. 13:1–14). But believers in the present age will not attempt the overthrow of unjust governments or societies, or establish new ones *as a church or as a part of its mission.* As Franson often preached,

> God is doing what he promises to do in this age: letting his Gospel be preached among the peoples and calling out from among them one people, a small flock—His Church, His Bride—whom he will be lifting up now any day to meet him in the air.
>
> It is not before the next age that we shall see nations as such be saved. Any attempt during this age to produce a Christian nation is merely an attempt to go ahead of God. . . . The only option open now is for individuals to become Christ's people.[18]

This focus on individual salvation and incorporation into the body of Christ certainly squares with Christ's priority. "I will build My church and the gates of Hades shall not overpower it" (Matt. 16:18). The same is true of Ephesians 5:25–33, where Paul said Christ's purpose in sacrificially dying on Calvary was to bring the church into being, to make that body holy through the application of the Word, and to present the church as a spotless bride to Himself.

Because of this importance placed on salvation and the church, premillennialists are concerned about her formation and concentrate on that rather than on the redemption of societies that are nowhere said in the Word to be the objects of redemption. The Bible envisions the salvation of *peoples,* not *countries*. The Bible sees believers acting as *salt*, agents that slow the putrefaction of the world to allow for the work of calling out Christ's body.

Many amillennialists have been missionaries. Many have done fine work in leading individuals to Christ and planting churches. But there are disturbing possibilities in amillennialism into which some of its adherents have fallen. These possibilities include the identification of the church with the kingdom to the extent that in societies where the church predominates, both society at large and the church in particular have become confused, mixed multitudes. Evangelism has faltered and complacency has set in. This has been especially true in Europe and Latin America, and has occurred in large segments of Christendom under both Roman Catholic and Protestant situations. In both cases the eschatological position is amillennialism. State churches and amillennial eschatology have historically gone together.

Liberation theology in Latin America has made a major play for the redemption of Latin societies. On the Latin scene two amillennial entities, the traditional Roman Catholic Church (closely identified with many repressive governments) and Catholic orders like the Maryknolls, are present. The latter are identified with the oppressed masses and advocate a mixture of personal piety and devotion with radical discipleship aimed at the overthrow of repressive regimes backed by the traditional church. Liberationists, whose literature is eagerly translated and circulated by the Maryknolls and Orbis Books in North America, are Marxist-oriented. They have accepted the possibility of Christianity at the personal devotional level with Marxist socialism at the socio-economic-political level.[19]

Liberationists are disposed to violence in their quest for liberation in Latin America. This violent role has been, they would say, thrust on them by the violence of the entrenched establishment. But liberationists—both Roman Catholic and Protestant—view the destruction of the old social order and establishment of a new one as the main element of their *mission,* an element without which, they say, personal salvation is meaningless. Eschatology is at the heart of the liberationist struggle and is frequently referred to by Moltmann,[20] Alves, Assmann, and Gutiérrez. The latter notes, "The Bible presents eschatology as the driving force of salvific history radically oriented toward the future. Eschatology is thus not just one more element of Christianity, but the very key to understanding the Christian faith."[21]

What has happened eschatologically in the thinking of established Roman Catholic Church leaders and radical new thinkers in Roman Catholicism? How could they be on opposite ends of the spectrum, with one defending an existing oppressive order and the other seeking its violent overthrow? The answer is that the traditional Roman Catholics in Latin America, like their brethren elsewhere, view the church as the kingdom. In situations where the majority of the population is considered a part of the church, the kingdom of God is viewed as inseparable from the political kingdom. Those who are in control have a vested interest in supporting one another on theological grounds as well as pragmatic grounds. An amillennial eschatology coupled with other shortcomings has in some cases ruined the established church and made it an integral part of repressive societies, rather like Israel as a theocracy in its worst moments.

The liberationist branch of the church is also controlled by its eschatology. "The Gospel does not get its political dimension from one or another particular option, but from the very nucleus of its message. If this message is subversive, it is because it takes on Israel's hope."[22] Gutiérrez does not attempt, as do many amillennialists, to spiritualize away the concrete promise of the kingdom to Israel. He, like many Marxists, is utopian, but nevertheless he is in a sense amillennial. He believes the only time the kingdom can be fully realized is now. There will be no return of Christ to set things straight in an earthly kingdom. All that can and must be rectified must be accomplished now. A liberationist struggles to *realize* the kingdom now. His failure is that he minimizes the spiritual aspect of conversion and the mystical aspect of the kingdom in the church today. To a liberationist, personal salvation and growth in the church are escapism. Lack of involvement in the struggle to produce a just society is viewed as truncated Christianity.

How can evangelical premillennialists—who are generally despised by liberationists for leading the evangelicals into an "escapist" nonconfrontational political stance—respond to the legitimate need for more just societies here and now? Paradoxically, the answer is found in the grain of wheat analogy (John 12:24–26).

A liberationist will fail in this age, just as the traditional church-as-kingdom-of-God view has failed, because he is getting ahead of God's program and attempting to build what cannot be constructed without a totally regenerated man and society. When a person, like a grain of wheat, falls into the political, social, and economic ground and dies to self-reliance and confidence in mankind, and when he throws himself on God for salvation from sin, he is personally reborn; he really does enter the kingdom that matters (John 3:3)—and he rises with Christ to multiplied fruitfulness. In Christ a person finally has the capacity to overcome his human, fallen problems that constitute the stumbling block to utopian societies. What is it that plagues society in Latin America?

Is it the system or the people? Do not the rich oppress by their covetousness, their thievery, their violence? Are not these cared for adequately only in the new man? Why is it that across Latin America, to say that one is an evangelical is to say that one is *sano, sin vicios, confiable* ("clean, without vices, and reliable"). Does this not give a clue as to what is really meaningful in effecting larger social gains, namely, the proliferation of individual conversions and growth within the body of Christ? Is this not exactly what Christ ordained believers to do in this age?

Evangelicals are indeed concerned about the social disjunction around them. They have been historically involved at every level of literacy, education, health, prison reform, abolition of slavery, and the right to life itself. But an evangelical, and particularly a premillennial one, is a realist. His realism does not make him a pessimist, because he is a witness to the power of Christ to deliver individuals and families from the worst of human conditions, and he knows the truth of 2 Corinthians 5:17. His realism makes him patient. He knows whole societies will not be set right until Christ returns, but individuals can be given the power to respond to the situations they face, and they can find equity, brotherhood, and supportiveness within the Christian community.

Liberationists would charge dispensationalists with "reformism and developmentalism," twin futilities to which the only answer, according to liberation theology, is revolution. According to premillennialism, the revolution is *personal,* not *societal,* in the present age, and Christ, not the church, will be the Head Revolutionary when He sets up the kingdom in its fullest earthly manifestation. A premillennial missionary knows what his most important contribution should be—and it is largely dictated by his eschatology.

THE ETERNAL STATE

All true believers hold in common the reality of heaven and hell, of paradise and reprobation. In spite of the wonderful and yet horrendous reality of these polarities, they are seldom addressed in reference to the modern missionary endeavor. Doug Wicks pointed out in *Wherever* magazine:

> In our witnessing attempts today we tend to focus strictly on the good news of the Good News. Rarely is the bad news part of the gospel message mentioned: that eternal damnation is in line for those who do not acknowledge Jesus Christ as the Son of God. . . .

> Without question, hell is real (Mark 9:43, 45), terrible (Isa. 66:24), and eternal (Dan. 12:2).
>
> Whatever wishful-thinking trap we fall into, the fact won't change: lostness is forever.
>
> The Book of Romans states that God reveals Himself to all people through creation (1:20) and through their conscience (2:25); therefore, people are without excuse (2:1), and their salvation lies in their acceptance of Christ as Savior (Acts 4:12). That involves us. It's our job in God's divine plan to lead others to Christ (Rom. 10:14).[23]

The possibility of eternal loss or gain must be kept in focus. It is clear that among denominations and mission societies where the concept of eternal damnation has been lost, and where appreciation for the real wonders of heaven have been minimized, the *motivation* for continued missionary endeavor has been diminished and the type of work that remaining workers have done has been changed. Works of temporal benefit and assistance, admittedly much needed, have taken the place of evangelistic enterprise. Where the forerunners of the modern ecumenical movement cried out for "the evangelization of the world in this generation," their modern counterparts within that movement now seek the political kingdom and horizontal reconciliation.

> Salvation to them is a force that "works in the struggle for economic justice against the exploitation of people by people. Salvation works in the struggle for human dignity against political oppression by their fellow men. Salvation works in the struggle for solidarity against the alienation of persons from persons. Salvation works in the struggle of hope against despair in personal life."[24]

Some observers sensed a return by liberal theologians to certain evangelical values at the Sixth World Council of Churches at Vancouver, July-August 1983,[25] but the concern for personal salvation in the light of eternal realities is still at a low ebb in ecumenical circles.[26]

It is a blessed thing to have a personal walk with God here and now and a tragedy to pass through life unforgiven and without reference to the One who makes all things come alive with meaning. It is also a tragedy to live life in an oppressed society. At the same time, what makes missions and evangelism doubly significant is the eternal state of man after this life is finished.

Who has not been profoundly moved at the description in Revelation 21 of the heavenly state? God will be with His people forever. He will wipe away all tears. He will wipe away all the old order with the repeated failures of fallen beings. No church buildings and no temple will be needed because God and the Lamb *are* the temple. There will be no need of sun or moon, for God is the light. No fear for safety and security will be experienced; the saints may come and go as they please, for the picture is one of open doors and open communion with God and His saints.

The thrill of this prospect for the future and the present reality of a walk with God provide enough incentive to drive any believer forward, not to obtain it for himself alone, but for the uncounted numbers from every people group—every tribe, language, people, and nation (Rev. 5:9; 7:9) who will one day cry out around the throne of God, "Salvation belongs to our God, who sits on the throne, and to the Lamb. . . . Amen! Praise and glory and wisdom and thanks and honor and power and strength be to our God for ever and ever. Amen!" (7:10–12 NIV).

CHAPTER 6

Paul's Approach to the Great Commission in Acts 14:21–23

David F. Detwiler

In anticipation of the Cross, Jesus declared to His Father, "I have brought you glory on earth by completing the work you gave me to do" (John 17:4).[1] On reaching the end of their days, in this world, followers of Christ should be able to say the same words, knowing that they have done their part in completing the work God has given them to do, namely, to "make disciples of all nations" (Matt. 28:19).

But what is involved in fulfilling this task? How are believers to carry out this "Great Commission" of the Lord Jesus Christ? This article explores the possibility that Acts 14:21–23 serves as an outline of—and brief commentary on—the discipleship process Jesus has called His followers to pursue in their own lives and to encourage in the lives of others.

The passage briefly describes the latter part of Paul's first missionary journey:

> They preached the good news in that city and won a large number of disciples. Then they returned to Lystra, Iconium and Antioch, strengthening the disciples and encouraging them to remain true to the faith. "We must go through many hardships to enter the kingdom of God," they said. Paul and Barnabas appointed elders for them in each church and, with prayer and fasting, committed them to the Lord, in whom they had put their trust.

Commentators assess the importance of these verses variously. A few, such as Stott, feel a pattern or policy for fulfilling the Great Commission is evident in the passage.[2] Others focus on the emphasis given to the role of suffering in the Christian life (v. 22). Marshall, for example, says of the passage, "Its importance lies in its teaching about the way in which the church must live in a hostile environment and equip itself accordingly."[3] Still others seem primarily interested in what verse 23 reveals about elders in the local church.[4] While none of these emphases is necessarily incorrect or unimportant, this study seeks to draw these strands together into a unified whole in Luke's summary of Paul's remarkable ministry in southern Galatia.

Making Disciples: The Fruit of Proclaiming the Good News

The passage begins with what is essentially a passing note on Paul and Barnabas's successful evangelism in the city of Derbe: "They preached the good news in that city and won a large number of disciples" (v. 21).[5] Little else is known about the Christians in Derbe, except that Paul eventually returned to strengthen the church there (Acts 15:36, 41; 16:1, 5, and perhaps again in 18:23), and that Gaius, a member of that congregation, later accompanied Paul on part of his third missionary journey (20:4).

What is highly significant concerning the ministry in Derbe, however, is Luke's use of the verb μαθητεύω ("make disciples") in describing the results of Paul and Barnabas's preaching. The only occurrence of this word other than in Matthew (13:52; 27:57; 28:19) is in Acts 14:21, where it is an aorist participle translated in the NIV as "won . . . disciples." Why did Luke use this verb here? Was he in fact aware of Christ's command to "make disciples of all nations"?

Disciples (μαθηταί) had been made before this time, for, as Wilkins explains, "Throughout the book of Acts, *disciples* is a title for those who have placed their faith in Jesus and are now followers of Jesus, converts."[6] To illustrate, those who are identified as "believers" in Acts 4:32 are also called "disciples" in 6:2 and "the Lord's disciples" in 9:1. Further, those in Syrian Antioch who "believed and turned to the Lord" (11:21) are referred to as "disciples" and later are designated "Christians" (11:26). Thus it is no surprise that in 14:21 those who responded to the preaching of the good news (εὐαγγελισάμενοι) are identified as "disciples," for "evangelism is the starting point for making disciples."[7] Whenever people "turn to God in repentance and have faith in our Lord Jesus" (20:21), they become disciples of Jesus.

However, as noted above, the verb "make disciples" had not been used previously in the Book of Acts to describe the fruit of proclaiming Christ, and there is surely a reason for this. Luter suggests that Acts 14:21–23 is "a crucial moment for Luke to comment on the apostle's disciple-making ministry in fulfillment of the Great Commission."[8]

In light of the summary nature of the narrative, one may rightly speculate that Luke deliberately used the word in order to show the scope of its fulfillment in Paul's ministry. Luke had previously recorded in Acts 2:41–42 that Peter was essentially "making disciples" at Pentecost (though the term is not used) through evangelistic preaching, baptism, and teaching (the scope of the Great Commission as outlined by Jesus; Luke 24:47; Matt. 28:18–20). Apparently in Acts 14 Luke explicitly stated how the apostle began to "make disciples of all nations" by "preaching the good news" in a pagan city (with baptism likely to follow, as was Paul's custom; cf. Acts 16:15, 33; 19:5).[9] However, this only brings the reader through the first step in the process of fulfilling the Great Commission, and so Luke continued.

Nurturing Disciples: The Emphasis on Spiritual Growth

After spending some time with the "large number of [new] disciples" in Derbe (Acts 14:21a), Paul's missionary team "returned to Lystra, Iconium and [Pisidian] Antioch, strengthening the disciples [previously made in those cities] and encouraging them to remain true to the faith" (vv. 21b-22a).

Lystra, Iconium, and Antioch had indeed been ripe for harvest (13:48–49; 14:1, 7, 20), but they were also (and apparently more so) hostile to the gospel and those who proclaimed it (13:50; 14:2, 5–6, 19; cf. 2 Tim. 3:11). "It took courage to return to the very places that had resisted the gospel and mistreated the messengers, yet the decision to return was not dictated by bravado but by the practical necessity of shepherding the converts"[10] (Longenecker, among others, notes that these cities experienced an annual change of administrators, and thus the danger may have subsided if such a change had occurred.[11]).

This "shepherding of converts" was central to Paul's understanding of his mission, as Bowers explains.

> Insofar as the pattern of Paul's plans and movements is available to us, there is no restless rushing from one new opening to another but rather a methodical progress concerned both with initiating work in new areas and at the same time with bringing the emergent groups in those areas to stable maturity.[12]

Thus it should not be surprising to find the strengthening and encouraging of young disciples as the gospel progresses in the Book of Acts, and this is exactly the case. For example, as the gospel spread from Jerusalem to Antioch of Syria, Barnabas "encouraged [the new disciples there] to remain true to the Lord with all their hearts" (11:23) and "for a whole year [he] and Saul met with the church and taught great numbers of people" (v. 26). Further, at the outset of Paul's second missionary journey, the apostle "went through Syria and Cilicia [and Galatia] strengthening the churches" (15:41; cf. 16:1, 5). Similarly on his third journey Paul "traveled from place to place throughout the region of Galatia and Phrygia, strengthening all the disciples" (18:23).

Such nurturing was far more than an afterthought in the wake of successful evangelism. It was (and is) central to the process of "making disciples," as is seen in Acts 14:22a, and in the insightful analysis of this verse by Wilkins.

> Luke's wording suggests a connection with the discipleship process outlined by Jesus in the Great Commission, because "strengthening the souls of the disciples" and "encouraging them to remain in the faith" implies the kind of "teaching them to observe all I commanded you" that Jesus gave as the ongoing process of growth in discipleship.[13]

What is perhaps not expected is the summary of the encouragement given to the disciples in Lystra, Iconium, and Antioch: "We must go through many hardships to enter the kingdom of God" (Acts 14:22b). As Bruce notes, "It is almost taken for granted throughout the New Testament that tribulation is the normal lot of Christians in this age."[14] (Note the word "must" [δεῖ] in the verse.) This is not to say that suffering is the means to obtaining salvation (for the Bible teaches otherwise), but rather that suffering is to be expected by those traveling along the narrow way of faith in Christ.[15] Reflecting on his first missionary journey, Paul made this abundantly clear to Timothy: "You, however, know all about my teaching, my way of life, my purpose, faith, patience, love, endurance, persecutions, sufferings—what kinds of things happened to me in Antioch, Iconium and Lystra, the persecutions I endured. Yet the Lord rescued me from all of them. In fact, everyone who wants to live a godly life in Christ Jesus will be persecuted" (2 Tim. 3:10–12).

Paul was realistic as he nurtured new believers in the faith. While he certainly taught that the life of God's kingdom consists in "righteousness, peace and joy in the Holy Spirit" (Rom. 14:17), he nevertheless emphasized the certainty of suffering (Phil. 1:29; 1 Thess. 3:2–4; 2 Thess. 1:5). The life of discipleship, according to the apostle, is not an easy one.

Organizing Disciples: The Provision of Spiritual Leadership

Such an emphasis on suffering might well lead to despair were it not for the "encouragement from being united with Christ, [the] comfort from his love, [and the] fellowship with the Spirit" that is experienced in the body of Christ (Phil. 2:1). And Paul was concerned with supplying new disciples with this very dynamic. In other words Paul's goal was to plant churches that could provide ongoing nurture through qualified leaders. "Paul and Barnabas appointed elders for them in each church" (Acts 14:23).

"Disciples" are now explicitly identified as members of a "church," and this is what Paul had been working toward all along. As Bowers concludes,

> Paul's missionary vocation finds its sense of fulfillment in the presence of firmly established churches. What lies, in effect, within the compass of Paul's familiar formula "proclaiming the gospel" is, I suggest, not simply an initial preaching mission but the full sequence of activities resulting in settled churches.[16]

The importance of this approach can hardly be overstated with regard to fulfilling the Great Commission. The local church is vital in the process of making disciples.

> Perhaps the single, most important development of discipleship illustrated in the book of Acts is the establishment of the community of disciples, the church. The community is what focuses the life of discipleship, provides the opportunities for growth in discipleship, and creates the environment for reproducing new generations of disciples.[17]

Spiritual leadership is key to effective local church ministry, and Paul and Barnabas provided for this need as they established churches in Lystra, Iconium, and Antioch. In an apparently relatively short time, they were able to appoint in each church "elders"[18]—those who had reached a certain level of spiritual maturity that enabled them to serve the church by strengthening and encouraging the disciples just as Paul and Barnabas had done.

While one may question whether such maturity could have been gained so quickly, it must be remembered that many Jews and God-fearing Gentiles were likely among the converts (cf. Acts 14:1), and their growth would have been understandably advanced. Further, as Bruce suggests, "perhaps Paul and Barnabas were more conscious of the presence and power of the Holy Spirit in the communities,"[19] enabling them to identify God's provision for leadership in each church. Whatever the case, it appears that

Paul was not content to leave these cities until leaders were in place (cf. Titus 1:5).

One final observation, made by Stott, may be added concerning the provision of spiritual leadership: "We notice that [the leadership] is both local and plural—local in that the elders were chosen from within the congregation, not imposed from without, and plural in that the familiar modern pattern of 'one pastor one church' was simply unknown."[20]

Entrusting Disciples: The Commitment to God's Care

Luke concluded his outline of Paul's ministry through southern Galatia by noting that "with prayer and fasting, [Paul and Barnabas] committed them [the elders and, by implication, the churches] to the Lord, in whom they had put their trust" (Acts 14:23b).[21]

The word translated "committed" (παρέθεντο) was used by Jesus as He breathed His last words on the cross, "Father, into your hands I commit my spirit" (Luke 23:46), and later by Paul as he bade farewell to the elders of the Ephesian church, "Now I commit you to God and to the word of his grace" (Acts 20:32). This verb carries the sense of entrusting something to God's care,[22] and this is exactly how Paul left the churches he had founded on his missionary journey.

Having provided for the ongoing teaching of (and obedience to) everything Jesus commanded by appointing leaders in each community of disciples, the apostle then moved on.

> Paul cast [disciples] entirely on God for their personal and corporate life. He would not have them tied to his apron strings. He visited them, wrote to them, and sent some of the missionary team to encourage them, but Paul never made the churches dependent on him.[23]

The Apostle Paul surely understood, even in those early days of his ministry, that Jesus is the Head of the church (Col. 1:18), that each believer is indwelt by the Spirit of God (1 Cor. 3:16; Eph. 2:22), and that the Lord, who began a good work in each community of disciples, would "carry it on to completion" (Phil. 1:6). In other words, as Allen observed, Paul "believed that Christ was able and willing to keep that which he had committed to him."[24]

Having reached this point, Paul's work of fulfilling the Great Commission in southern Galatia was over. The task of "making disciples" could now begin anew in each church that was nurtured, organized, and entrusted to the Lord.

Implications of This Study

The most obvious implication of this study concerns the nature and strategy of missionary work. A commitment to the Great Commission means little if one fails to understand the scope of Jesus' command to "make disciples." Acts 14:21–23 provides the clarification that is needed.

Just over a decade ago Engel rightly asked, "Where is the local church in all our strategizing? How closely are our slogans and evangelistic methods tied to the creation of strong and vital local churches?"[25] His question remains valid today. Paul's missionary activity in Acts 14:21–23 makes a strong case for fulfilling the Great Commission not only by preaching the good news (although this is the necessary first step), but also by nurturing new disciples and organizing them into churches that can eventually provide for their own growth in discipleship. The apostle refused to stop short of this, and missionaries today should do likewise.[26]

But what of those who are not involved in missionary work (in the sense of cross-cultural church planting)? What can be learned and applied from Acts 14:21–23? A few brief implications may be offered, following the general structure of this study.

First, the discussion of verse 21 should make it abundantly clear that people become disciples the moment they believe the good news about Jesus Christ—not at some later point. As Willard creatively puts it,

> The disciple of Jesus is not the deluxe or heavy-duty model of the Christian—especially padded, textured, streamlined, and empowered for the fast lane on the straight and narrow way. He stands on the pages of the New Testament as the first level of basic transportation in the kingdom of God.[27]

The idea that one who has trusted in Christ for salvation is not yet a disciple of Jesus is not found in the Book of Acts. Rather, when a person becomes a Christian he or she embarks on the life of growing in the Lord as His disciple.

Second, following the example of Paul, older (i.e., more spiritually mature) disciples should be committed to strengthening and encouraging those who have begun the life of discipleship. It is not enough to rejoice in the decision people make to trust in Christ; older disciples must do all they can to help new disciples along in this commitment (and they should seek ongoing help for themselves as well).

Jesus made this clear when He declared that His followers should be "teaching them to obey everything I have commanded" (Matt. 28:20), including (and, according to Paul, especially) how to respond to the reality of suffering in the Christian life (Acts 14:22; cf. Matt. 5:10–12, 38–48; 1 Peter 4:12–19). Therein lies a challenge—and a word of encouragement—for all those engaged in teaching others to know and live biblical truth (whatever the context). Such ministry, according to both Jesus and Paul, is vital to fulfilling the Great Commission.

Third, it should be kept in mind that "to believe on Jesus draws a person into community, a community that defines its expectations, responsibilities, and privileges in terms of discipleship."[28] Spiritual leadership is crucial to the success of such a community, and therefore older disciples should not fail to shepherd new disciples into (and commit themselves to) a well-led church. It is virtually impossible to grow as a disciple apart from the loving fellowship and pastoral leadership provided by a strong local church. Paul understood this clearly, and so should believers today.

Fourth, older disciples should trust the Lord with their lives—and with the lives of others. While they may play a significant role during certain stages of the spiritual growth of other followers of Christ, they should be content to let these disciples go (or urge them on) as God provides for their strengthening and encouragement in other ways. As Paul's ministry indicates, this too is an important part of fulfilling the Great Commission.

CHAPTER 7

Paul's Corporate Evangelism in the Book of Acts

George W. Murray*

In 1971 my wife and I went to the largely unevangelized country of Italy as church planters with a mission agency that at that time had six church-planting couples in the country. Each couple was located in a separate city. Because so many Italian cities and towns were (and are) totally unevangelized, our mission leadership reasoned that its personnel should be spread out to cover more unreached territory. We, however, resisted this strategy, because we felt inadequate to do the work of evangelism and church planting by ourselves. After much discussion we persuaded our mission leadership to let us recruit a team of eight other missionaries to work with us in the unreached province of Pordenone, with a population of 300,000. We had a wonderful experience with that team, evangelizing together in a way that none of us was capable of doing alone, and planting a church in the capital city of the province.

During that time articles about teamwork in pioneer evangelism began appearing in missionary publications. Some articles questioned its validity,[1] while others strongly supported the concept.[2] Reading other missionary literature, I discovered that Jonathan Goforth, at the turn of the century, was convinced of the importance of doing evangelism corporately. "Now we have proved it so often that we have the conviction that we could go into any unevangelized center in North China with an earnest band of male and female workers and within a month have the beginning of a church for Jesus Christ."[3]

But most of all, my own experience in Italy convinced me of the importance of engaging in evangelism and church planting corporately. During that time, however, I kept asking myself if we had a strong biblical basis for how we were working. I was sure teamwork was good, because it worked! But does the Bible say anything about corporate evangelism? I decided to take a closer look.

Besides looking at data concerning corporate spiritual activity in the Old Testament and at Jesus' practice of having disciples and sending them out two by two, I examined the practice and teaching of Paul, the prominent New Testament missionary apostle. I concentrated my biblical research on Paul's practice of corporate evangelism in the Book of Acts and on his teaching about corporate witness in his Epistle to the Philippians. This article discusses the relevant data about Paul's practice in the Book of Acts.

An examination of Acts reveals that Paul was certainly not a "loner," but had extensive association with others during his life and ministry. There are a number of reasons why Paul lived, traveled, and worked together with other believers, one of which was to engage in the ministry of evangelism (Acts 9:28–30; 13:1–5, 13–16, 44–46; 14:1, 7, 20–21, 25; 17:1–15; 18:5–8). A close look at Acts reveals that other believers were often present when Paul engaged in evangelism, and in quite a few cases he and other believers actually evangelized corporately.

Paul's Association with Others in Acts

Although the Bible never states that Paul had disciples, clearly he had many close friends and associates with whom he lived and worked. Ellis points out that in the Book of Acts and Paul's epistles approximately one hundred individuals were associated with the apostle.[4] "In summary, the picture that emerges is that of a missionary with a large number of associates. Indeed, Paul is scarcely ever found without companions."[5] In the concluding reflections of his overall treatment of Paul's life, Bruce says,

> Paul has no place for the solitary life as an ideal; for all his apostolic energy he would have scouted the suggestion that "he travels the fastest who travels alone." He emphasizes the fellowship, the togetherness, of Christians in worship and action; they are members one of another, and all together members of Christ.[6]

A chronological survey of the Book of Acts makes Paul's emphasis on togetherness clear.

After conversion Paul spent several days with believers in Damascus (Acts 9:19).[7] Later, when he went to Jerusalem, he tried to join the disciples (v. 26). There he stayed with some apostles (v. 28)—namely, Barnabas, Peter, and James (v. 27; Gal. 1:18–19)—until they were constrained to send him off to Tarsus for his own protection (Acts 9:29–30).[8] He ministered together with Barnabas for a year among the believers in Antioch (11:25–26), went with Barnabas to Jerusalem with the famine relief (v. 30), and then went out on his first missionary journey with Barnabas and John Mark (13:2–5). Then he traveled with Barnabas and other believers to the Jerusalem Council (15:2).

On his second missionary journey Paul set out with Silas (15:40) and recruited Timothy in Lystra to join their team (16:3). In Troas, Paul and his companions were joined by Luke—attested by the abrupt change in the Lucan narrative from "they" (v. 8) to "we" (v. 10)—and all four of them went to Philippi together (16:12–18).[9] From Philippi, Paul, Silas, and Timothy went together to Thessalonica, leaving Luke in Philippi, as attested by the return to the use of "they" in the narrative (17:1–15). The three men ministered together in Thessalonica and Berea until the believers were compelled to send Paul to Athens in order to escape danger (vv. 13–15). Arriving in Athens, Paul instructed those who accompanied him, asking "for Silas and Timothy to come to him as soon as possible" (v. 15). Though Paul ministered alone in Athens, he did so while waiting for Silas and Timothy to join him (v. 16). Paul went on to Corinth, where he stayed with Aquila and Priscilla, perhaps for reasons of ministry as well as material reasons (18:1–3).[10] Silas and Timothy eventually joined Paul in Corinth (v. 5).[11] From 1 Thessalonians 3:6 it seems that when Silas and Timothy arrived in Corinth, they brought Paul a good report of the situation in Thessalonica, occasioning Paul's first letter to the church there. Paul's second letter to Thessalonica was probably also written from Corinth, not too long after the first letter.[12] Both of these letters were sent by Paul, Silas, and Timothy, as seen from the opening verse of each letter, and from the fact that both letters were completely written in the plural (with the exception of 1 Thessalonians 2:18 and 2 Thessalonians 2:5; 3:17). In fact in all but two of his letters to churches (Romans and Ephesians), Paul included others with him in the opening salutations. Even in his letter to Philemon, Paul included Timothy in the salutation (Philem. 1). Aquila and Priscilla accompanied Paul to Ephesus, where he left them and went on to Antioch via Caesarea (Acts 18:18–22).

On Paul's third missionary journey he went through Asia Minor to Ephesus (18:23; 19:1).[13] Because of opposition in Ephesus he moved from the synagogue to the lecture hall of Tyrannus, taking the disciples with him (19:9). Timothy and Erastus were with Paul in Ephesus where they "ministered to him" (v. 22). Gaius and

Aristarchus were also with Paul in Ephesus and were called his "traveling companions" (v. 29). When Paul went from Greece to Macedonia, he was accompanied by seven men (Sopater, Aristarchus, Secundus, Gaius, Timothy, Tychicus, and Trophimus; 20:4). Joining Paul again at Philippi (20:5–6), Luke stayed with Paul on his trip back to Jerusalem (21:15) and on to Rome (27:1; 28:16). In his farewell discourse to the Ephesian elders Paul referred to "my companions" (20:34 NIV), for whom he provided by working with his own hands.

Arriving in Jerusalem, Paul was received by the brethren, James, and the elders (21:17–18). Later in Caesarea, Felix told a guard to "permit [Paul's] friends to take care of his needs" as a prisoner (24:23 NIV).[14] Besides Luke, Aristarchus accompanied Paul on his trip to Rome (27:1–2).[15] In Sidon the centurion guard allowed Paul to go ashore so that "his friends . . . might provide for his needs" (27:3 NIV). In Italy Paul was met and cared for by the brethren in Puteoli (28:14), and on his trip to Rome he was met by brethren who came down from the capital city to accompany him (v. 15). At the sight of these companions Paul thanked God and was encouraged (v. 15). Although the Acts narrative ends with Paul in Rome, Paul's epistles reveal three other people who were closely associated with Paul in his first Roman imprisonment. They were Epaphras (Col. 1:7; Philem. 24), Onesimus (Philem. 10, 16), and Epaphroditus (Phil. 2:25–30; 4:18).[16]

From this brief survey of Paul's ministry the picture emerges of a man who spent much of his Christian life and work in the company of other Christians. Paul's love and need for the company of others are evident in his own words in 2 Timothy 4:9–11, written during his second Roman imprisonment: "Do your best to come to me quickly, for Demas, because he loved this world, has deserted me and has gone to Thessalonica. Crescens has gone to Galatia, and Titus to Dalmatia. Only Luke is with me. Get Mark and bring him with you, because he is helpful to me in my ministry."

Reasons Paul Joined with Others

From the Acts narrative a number of reasons for Paul's corporate relationships can be observed. He lived and worked with others for these reasons: (a) to have fellowship (Acts 9:19, 26–28); (b) to have companionship (18:18; 19:29; 20:34; 27:1–2; 28:15; (c) to have protection (9:30; 17:15; 20:2–4);[17] (d) to have encouragement

(28:15); (e) to form an official delegation to attend the Jerusalem Council (15:2) and to deliver famine relief (11:30; 20:4);[18] (f) to provide for material needs (18:1–3;[19] 24:23; 27:3; 28:14); (g) to engage in the ministry of edification (11:25–26; 14:21–23; 15:35; 15:40–41; 16:4–5; 19:9; 20:6–38); and (h) to engage in the ministry of evangelism (9:28–30; 13:1–5, 13–16, 44–46; 14:1, 7, 20–21, 25; 17:1–15; 18:5–8).[20]

Paul and Corporate Witness in Acts[21]

Paul's practice of corporate witness as seen in Acts[22] includes instances in which he evangelized when others were present, and instances in which he and others evangelized together (though it is sometimes difficult to distinguish these two).

PAUL EVANGELIZING WITH OTHER CHRISTIANS PRESENT

Acts 9:27–28. When Paul went from Damascus (where he had been proclaiming in the synagogues that Jesus is the Son of God, v. 20) to Jerusalem, he was with the apostles (v. 27) and was "moving about freely in Jerusalem, speaking out boldly in the name of the Lord" (v. 28). The words "moving about freely" are literally "going in and going out." This may suggest that he ministered in the presence of the apostles.

Acts 13:16–41. In Pisidian Antioch (v. 14) Paul stood up in the synagogue (v. 16) and preached an evangelistic message. He told the Jews that "through [Jesus] forgiveness of sins is proclaimed to you" (v. 38). Though Paul was the only one who spoke, it is clear that Barnabas was with him (v. 42).

Acts 14:8–20. In Lystra Paul was the one who spoke (v. 12). That Paul was preaching the gospel can be seen by the immediate context ("they continued to preach the gospel," v. 7) and from the apostles' words to the crowd: "We are bringing you good news, telling you to turn from these worthless things to the living God" (v. 15 NIV). Although Barnabas was present (vv. 1, 12, 14, 20), Paul did the speaking. In fact the people called him "Hermes" because "he was the chief speaker" (v. 12).

Acts 17:1–5. In Thessalonica Paul went into the synagogue, as was his custom, and reasoned from the Scriptures regarding Christ's death and resurrection (vv. 2–3). That his intent was evangelistic can be seen from his statement, "This Jesus whom I am proclaiming [καταγγέλλω] to you is the Christ" (v. 3). That Silas was present is clear from 16:40 and from the fact that those who were persuaded by Paul's preaching joined Paul and Silas (17:4).[23] Although the text does not say that Silas verbally evangelized, it is significant that the people identified the gospel message with both Paul and Silas.

Acts 17:10–12. In Berea Paul again spoke in the synagogue (vv. 10–11). That his intent was evangelistic can be seen by the result that many believed (v. 12). Both Silas and Timothy were present (vv. 10, 14).[24]

Acts 18:1–18. In Corinth Paul again engaged in evangelistic activity. Every Sabbath he was in the synagogue "trying to persuade Jews and Greeks" (v. 4). He devoted himself to preaching, "testifying to the Jews that Jesus was the Christ" (v. 5). Many of the Corinthians believed and were baptized (v. 8). Only Paul is mentioned as being involved in direct evangelistic activity. However, he was not alone. Aquila and Priscilla were there, working with Paul in his trade of tentmaking (vv. 2–3).

Acts 19:8–10. In Ephesus Paul again engaged in evangelism in the synagogue, "arguing persuasively about the kingdom of God" (v. 8 NIV). When opposition arose, he took the disciples with him to Tyrannus's lecture hall where he ministered for two years (vv. 9–10). Although "disciples" were with him, nothing is said about whether they too did evangelistic work. At any rate, they were present with Paul.

All these passages reveal that the apostle Paul often evangelized in the presence of other believers and in most cases in the presence of other Christian workers.

PAUL EVANGELIZING TOGETHER WITH OTHER CHRISTIANS

Acts 13:1–5. The calling of Barnabas and Saul and their first missionary activity in Cyprus reveal the importance of corporate witness. Their call came from God, for the Holy Spirit said, "I have called them" (v. 2).[25] The fact that God called them to joint participation in a common activity is clear, for He called them (αὐτούς, plural) to the work (τὸ ἔργον, singular). The work to which they were called was evangelism. This can be seen not only from their actual involvement in evangelism during the trip, but also from their report when they returned. Arriving in Antioch they reported all "that God had done with them and how He had opened the door of faith to the Gentiles" (14:27). And later in

Phoenicia and Samaria they told how the Gentiles had been converted (15:3).

Recognizing this call of God to evangelistic work, the spiritual leaders in Antioch sent Barnabas and Saul on their first missionary journey (13:3). At Salamis they proclaimed (κατήγγελλον) the Word of God together (13:5). John Mark was with them as their helper (ὑπηρέτην).[26] Paul expected John Mark to be involved with them in evangelism, as seen from his later accusation in 15:38 that John Mark had not continued with them in "the work" (τὸ ἔργον; cf. 13:2).[27]

Acts 13:13–52. Corporate witness is evident in this account of Paul and his companions in Pisidian Antioch.[28] That their intent was evangelistic can be seen from Paul's message, particularly the statement, "Therefore let it be known to you, brethren, that through Him forgiveness of sins is proclaimed to you" (v. 38). This is also revealed by the Lord's instruction, which they related to the people: "I have placed you as a light for the Gentiles, that you should bring salvation to the end of the earth" (v. 47).

That they were corporately involved in witness can be seen from the fact that they entered the synagogue, and the fact that the synagogue rulers addressed them in the plural ("brethren"), asking them to speak a message of exhortation (vv. 14–15). Though Paul was the one who preached at the end of the synagogue service, the people invited them to speak further about these things (v. 42). When the crown was dismissed, many of the people followed Paul and Barnabas, who talked with them and urged them to continue in the grace of God (v. 43).[29] On the next Sabbath Paul and Barnabas boldly told the Jews that since they rejected the gospel, Paul and Barnabas were "turning to the Gentiles" (v. 46), for that was what "the Lord has commanded us [plural]" (v. 47). Persecution was stirred up against both of them, and they were expelled from the region (v. 50).

Acts 14:1–7. In Iconium Paul and Barnabas went together into the synagogue (v. 1) and spent considerable time there speaking boldly for the Lord, who enabled them to do miraculous signs and wonders (v. 3). Discovering a plot to stone them, they went to Lystra and Derbe (vv. 6–7), where "they continued to preach the gospel [κἀκεῖ εὐαγγελιζόμενοι ἦσαν]," (v. 7).

Acts 14:20–28. In Derbe Paul and Barnabas preached the good news (εὐαγγελισάμενοι) and won a large number of disciples (v. 21). Then they returned to Lystra, Iconium, and Antioch for a ministry of edification. In Perga, they preached the word (λαλήσαντες . . . τὸν λόγον) again (v. 25). These Greek verbs that describe their activity in Derbe and Perga denote evangelism and both verbs are in the plural. Back in Antioch, Paul and Barnabas reported to the church what God had done through them (v. 27).

Acts 15:35. This verse gives a clear picture of Paul and Barnabas evangelizing together in Antioch. They were teaching (διδάσκοντες) and preaching (εὐαγγελιζόμενοι) the word of the Lord.[30] "Many others" also engaged in this work.[31] The fact that this verse is a summary statement indicates that evangelism and edification were being carried out regularly.

Acts 15:40–16:12. On his second missionary journey Paul took Silas with him (15:40) and later he took Timothy along (16:1–3). When this missionary team was in Troas, Paul was led by God through a vision to go to Macedonia (v. 9). Of interest here is the fact that Luke was also part of this group, for he used "we" and "us" in 16:10–11, 13, and 15–17. In verse 10, Luke wrote, "And when [Paul] had seen the vision, immediately we sought to go into Macedonia, concluding that God had called[32] us to preach the gospel to them."

Acts 16:13–33. Three incidents in Philippi demonstrate the apostle's corporate evangelistic work. On the Sabbath Paul and his companions went to the riverside, where they assumed some Jews would be gathered for prayer.[33] Luke recounted, "We sat down and began speaking to the women who had assembled" (v. 13). All of them—Paul, Silas, Timothy, and Luke—were involved in witnessing. After she responded to Paul's message (v. 14), Lydia invited the entire group to stay in her home (v. 15). That their message was evangelistic is seen from the results: Lydia believed, and she and her household were baptized.

A slave girl with a spirit of divination shouted, "These men are bond-servants of the Most High God, who are proclaiming [καταγγέλλουσιν] to you the way of salvation" (v. 17). She (or the demonic spirit in her) acknowledged the witness of the men as a group. It was Paul, however, who commanded the demon to come out of her (v. 18). Then Paul and Silas were arrested, having been accused of advocating unlawful customs (v. 21).[34] At midnight Paul and Silas prayed and sang hymns to God, as the other prisoners listened (v. 25).

After an earthquake the jailer rushed in and addressed Paul and Silas. "Sirs, what must I do to be saved?" (v. 30). Luke recorded that they replied, "Believe in the Lord Jesus, and you shall be saved, you and your household" (v. 31). Then they spoke "the word of the Lord" to the jailer and his family, and immediately they were baptized (vv. 32–33).

From this brief survey of Paul's activities recorded in the Book of Acts, several things stand out. First, Paul lived and worked closely with others. He seldom ministered alone. On numerous occasions he engaged in team evangelism. He was burdened to share the good news of salvation through Christ with as many people as he could possibly reach. Third, divine initiative was behind the apostle's corporate witness activities. Twice Luke wrote that God called Paul and his companions to evangelize together (13:2; 16:10). On their first missionary journey Paul and Barnabas told the people God was the one who commanded them to "bring salvation to the end of the earth" (13:47). Twice Paul and his fellow workers reported back to the church everything God had done through them (14:27; 15:4).

Reasons for Team Evangelism

Why did Paul engage in corporate evangelism? What scriptural and practical reasons suggest this kind of evangelistic activity should be carried out in missions today? One answer some give is that corporate witness models the end product being sought, namely, the corporate community and fellowship of believers in local churches.[35] The increased credibility that stems from multiple witnesses is another reason for corporate evangelism.[36] Other reasons for carrying out evangelism by teams include the sharing of spiritual gifts,[37] mutual support among the evangelizers,[38] accountability to each other,[39] and increased results because of additional workers.[40]

Is the Evidence in Acts Enough?

It is clear from the Book of Acts that Paul engaged in corporate evangelism as part of his missionary strategy. But is that reason enough for missionaries now to do it? Some would question the wisdom of using the historical account of the early church in Acts as a guide for normative experience in the church today. While a case can be made for recognizing that Luke wrote the Book of Acts with didactic intent as well as to give an accurate account of history,[41] it is always helpful if the rationale for ministry practice can be buttressed by teaching given in the New Testament epistles.

A subsequent article will examine Paul's clear teaching about the importance of corporate ministry in the Book of Philippians, as well as sharing some reasons for such a practice and how it is being implemented in missionary work today.

CHAPTER 8

Paul's Corporate Witness in Philippians

George W. Murray

As noted in the previous chapter, the apostle Paul often ministered with others in his evangelistic efforts. He seldom worked alone. Luke reported in the Book of Acts numerous occasions when Paul served with fellow workers, actively engaging in corporate evangelism.

The book of Philippians, too, highlights Paul's emphasis on fellowship in evangelism. The themes of unity and witnessing are seen, as Martin observes, in the two words "gospel" (εὐαγγέλιον) and "fellowship" (κοινωνία).[1] In Philippians "gospel" denotes the work of evangelism and "fellowship" points to active partnership in that activity.[2]

At the beginning of this epistle Paul thanked the Philippians for their "partnership in the gospel" (1:5 NIV).[3] He spoke of their "defending and confirming the gospel" with him (v. 7) and about his circumstances that served to advance the gospel (v. 12). He mentioned the brethren who spoke "the word of God" (v. 14), he referred to those who "preach Christ" (vv. 15, 17), and he rejoiced because "Christ is preached" (v. 18).[4] He exhorted the Philippians to live a life "worthy of the gospel of Christ" and to be "contending as one man for the faith of the gospel" (v. 27).

Believers are to "shine like stars" and to "hold out the word of life" in a "depraved generation" (2:15–16). Paul commended Timothy because he served with me in the work of the gospel" (v. 22). Euodia and Synteche shared with Paul and others "in the cause of the gospel" (4:3). Near the end of the letter, Paul referred to the time when the gospel was first preached to them (v. 15).

These references reveal that the gospel weighed heavily on the heart of Paul as he wrote this letter. His concern for the propagation of the good news shows up in his use of a number of words in connection with the gospel: "defending" (1:7), "confirming" (v. 7), "advance" (v. 12), "speak" (v. 14), "preach" (κηρύσσω v. 15; καταγγέλλω in v. 18), "contending for" (v. 27), "hold out" (2:16), "served . . . in the work of" (v. 22), and "contended . . . in the cause of" (4:3).

Concerned for the unity of the Philippian believers, Paul urged them to be "standing firm in one spirit, with one mind [lit., soul] striving together" (1:27 NASB), to be "of the same mind, maintaining the same love, united in spirit, intent on one purpose" (2:2 NASB), and to "live in harmony in the Lord" (4:2 NASB). Recognizing that true humility is the key to unity, Paul cited the example of Jesus Christ (2:5–11). Unity is indeed a major emphasis of this letter. Commenting on Paul's purposes for writing the epistle, Foulkes says, "News brought to him indicated the dangers of divisions and party spirit among the Philippian Christians, and he wanted to exhort them to live and act and witness in the unity of the Spirit."[5] He spoke of the fellowship (κοινωνία) of believers in 1:5 ("your partnership in the gospel") and in 2:1 ("fellowship of the Spirit" [NASB], i.e., fellowship that comes from the Holy Spirit).[6]

Several times Paul indicated the importance of unified witnessing: 1:5; 1:7; 1:27–28; 2:14–16; 2:22; 2:25–30; 4:3; and 4:21.

Philippians 1:5

In this verse Paul spoke of the Philippians' partnership (κοινωνία) with him in furthering the gospel. This was not simply a common enjoyment of the benefits of the gospel. Rather, it denoted an active partnership in propagating the gospel. The Philippians indicated the reality of their partnership in the gospel not by "a quiet enjoyment of it, but [by] a keen activity in the interest of it."[7]

Κοινωνία occurs fourteen times in Paul's writings.[8] Before the New Testament era the word signified the "close union and brotherly bond between men,"[9] and the close relationship between God and human beings.[10] Paul used the word in both ways.[11] In both cases the word refers to two or more persons sharing something in common.[12] In 1:5 the idea of partnership (κοινωνία) and gospel propagation (εἰς τὸ εὐαγγέλιον) are linked.

Friedrich says κοινωνία in this verse refers not to the Philippians' partnership in spreading the gospel, but to their fellowship in the gospel itself, that is, their fellowship as believers.[13] Lightfoot believes the fellowship includes sympathy with Paul's sufferings, but he does not exclude the possibility of corporate witness.[14] Eadie, however, rejects these ideas for a more general view. "The noun is followed by the genitive of the thing participated in, or with εἰς, denoting its object. We, therefore, take κοινωνία in a general sense, and the following clause so closely connected with it, through the nonrepetition of the article, as assigning its end or purpose. Thus understood, it denotes participation, or community of interest in whatever the gospel had for its object."[15]

Eadie adds that everyone pertaining to the defense and propagation of the gospel was a matter of concern to the Philippians, and he calls their common participation with Paul "a palpable co-partnery" in gospel witness.[16] Müller points out that εἰς with the accusative includes the idea of motion, direction, and a "striving toward," thus denoting definite activity in gospel witness.[17] Hendricksen concurs by referring to the partnership of Philippians 1:5 as "an active participation in gospel activity."[18] Κοινωνία, then, in this verse refers not only to what believers do for each other, but also what they do together for others.

This partnership in evangelism took place between Paul and the Philippian believers when they were together ("from the first day") and when they were apart ("until now"). Therefore partnership in evangelism does not always involve physical presence. However, even when Paul was apart from them, the believers at Philippi were one with him in the task of evangelism through their prayers (1:19) and gifts (4:15), and by sending Epaphroditus to take care of the apostle's needs and to be his "fellow worker" (2:25). The Philippians, Paul pointed out, sent Epaphroditus not just to take him a financial gift, but also to help him in his ministry as they themselves would have done had it been possible for them to be there.

Since κοινωνία εἰς τὸ εὐαγγέλιον denotes active partnership in gospel witness, Paul's thankfulness expressed in 1:3 takes on greater significance. He was grateful for their partnership in evangelism. Viewing verse 4 as parenthetical,[19] Paul wrote in verses 3 and 5, "I thank my God . . . because of your partnership in [the furtherance of] the gospel." Lightfoot points out that the "good work" in verse 6 refers to the Philippians' cooperative evangelism with Paul.[20] On the surface it would seem that the "good work" of verse 6 refers generally to God's work of salvation in the Philippians. However, verse 6 continues the thought of verse 5. This cooperative evangelism, then, was not primarily the idea of Paul or the Philippians; it was a good work begun and continued by God.

Philippians 1:7

In this verse Paul wrote of defending and confirming the gospel. Based on his words "in chains" in this same verse, some writers believe this refers to his suffering and defense as a prisoner, rather than to his preaching ministry.[21] However, Paul seemed to make a distinction between being "in chains" and defending and confirming the gospel. Seeing this distinction, Eadie points out that this phrase cannot be restricted to suffering, since the speaker's reference to God's grace at the end of the verse refers equally to his ἀπολογίᾳ ("defense") and his δεσμοῖς ("chains").[22] The phrase "the defense and confirmation of the gospel" clearly refers to evangelistic activity. As Lightfoot points out, "ἀπολογίᾳ implies the negative or defensive side of Paul's preaching" and "βεβαίωσις [confirmation] denotes the positive or aggressive side, the direct advancement and establishment of the Gospel."[23]

Paul then linked the Philippian believers with him by stating that in both of these things they were "partakers" (συγκοινωνούς) with him of God's grace, that is, partners in activities (suffering and evangelism) connected with God's grace. They were "copartakers of his [Paul's] grace in evangelical labor."[24] That is, they joined with Paul in defending and confirming the gospel, and that joint activity evidenced God's grace.[25]

Philippians 1:27–28

Paul exhorted the Philippians to "stand firm in one spirit . . . for the faith of the gospel." Here again he spoke of united witness. Besides commending these believers for their participation with him in evangelism (v. 5), he urged them to join in the same cause even in his absence.

Συναθλέω (lit., "striving together") is used only twice in the New Testament, and both occurrences are in Philippians (1:27; 4:3). "The unity here envisioned is one of striving or struggling side by side, like gladiators, against a common foe. This struggle, moreover, is not only against a foe, but for the gospel-truth."[26]

In the phrase "for the faith of the gospel" πίστις is objective, denoting the contents of belief (as in Jude 3). This phrase τῇ πίστει τοῦ εὐαγγελίου, occurring only here in the New Testament (Phil.

1:27), could be translated "with the faith of the gospel." But the idea of "on behalf of the gospel"[27] seems preferable, since the same word for striving (συναθλέω) in 4:3 clearly denotes work for the gospel, as seen by its link with the phrase ἐν τῷ εὐαγγελίῳ.

The words "contending as one man for the faith of the gospel" is part of a long sentence that begins with a command ("conduct yourselves in a manner worthy of the gospel of Christ," v. 27) and ends with a theological statement ("This is a sign to them that they will be destroyed, but that you will be saved—and that by God," v. 28). Both the command and the theological statement relate to the words "contending as one man for the faith of the gospel."

The command "conduct yourselves" (πολιτεύομαι) can be translated, "discharge your obligations as citizens."[28] The Philippians were to act as citizens of the gospel. "The *polis* of ancient Greece was not merely a place of human habitation, but was the theatre of corporate activity of every kind, in which the individual citizen found scope for the use of all his gifts and the realization of all his potentialities; it was 'the highest of all fellowships or associations, which embraces all the others and exists for the attainment of the highest of all goods' (Aristotle, *Politics,* A. 1252a). The verb (πολιτεύεσθαι) as used here by Paul rests upon the transfer of these general conceptions to the church, and bears upon the corporate life of the Christian community of Philippi."[29]

The verb πολιτεύεσθαι "seems always to refer to public duties devolving on a man as a member of a body."[30] Just as a person living in Philippi, a Roman colony, would betray the fact that he is a Roman citizen by his behavior, so a Christian by his conduct should betray the fact that he is a citizen of the gospel.[31] True citizens of the gospel seek to propagate that gospel in the context of unified cooperation with other believers. In effect, Paul was saying that by their behaving as citizens of the gospel he would know (even if he never got back to Philippi) that they would be standing "firm in one spirit" together for the gospel.

The theological statement points back to what Paul already had said. Their united and courageous witness (v. 27) evidenced their saving relationship with the Lord (v. 28). The phrase "and that by God" shows that the apostle's exhortation to show their gospel citizenship by united, courageous witness was God's will. Some commentators say τοῦτο ἀπὸ θεοῦ refers only to "salvation" (σωτηρίας),[32] whereas others say it refers to the word "sign" (ἔνδειξις).[33] However, both of these words are feminine, whereas τοῦτο is neuter. Thus τοῦτο refers not to "salvation" or "sign" but to the fact of their courageous witness and its results.[34]

Philippians 2:14–16

These verses also indicate the importance of unified witness. Paul pleaded for unity between believers ("do everything without complaining or arguing") in order to carry out an effective witness ("in which you shine like stars . . . as you hold out the word of life"). This appeal for unity is so that (ἵνα) they will be effective witnesses—"blameless and pure . . . without fault" in an evil world in which they are to "shine like stars," holding forth God's Word (v. 15). By their unity they could "present an unbroken front in their conflict for the faith."[35]

As stars, believers are to dispel spiritual darkness by enlightening the hearts of the unsaved.[36] They are to hold out or hold forth[37] the word of life (λόγον ζωῆς), an expression the believers would clearly understand as a reference to the gospel.

Philippians 2:22

In Philippians 2:22 Paul said that Timothy was like "a son with his father" who had "served with me in the work of the gospel." Εἰς τὸ εὐαγγέλιον ("in the gospel") clearly denotes evangelistic proclamation,[38] as it does in 1:5 and 4:3. In 1 Thessalonians 3:2 Paul called Timothy "our brother and God's fellow worker in spreading the gospel of Christ [ἐν τῷ εὐαγγελίῳ τοῦ Χριστοῦ]." By using the father-son image, Paul was not saying Timothy was subordinate to him. (Paul did not say Timothy served him, but that Timothy served *with* him.) Paul and Timothy were partners together in the business of the gospel. Also Timothy's intimate union with Paul in gospel witness was proof of his worth as a Christian worker ("Timothy has proved himself").

Philippians 2:25–30

In 2:25–30 Paul commended Epaphroditus for his partnership in the work of the Lord. Epaphroditus was Paul's "fellow worker" (συνεργός) and "fellow soldier" (συστρατιώτης).[39] Συνεργός refers "to a work or achievement which is more or less equally divided among fellow-workers. . . . Their assistance in proclaiming the gospel means they share with the apostle the burden of the ministry of reconciliation."[40]

However, did not Epaphroditus come to minister to Paul, rather than with Paul, since he is called the one "whom you sent to take care of my needs"? While it is true that Epaphroditus ministered to Paul, the terms "brother," "fellow worker," and "fellow soldier" reveal that he was involved in joint ministry with Paul. These three words are arranged in an ascending scale, denoting "common sympathy, common work, common danger and toil and suffering."[41]

The fact that Epaphroditus almost died for the work of Christ indicates this involvement in service. At the end of this passage Paul wrote that Epaphroditus risked his life "to make up for the help[42] you could not give me" (v. 30). Since the Philippian believers were helping Paul through their prayers (1:19) and gifts (4:18), the help they could not give may have been the "partnership in the gospel" which Paul had experienced with them in Philippi "from the first day" (1:5).

Philippians 4:3

In this verse the apostle mentioned three examples of corporate activity, at least one of which involves evangelism. They are (a) the person Paul called his "loyal yokefellow" who worked with Paul, (b) the "yokefellow's" help to Euodia and Syntyche, and (c) Euodia and Syntyche, who contended at Paul's side in the cause of the gospel, along with Clement and Paul's other associates.

Paul addressed someone whom he called σύζυγε, an adjective denoting "yoked together," which is used here as a noun.[43] This expression clearly portrays the idea of working together, "a person who pulls well in a harness for two."[44]

Paul then asked this "loyal yokefellow" to "help" Euodia and Syntyche. In the middle voice with the dative of a person the word "help" (συλλαμβάνω) occurs only here and in Luke 5:7.[45] In the "latter verse the word describes fishermen who were helping each other bring in a net of fish. Perhaps Paul was asking this comrade to engage in gospel activity with these women. However, more likely Paul was asking him to help these women resolve their differences. These women had previously engaged in joint evangelistic activity with the apostle Paul; they "contended at my side" (συνήθλησάν). The effectiveness of any continuing witness by these women would be hampered unless their differences were settled. Therefore Paul's plea for unity should be seen not only as an end in itself, but also as a means to effective witness.

"Contended at my side" translates συναθλέω, which occurs

only here and in 1:27. In both cases it denotes corporate activity in the spread of the gospel. Here again ἐν τῷ εὐαγγελίῳ, a phrase noted earlier, signifies gospel proclamation. There is no reason to believe these women did not play an active partnership role in gospel witness with the apostle Paul. The Book of Acts reveals that women of the Hellenistic culture to which Paul ministered played a prominent role in society (see, e.g., Acts 16:13; 17:4; 12). "If Macedonia produced perhaps the most competent group of men the world had yet seen, the women were in all respects the men's counterparts; they played a large part in [business] affairs, received envoys and obtained concessions for them from their husbands, built temples, founded cities, engaged mercenaries, commanded armies, held fortresses, and acted on occasion as regents or even co-rulers."[46]

The command to Paul's "yokefellow" to help restore Euodia and Synteche's broken unity suggests that he wanted to see them restored to the corporate witness in which they once had been engaged.

Philippians 4:21

Paul's statement, "The brothers who are with me send greetings," seems at first glance to be a salutation from the Christian community in Rome. However, in the next verse Paul sent greetings from "all the saints." Thus a distinction is made between "the brothers" and "the saints." This distinction can be seen elsewhere in the New Testament. "The churches in the province of Asia send you greetings. Aquila and Priscilla greet you warmly in the Lord, and so does the church that meets at their house. All the brothers here send you greetings" (1 Cor. 16:19–20). "Peace to the brothers, and love with faith from God the Father and the Lord Jesus Christ. Grace to all who love our Lord Jesus Christ" (Eph. 6:23–24). "Give my greetings to the brothers at Laodicea, and to Nympha and the church in her house" (Col. 4:15).

"From such passages one may regard it as probable that when used in the plural with the article, 'the brothers' in Pauline literature fairly consistently refers to a relatively limited group of workers, some of whom have the Christian mission and/or ministry as their primary occupation."[47] Ellis also notes that "the brothers" in 2 Corinthians 9:3, 5 and 3 John 3, 5, 10 were traveling workers, probably preachers or teachers associated with or led by an elder.[48] Thus "the brothers" in Philippians 4:21 may well refer to workers engaged in evangelism. In this particular instance, Paul pointed out that they were "with me," in keeping with his common practice of evangelizing in company with others.

Summary

Paul's letter to the Philippians demonstrates the importance of "unity in the propagation of the gospel."

Philippians includes three clear cases of others who worked together with the apostle Paul in evangelism: the Philippian believers (1:3–6), Timothy (2:22), and Euodia and Syntyche (4:3). Also there is evidence that Paul worked together in evangelism with Epaphroditus (2:25–30), Clement and other fellow workers (4:3), and "the brothers" (4:21).

In connection with the passages studied in Philippians, the following observations can be made: Paul thanked God for corporate witness (1:3–5). Paul said God is the Initiator and Perfecter of corporate witness (1:6). Corporate witness is a token of God's grace (1:7). Corporate witness characterizes those who are "citizens of the gospel" (1:27). Twice Paul urged unity in the context of gospel witness (2:14–16; 4:3). Involvement in corporate witness demonstrates that Christian workers have been tried and stood the test (2:22). Paul said to welcome and honor the person who worked together with him in corporate witness (2:25–30).

Although in varying degrees, these passages all show the importance of working together in evangelism. This points up the value of the missions principle that evangelistic work be carried out with coworkers and not in isolation.

CHAPTER 9

Soteriological Inclusivism and Dispensationalism

Ramesh P. Richard

Explosive growth in the world's population forces an important question on all evangelicals: Are the masses of the world condemned to eternal conscious punishment even though they have not heard the gospel of Christ in this life? The emotional pain the question evokes cannot be masked, and the theological stress is steady. Evangelicals insist that explicit knowledge of Christ is necessary for personal salvation. But they also know that vast numbers of mankind are inhibited or prohibited by history, geography, religion, culture, and Christian failure from having access to knowledge of Christ. When these realities are combined with God's stated desire for all men to repent (2 Peter 3:9), the question attains enormous complexity.

The Options

For many it seems that to achieve a theologically and emotionally satisfying answer one must either deny or broaden the exclusive condition of salvation to which evangelicals have traditionally subscribed. On theological grounds, however, the former is not an evangelical option.[1] Would an emotionally acceptable broadening of the exclusive condition of salvation be a biblically, theologically, and evangelically permissible alternative?

Clark Pinnock and John Sanders think so. They propose a broadening of the salvific condition so that evangelicals may adequately grapple with the question while maintaining orthodoxy.[2] They marshal several theological and historical arguments in support of their proposal.

This article ponders that critical question from the perspective of dispensationalism.[3] Need for this arises from certain arguments that Pinnock and Sanders put forth in defense of an inclusivist or "wider-hope"[4] position. A few of these arguments will be examined before presenting interaction from the viewpoint of dispensational evangelicalism.[5]

One argument for the "inclusivist" position is that Jews in the Old Testament were saved without actually confessing Christ.

> Another class of people saved without professing Christ were the Jews who lived before Jesus was born. . . . The Old Testament describes a large number of believing Israelites who trusted in God, though the Messiah had not yet come to them. Yet they exercised saving faith, as did Abraham, and experienced forgiveness, as did David. Their theological knowledge was deficient, measured by New Testament standards, and their understanding of God was limited because they had not encountered Jesus, in whom alone one sees the Father. Nonetheless, they knew God and belonged to the great cloud of witnesses who encourage us (Heb. 12:1). Without actually confessing Jesus Christ, they were saved by his work of redemption.[6]

Another support for "wider hope" comes from the "holy pagan" tradition of Melchizedek, Abimelech, and other pre-Israelite or non-Israelite people who experienced Old Testament salvation. "Abel, Noah, Enoch, Job, Jethro, the queen of Sheba, the centurion, Cornelius—all stand as positive proof that the grace of God touches people all over the world and that faith, without which it is impossible to please God, can and does occur outside as well as inside the formal covenant communities."[7]

The conclusion to this sampling of arguments[8] is clear. According to Pinnock and Sanders, people may be saved today without actually confessing Jesus Christ, even as people were saved before Christ without actually confessing Christ.

> While everyone will grant that it was possible to respond to God the way Job did in premessianic times, not everyone thinks that the possibility still exists. This latter hesitation needs to be confronted. Why would it make any difference if Job were born in A.D. 1900 in outer Mongolia? Why would God not deal with him the same way he dealt with him in the Old Testament? A person who is informationally messianic, whether living in ancient or modern times, is in exactly the same spiritual situation.[9]

Evangelical Responses to the Critical Question

Evangelicals rightly spurn the conclusion of these "inclusivist" hope premises. Many covenant theologians counter that people before Christ did actually confess Him, in an embryonic but developing way. Therefore people today must actually confess Christ for salvation. Dispensationalists rebut the inclusivist premise in another way.[10] True, individuals before Christ were saved without actually confessing Him, but that does not mean that they did not confess anything specific. Every dispensation has a specific and exclusive content to faith. In the present dispensation the confession of Christ is necessary for eternal salvation.[11] Both the covenant and dispensational answers reject the "inclusivist" premises and conclusion.

THE CRITICAL QUESTION

The critical question is this: *Can the quality, reality, and vitality of Old Testament salvation be affirmed to be as valid as New Testament salvation in the face of the lack of knowledge of Christ in the Old Testament, while at the same time preserving the New Testament necessity of explicit knowledge and trust of Christ for eternal salvation?* Only by recognizing the historical distinctiveness of Old Testament salvation without widespread and explicit content of Christ—while emphasizing the epistemological exclusivity of Christ in New Testament salvation—can one effectively discount the inclusivist position.

COVENANT THEOLOGY AND THE CRITICAL QUESTION

Covenant theologians question the first part of the critical question. For them no material difference exists in the content of faith between the Old and New Testaments. Incipient, Old Testament Christocentric knowledge of the One to come is a necessary postulate of the position. Many would hold that Old Testament saints knew enough about the Seed of Abraham, the Greater Moses, the Lion of Judah, the Son of David, or the Servant of Isaiah to be saved. Messianic themes, shadows, allusions, prefigurements in typological prophecy, and other connections between the Old and New Testaments are strong testimony to this line of specific knowledge of Christ by Old Testament believers. This may be called the Christocentric "continuity" position.[12]

Nicole addresses the question of the "heathen" and the uniqueness of Jesus from a covenant perspective. He notes that Abraham (John 8:56), Moses (John 5:46), and the Old Testament prophets (1 Peter 1:10–11) "sensed they were speaking about the salvation to come through the work of Christ."[13] Or as Hodge wrote, "It was not mere faith or trust in God, or simple piety, which was required, but faith in the promised Redeemer, or faith in the promise of redemption through the Messiah."[14] Calvin wrote that "the people of God before Christ were 'adopted into the hope of immortality' and had full assurance of their salvation (II.x.2), because of God's grace and because their hope was in Christ, 'the Mediator, through whom they were joined to God and were to share in his promises' (II.x.2)."[15]

INCLUSIVISM AND THE CRITICAL QUESTION

The "wider-hope" position plays up the lack of knowledge of Christ in the Old Testament to deny the second part of the critical question. It follows for inclusivists that, contrary to covenant theology, explicit knowledge of Christ was and is not necessary for eternal salvation at any time. Inclusivists argue that since it was impossible for individuals in Old Testament times to know of Christ and yet they experienced salvation, no specific knowledge of Christ is necessary now. This may be called the "faith principle" position.[16] "In my judgement," Pinnock writes, "the faith principle is the basis of universal accessibility. According to the Bible, people are saved by faith, not by the content of their theology."[17] Or as Sanders says, "Inclusivists do not claim that people are saved by their righteousness; they contend that people like Cornelius are saved because they have the 'habit of faith,' which involves penitence. But inclusivists do claim that it is not necessary to understand the work of Christ in order to be saved."[18]

Questions and Responses of Dispensationalism

Covenant theology, inclusivist theology, and dispensational theology agree on the atoning work of Jesus Christ. They differ about whether faith explicitly in Christ is necessary for salvation.

DISPENSATIONALISM CONSIDERS COVENANT THEOLOGY

Dispensationalists, including Ryrie,[19] affirm that "it is very difficult if not impossible to prove that the average Israelite understood the grace of God in Christ."[20] Ross adds, "It is most improbable that everyone [in the Old Testament] who believed unto salvation consciously believed in the substitutionary death of Jesus Christ, the Son of God."[21]

So dispensationalism raises major questions[22] about the amount and content of Christocentric, salvific truth available during Old Testament times. Even if one agrees that certain Old Testament personalities had a degree of Christocentric knowledge by divine revelatory initiatives such as covenants, visions, dreams, and other personal means of revelation, the number of individuals who had access to such extraordinary salvific content is rather insignificant to make it the general content of widespread salvation during the Old Testament.[23]

DISPENSATIONALISM CONSIDERS INCLUSIVISM

Along with covenant theology,[24] dispensationalism questions the inclusivist view of a generic, contentless, salvation-bringing faith principle in the Old Testament, let alone the New Testament. While inclusivists are eager to use Ryrie's words to emphasize the basis, requirement, and the object of faith in salvation, they overlook a structural characteristic of a dispensational theology of salvation—the specific content necessary in each dispensation. "It is this last point, of course, which distinguishes dispensationalism from covenant theology."[25] It may be added that this last point also distinguishes dispensationalism from the inclusivist view. As Ross puts it,

> Ultimately the content of saving faith in any age must be God and his revelation concerning participation in his covenant (what we call salvation). Believers were ultimately taking God at his word when they responded to the truth in their situations. But as revelation continued, the content of faith grew.[26]

Old Testament saints did not have a contentless faith. Their faith-content was specified, required, and therefore exclusive. That is, exclusivity is not just a New Testament phenomenon introduced in Jesus Christ. When one takes the Old Testament's exclusivity and adds the fuller, clarified New Testament insistence on explicit, conscious knowledge and belief in Jesus Christ as the means of receiving eternal salvation, the inclusivist, wider-hope view is inadmissible.

As already noted, the problem with the covenant position (the continuity view) is that it assumes a great amount of Christological knowledge by the typical Israelite. It argues from the few to the many.[27] The fact that Job, Abraham, Moses, and David knew much about the Coming One, does not mean that all who were saved knew much about Him.

The problem with the faith-principle position is similar to the problem with the continuity position. The inclusivist opinion has to assume a great amount of faith in the right object on the part of many unmentioned non-Israelites on the basis of a few non-Israelites who are named to salvation. The fact that Abel, Melchizedek,

Noah, Jethro, and Naaman were saved does not mean most of those outside contact with and knowledge of Yahweh were saved or had access to salvation.

Both continuity and faith-principle theologies commit the fallacy of the general rule. They argue for a general rule from a small sample.[28] In the covenant scheme a few cases of definite Christocentric knowledge become the basis for a widespread availability of specific Christocentric knowledge. In the inclusivist scheme a few cases of non-Israelite salvation become a case for the general availability of salvation without an exclusive content condition. Several "neglected factors" and "disconfirmatory instances" exist in both of these theologies of salvation.[29]

While the arguments of covenant and inclusivist theologians are similar, their conclusions differ.[30] A major dividing line between these two theologies is the application of the generalizations. Some Old Testament saints (e.g., Abraham, Moses, David) had greater insight than others into the promised Redeemer. The question is whether this sampling is representative and proportionate to the entire Old Testament population of saints. On the other hand the inclusivist view has not established one solid biblical instance of salvation by "the direction of heart rather than the content of theology."[31] There is no biblical evidence of an abstract faith principle toward God without specific theological truth bringing salvation. Consequently Pinnock and Sanders must make an enormous inductive leap, a leap that is exegetically unsound and logically questionable.[32]

Dispensationalism preserves pre-Christ salvation outside explicit knowledge of Christ while insisting that explicit knowledge of Christ is an exclusive, universal condition now. A normal historical and hermeneutical distinction[33] between dispensations[34] makes a broadened condition for salvation impossible.

Some Directions from a Theology of Discontinuity

The "historical location" and the epistemological content of salvation become critically important. Theologies of salvation configure the relationship between these two elements in different ways. For universalists neither time nor content is critical to salvation. For inclusivists content is inconsequential. For covenant theologians a Christocentric epistemology provides unity to the progress of redemption with differences in historical location being less important.

However, for dispensationalists,[35] historical location is integrated with epistemological content. One of the distinctives of dispensationalism may well focus on this point that the specific content of saving faith distinguishes a dispensation. Such a distinctive is important in relation to the inclusivist question. That is, it is possible for people to be saved without explicit knowledge of Christ before Christ came, but not after He came. In this way, the truth and adequacy of Old Testament revelation for salvation is preserved, while emphasizing that in this age a personal relationship with God is "mediated exclusively through the Son."[36]

This "integrative" dispensational view of the time and content of salvation provides several points of argumentation against inclusivism. These dispensational resources are viewed soteriologically, ecclesiologically,[37] and eschatologically.

SOTERIOLOGICAL IMPLICATIONS

First, in dispensationalism the details of Old Testament salvation are given equitable weight in the linkage between historical location and salvation epistemology. Pre-Israelites, non-Israelites, and nominal Israelites could be saved as they were rightly related to God by exercising faith in the specifically and divinely revealed content for that epoch. During Old Testament times salvation was possible even if Christ was not explicitly known by most Old Testament saints. Embryonic or mature salvific knowledge of Christ is attributed to divine revelatory initiatives which dispensed insight into the messianic promise to significant patriarchs and prophets (Abel, Noah, Abraham, Moses, David, Isaiah, Jeremiah, Daniel, etc.; cf. Heb. 11). And yet these individuals did not necessarily understand many dimensions of what they stated (cf. 1 Peter 1:10–11). Also any non-Israelites who were saved came into contact with Israelites and had to acknowledge the God of Israel (e.g., the queen of Sheba and Solomon, Naaman and Elisha, Nebuchadnezzar and Daniel).

Second, in dispensationalism the details of New Testament salvation are given equitable weight in the linkage between historical location and salvation epistemology. Individuals in the present age can be saved as they become rightly related to God by exercising faith in the specifically and divinely revealed content for this epoch (John 3:16; Acts 4:12; 16:31; etc.) Even now, divine revelatory initiatives may dispense insight into the arrival of the messianic promise, but any such recipient (e.g., a Hindu or

Muslim seeker) must still relate to Jesus Christ (as, e.g., Cornelius, Acts 10:43). In other words divine revelatory initiatives are not independently salvific. A person must explicitly believe in the salvific content of this dispensation, namely, on the Lord Jesus Christ as his or her only God and Savior.

Third, while affirming the unchanging and unchangeable aspects of salvation (e.g., divine election, the atonement, and the necessity of faith), dispensationalism carries the truth of exclusivity throughout the epochs of history without diminishing the quantitatively lesser amount of messianic knowledge in the Old Testament as qualitatively inferior.[38]

For instance dispensationalism does not permit glossing over the pre-Israelite period as many tend to do. Sanders (like Porphyry, the neo-Platonist from Tyre who assailed early Christianity) discusses a legitimate concern.

> Porphyry was aware that some Christians attempted to meet his objection by claiming that people before Christ were saved by faith in the Christ to come. Pagans, before Christ, it was argued, were saved if they turned to the Jewish faith, which taught about the Christ who was to come. To this Porphyry said: "Let it not be said that provision had been made for the human race by the old Jewish law. It was only after a long time that the Jewish law appeared and flourished within the narrow limits of Syria. . . . It gradually crept onwards to the coasts of Italy; but this was not earlier than the end of the reign of Gaius. . . . What, then, became of the souls of men in Rome and Latium who lived before the time of the Caesars, and were destitute of the grace of Christ, because He had not then come?"[39]

Dispensationalists answer this objection from a time-content integration. Before the time of the nation of Israel, God had other divinely revealed, specific content for salvation. Once any such content was given, people everywhere had to relate properly to the God who was communicated in it. Pre-Israelite salvation was just as real and vital[40] as salvation offered at any other time in human history. In this way dispensationalism also protects against the inference that a pre-Israelite period was the archetypal dispensation for the paradigm of salvation—a necessary assumption of the inclusivist view.

Fourth, dispensationalism insists that the temporal, geographical, and epistemological extents of salvation are coterminous. This view is possible since the amount of messianic (salvific?) knowledge given to Abraham or David did not have to extend to all Old Testament saved people. Pinnock argues that Abimelech "was in fact another pagan who had a right relation with God outside the boundaries of Israel's covenant."[41] From this Pinnock deduces that the boundaries of Israel's covenant are similar to the boundaries of Jesus' salvation. Since Abimelech was outside Israel, Pinnock reasons, those today who do not know of Jesus can be saved.

Inclusivists suggest that Abimelech's dream of divine accountability, his protests of a clean conscience, his compensatory generosity, and his healing are synonyms of personal salvation. However, the coterminous view of the temporal, geographical, and epistemological extent of salvation demands that specific content be available to the human race at a given time regardless of circumstances. The "holy pagan" passages actually prove that Yahwistic salvation was for the whole world (as in, e.g., the Abimelech-Abraham interchange). This salvation was available before the beginning of the nation Israel and continued through the duration of Israel to be available to non-Israelites. This is also true in the New Testament. The temporal, geographical, and epistemological aspects of salvation are coterminous.[42]

If salvation were only for Israel[43] and *if* non-Israelites could be saved outside the boundaries of Israel, this would not indicate that people can be saved outside Jesus today. However one understands Israel's covenant geography, salvation since Jesus' first advent is clearly universal (as demonstrated even by inclusivist use of the universal texts). This fact is a point in favor of the discontinuity position in a theology of the history of salvation.

ECCLESIOLOGICAL[44] IMPLICATIONS

Believers and Christians. The inclusivist view requires a distinction between saved "believers" and "Christians."[45] Believers, Sanders says, are "all those who are saved because they have faith in God,"[46] and a Christian is "a believer who knows about and participates in the work of Jesus Christ."[47] Pinnock distinguishes between premessianic believers and messianic believers (Christians).[48] Both these groups are saved. Premessianic believers presently need Christ and missions for "full strength" salvation in this life. "Unevangelized believers need a clearer revelation of God's love and forgiveness, and the assurance that goes with love and forgiveness."[49]

Pinnock and Sanders say little if anything about the composition of the universal church. Presumably they view the church as composed of Christians (messianic believers) who participate in the mission of bringing Christ to the nations, including "unevangelized believers" who have not heard of Christ.

Inclusivism leads to two awkward ecclesiological options. The first option is to include only true Christians in the church. But in this case Pinnock has two categories of the saved in relationship to the church—the saved who belong to the church (and therefore are aware of it) and the saved who do not belong to the church (and therefore are unaware of it). Though Pinnock distances himself from Rahner,[50] the latter category sounds like a Rahnerian "anonymous Christian" view. This could be called an "anonymous church" view or "anonymous believer" view. That is, a person does not know he is a Christian (Rahner) or that he is in the church (Pinnock) and "saved non-Christians" do not know it either.

Inclusivism's second option on the composition of the church is to make both premessianic believers and messianic Christians part of the church, though Christians still have to evangelize believers. Here, strangely, those who have not believed in Christ are viewed as part of the church. That believers already in the church need to be evangelized not only sounds outlandish, but also reduces missions to a mere "conscientization" task with nonevangelical overtones of mission.[51]

A hint about the composition of the church may be found in the following statement by Pinnock: "A forward look characterizes the church age, and central to it is the ingathering of the Gentiles. . . . The central thrust of this present age is the ingathering of the Gentiles through the mission entrusted to us."[52] Whether these Gentiles include believers is not stated, though those who carry the mission are Christians. Seemingly Pinnock is suggesting that "the Church Age" comprises all present believers (messianic and premessianic) in a universal entity, the church, parts of which are identifiable (messianic believers) and parts of which are unidentifiable but authentic (premessianic believers). Only self-conscious Christians belong to what is identifiable as the church, and they are responsible to carry on its mission.

This point is discussed here under ecclesiology rather than soteriology because of the dispensational insistence that the church is composed of the saved in this age and is administratively discontinuous with Israel.[53] One of the essential (not just institutional) differences between the church and Israel is the constituents of these two entities. Though Israel and the church may be analogous,[54] how one becomes part of Israel or the church differs.

Everyone physically born within the sociopolitical orbit of Israel was a bona fide, ethnic Israelite.[55] But not all ethnic Israelites, Abrahamites of the flesh, were believers, that is, Abrahamites of the promise. To receive salvation, ethnic (children of the flesh) Israelites still had to express personal belief in Yahweh. "Faith found expression in the OT in two predominant ways: obedience to the Law, and worship through sacrifices."[56] In Israel some were saved and others were not.

Most evangelical ecclesiologies of salvation hold that it is not possible for the unsaved to belong spiritually in the church. People must personally believe in Christ to be spiritually born into the church. Unlike Israel, the church has no distinction between those who are spiritually related to it and those who are not. That is, in the church there are no levels of ethnic meaning or tiers of belonging. Consequently if Israel and the church are continuous or essentially the same, one not only runs into soterio-ecclesiological problems but also faces a major enigma that caters to the inclusivist view. Inclusivists could argue that just as "more-than-authentic" Israelites were in Israel, so "more-than-authentic" Christians are in the church. In dispensational discontinuity only the saved are in the church. And they are self-consciously the church with missionary responsibilities to the unsaved world.

Simultaneous dispensationalism. One of the powerful arguments for inclusivism is what may be designated "simultaneous or concurrent dispensationalism." In this approach more than one dispensation runs concurrently. Kraft "distinguishes between the chronological position of those who have never heard and their position with respect to revelational information."[57] This group is "chronologically A.D. and informationally B.C." The unevangelized are in the New Testament dispensation in reference to time and in the Old Testament dispensation in reference to the content of salvation.

This issue may be addressed in several ways. Dispensationalists again point out that Old Testament saints, in spite of their lack of knowledge of Christ, did have divinely revealed, specific content to believe (which content demarcates the dispensations). If Old Testament believers had nothing definite to believe, Kraft's point might be acceptable. People today are not in an Old Testament dispensation in reference to specific content. Furthermore what the religious masses in the populous regions of the world (e.g., China and India) believe today does not even remotely correspond to what Abraham and Melchizedek believed as the divinely revealed specifics of their day.[58] People today, like the unsaved of the Old Testament, affirm other (nonbiblical and therefore false) means of salvation.

Thus Kraft makes an erroneous crossdispensational link based on "shared ignorance" between the Old and New Testaments.[59] He confuses the specific content believed by saved people such as Melchizedek and Naaman (in spite of their ignorance of Christ), with the lack of specifics of Christ among unsaved chronologically A.D. people. People outside Jesus Christ today do not maintain neutral or blank religious minds.[60] While they may be deficient in information about Christ, they are not deficient in their information about God.[61] Too, the Bible points to a moral problem among all the unsaved. Their problems in relation to salvation are twofold. The negative angle relates to knowledge of Christ, but the positive angle relates to suppression of truth and rebellious action. So the transdispensational link is between the "unsaved" of both Old and New Testaments—both are guilty—and not between the non-Israelites who were saved in the Old Testament and non-Israelites in the present era who are not saved. The latter hold religious views that conflict with divinely revealed salvation content.

This feature of specific content of salvation for a period of time, affecting all humans in that time, actually opposes the "faith principle" of salvation. This approach seeks a common denominator for salvific content (the "faith principle") in the various ages. Once this content of salvation is abstracted and given a generic status, inclusivists then attempt to find suitable candidates in any given dispensation to fit the abstracted condition. But a newly defined specific for salvation thwarts their efforts.[62] So they posit concurrent dispensations to accommodate the abstracted generic content for premessianic believers and a concrete specific content for messianic Christians.

Dispensationalism's philosophy of history[63] does not allow for concurrent dispensations in any epoch. Salvific content includes divinely revealed specifics for each age. Intensive content and extensive reach distinguish the dispensations. Any period of salvific revelation in the Bible applies to the entirety of the human race for that time. Specific revelatory events had global dimensions as witnessed in Adam (global effect of the Fall, Gen. 3); Noah (the global Flood and the Noahic Covenant, Gen. 6–8); Abraham (global promise, Gen. 12); Israel (global orientation, Ex. 19:6;

Deut. 4:6–8; Ps. 67; Isa. 60–66); the Cross (global implication, John 3:16; 1 John 2:2) and the church (Matt. 28:19–20, global influence); the millennium (global reign, Ps. 2; Rev. 20:1–6); and eternity (global "summing up" and the new creation, 1 Cor. 15:27–28; Rev. 21–22). Can several dispensations be running concurrently now? Theologically this cannot be so, since such a view reduces the comprehensive, epochal, and global radicalness of the Cross and the comprehensive, epochal, and global uniqueness of the church in God's program.

For the present dispensation, the Cross is of global significance. This significance is more than merely ontological since it relates to all the inhabited earth. Otherwise the Cross might as well have happened in the realm of the ideal in an eternal form in God's mind.[64] Simultaneous dispensationalism diminishes the historical radicalness of the Cross by taking away its epistemological distinctive and thereby undermining its comprehensive global claim and coverage.

Also in this philosophy of history the church has comprehensive global significance. Christ's disciple-making mandate is noted for its internationality (Matt. 28:19–20). The church is to spread the message of Christ across the world. Unfortunately the church may cultivate an ingrownness as Israel did in confusing elective responsibility for selfish privilege.[65] However, in dispensationalism the church portrays a new universality that is discontinuous with Israel. To a large measure, the church was unforeseen in the Old Testament.[66] While salvation of Gentiles is highly evident in the Old Testament, the equality of Jews and Gentiles in a corporate body was a mystery revealed to the New Testament apostles and prophets.[67] So the church is not a limited, nationally constituted institution. By nature it is new, and by composition it is multiethnic. This nonnationalistic, indiscriminate, interracial composition of Christ's body, the church, does not allow for simultaneous dispensationalism. The fundamental event of the Cross and the composition of the church extend throughout the globe in this age. To provide a different content of faith for human salvation in the Church Age is to regulate post-Cross salvation by a pre-Cross model and to suggest pre-Pentecost descriptions for a post-Pentecost entity.

So a dispensational philosophy of history in its linear view of time and incremental view of revelation argues strongly against the idea of concurrent dispensations. Dispensationalism invalidates a "chronologically A.D. and informationally B.C." division as a model for salvation today. Such an ineffectual division is acknowledged by Kraft himself. "The discontinuity from our perspective is in fact that chronologically A.D. people could know whereas B.C. people could not know."[68] Certainly this kind of a person is not unique. Everyone in this dispensation, until he comes to know Christ, is "chronologically A.D. and informationally B.C." So this category of the unevangelized is not unique.[69] One's pre-Christ ignorance can be corrected in this post-Christ dispensation. But such a correction was not historically undertaken on a wide scale in a pre-Christ dispensation.

ESCHATOLOGICAL IMPLICATIONS

Perhaps dispensationalism is most popularly known for its eschatological thought.[70] The futurist orientation of dispensational premillennialism points to some implications that speak against an inclusivist interpretation of salvation.

This-worldly salvation. The Old Testament prospect of salvation was spiritual, immediate, and this-worldly. Ross regards the profile of Old Testament salvation as deliverance from enemies, rest in the land, and unbroken fellowship with God.[71] Though Pinnock does not discuss this concept, he could gain a certain Old Testament advantage by doing so since he wants to make the New Testament benefit of salvation spiritual, immediate, and this-worldly too. Of course to make the Old Testament understanding of salvation parallel to New Testament salvific benefits, some adjustments would be needed. Sociopolitical deliverance from enemies and literal rest in a geographically defined land would have to be adjusted to refer to sin, demons, heaven, and so forth.[72]

Dispensational premillennialism enables the prospects of Old Testament salvation to be taken in a plain, originally understood sense.[73] And the discontinuity in dispensationalism does not allow for New Testament salvation to be beneficial only in a spiritual, immediate, and this-worldly sense. Old Testament Israel, while finding spiritual salvation on earth along with short-term deliverance from enemies, still looked forward to the eschatological realization of their geographical hope. But New Testament salvation promises an eternal, ultimate, and otherworldly salvation. It refuses to give eternity second place to an earthly millennium, though the saved of all ages will enjoy the benefits of an earthly resolution of history and an eternal consummation of all things under Christ in a permanent conjoining of identities and destinies.

Criterion for truth. One of the difficulties in the inclusivist view is ascertaining a criterion for salvific truth that can be presently applied to non-Christian religions. Having seen the Bible as providing a generic principle for salvation (i.e., faith commitment to God), but not providing specifics for salvation (content for explicit trust), inclusivists face the question of how to evaluate truth components in non-Christian religions. A lack of such a criterion allows Pinnock to see Buddhists as in touch with God their own way[74] and Muslims as worshiping the same God as Christians and Jews.[75] Most evangelicals find these suggestions unacceptable since non-Christian religions do not measure up to the standard of the Scriptures[76] with reference to the condition and possibility for eternal salvation.

Dispensationalists look forward to a future time when all believers will participate in the millennial kingdom of Jesus Christ as the final earthly dispensation. This kingdom will be brought about by divine intervention and without human agency. This kind of a *historical* eschatological scenario contrasts with Pinnock's (and Hick's) notion of alleviating present decisions about absolute truth by aspiring to the eschatological verification of truth.[77] But if truth and falsehood cannot be resolved in the historical past or present, they cannot be resolved by a nonhistorical, eschatological maneuver. When the historical connection is cut, the criterion for truth becomes a nonhistorical, teleological ideal rather than a verifiable, historical absolute that discriminates between truth and error.

In Jesus' incarnation the King and kingdom were historically present.[78] Christ as King furnishes the historical criterion of truth for the exclusivity of Christ and the evaluation of whether other religions include salvific truth.[79] This is true because the dispensational view of history provides a past, present, and *future* of earthly, historical realities. The tight link between the future, earthly, historical form of the kingdom, made certain by its relationship to the past, earthly, historical presence of Jesus as King, supplies the critical evaluative criterion for world religions.[80] The *King* has come visibly in history and geography, but the millennial *kingdom* has not yet come visibly in history and geography. So the King provides the criterion by which anyone may be included in His kingdom.

Summary

The inclusivist view is a crucial issue in modern evangelicalism. Dispensationalism provides a New Testament epistemology of exclusivity against the inclusivist view. In connection with "historical location" and salvific epistemology, four inclusivist arguments[81] are cited below with appropriate responses from a dispensational viewpoint.

1. "Pre-Christ individuals have been saved without explicit knowledge of Christ." However, not having "explicit knowledge of Christ" is only part of the equation of salvation content. Dispensationalism insists that pre-Christ believers did have divinely revealed, specific content of which there had to be explicit knowledge in order to receive salvation.
2. "People, then, can be saved without explicit knowledge of Christ." This view disregards the content of salvation at any given time and arbitrarily gives universal status to that period which yields their principle. Inclusivists jump from one half of the fact (what Old Testament believers did and could not have) to a ubiquitous means of salvation. True, people in the Old Testament have been saved without knowledge of Christ. But it is improper to conclude from this that now anyone anywhere can and will be saved in the same way. Dispensationalism insists on the critical time factor and does not permit an archetypal faith principle that claims that people can and will be saved without knowledge of Christ in this era in human history.
3. "There are many post-Christ individuals without explicit knowledge of Christ now." No one disputes this fact.
4. "Therefore these too can be saved without explicit knowledge of Christ as were their pre-Christ counterparts." This conclusion is inadmissible. As already argued, pre-Christian times, like post-Christian times, had divinely revealed specifics for salvation. The legitimate universalizable principle is that there are divinely revealed specifics of salvation for all humans regardless of time and location. In the present dispensation the "specific" is knowledge of Christ. Indeed, circumstances of birth of individuals since the Cross are not any more or less advantageous for the unevangelized, since divinely revealed specifics for salvation were given in pre-Christian times as well.[82]

Dispensationalism rejects the conclusions of the inclusivist, wider-hope view. But dispensationalism is able to preserve continuity of faith toward God in both the Old and New Testaments while preserving the specificity of the content of faith in both Testaments. In answer to Pinnock's earlier question, "Why would it make any difference if Job were born in A.D. 1900 in outer Mongolia?" dispensationalists answer, "It would not, unless one draws on the definite resources of a discontinuity construct of the history and theology of salvation."

CHAPTER 10

Isaiah, Jonah, and Religious Pluralism

Wayne G. Strickland

With the church's concern for the lost, nagging questions such as these often have been raised: What about those in other cultures who have never heard the gospel of Jesus Christ? What about ancestors who never heard of Christ?[1] Do all roads lead to heaven? Can other religions provide salvation? Do non-Christian religions have any redemptive truth? Should Christians continue to insist on the uniqueness of Christ in the pluralist "global community"?

These questions seem to have led to a reevaluation of the traditional evangelical position known as exclusivism. The philosophical basis for this reevaluation is the relativism introduced by Immanuel Kant, who denied the possibility of validation of absolute truth claims regarding the metaphysical. This perspective was expounded in Hick and Knitter's *The Myth of Christian Uniqueness,* which demanded that Christians give up their claim to the uniqueness of Christ.[2] However, the question is more fundamental than the soteriological issue raised by pluralism. As Newbigin has noted, the central issue in the debate is the "abandonment of the belief that it is possible to know the truth."[3] Many who adopt inclusivistic or relativistic models reject the evangelical doctrine of the inspiration and authority of Scripture, including the claims of Jesus Christ.[4]

Don Richardson, who holds the evangelical doctrine of biblical inspiration, opened the door to such reevaluation in his book *Eternity in Their Hearts.* On the basis of general revelation he argued that non-Christian religions are redemptive (i.e., they contribute to the redemption of a people) and may lead to salvation although they are not in and of themselves redeeming, apart from the gospel of Jesus Christ.[5] Similarly Norman Anderson, who has worked for many years among Muslims, represents the growing trend toward reevaluation of the exclusivist model: "I cannot believe that *all* those who have never heard the gospel are *inevitably* lost."[6] Packer concurs that a devotee of another religion might through general revelation experience salvation without the explicit message of the gospel.

> The answer seems to be yes, it *might* be true, as it may well have been true for at least some of the Old Testament characters. If ever it is true, such worshippers will learn in heaven that they were saved by Christ's death and that their hearts were renewed by the Holy Spirit, and they will join the glorified church in endless praise of the sovereign grace of God.[7]

With these leaders within evangelicalism softly raising their voices against absolute exclusivism, it is prudent to examine their challenges. As Newbigin has suggested, "critical reflection is in order."[8]

The Models Surveyed

The traditional evangelical view on the lost condition of those who have never heard of Christ is called "exclusivism"[9] or "restrictivism."[10] According to this view there is only one way to God; salvation comes only through personal faith in Jesus Christ. This view necessitates the corollary that those who do not respond to the gospel of Jesus Christ in this Church Age are lost. More recently some have modified this allegedly "harsh" position, opting for an "implicit-faith" view, which allows for those who have not been introduced to the gospel to be saved by means of general revelation.[11]

The "inclusivist" model insists that Christianity is the sole true religion, but it allows for sincere followers of other religions to be saved. These individuals are viewed as "covert" followers or "anonymous Christians."[12] Contrary to the "implicit-faith" form of exclusivism, inclusivism allows for those who have consciously rejected the gospel of Christ still to be saved. Among those evangelicals who reject exclusivism, this view seems to be attractive, for it gives some measure of absoluteness to Christianity in that it maintains the finality of Christ as the basis of salvation.

The more extreme religious position is relativism, most commonly called "pluralism" or "unitive pluralism."[13] This view rejects the uniqueness of Christianity or of Jesus Christ, holding that God may be reached through major non-Christian religions. Since there is no unique absolute revelation in history, all expressions of religion are relative and are thus equally valid avenues of approach to the divine. Hick and Knitter have pioneered a shift from a Christ-centered paradigm to a more general God-centered paradigm, which levels all major religions. They call this shift a "Copernican revolution" in theology.[14]

Which view harmonizes best with Scripture? While this article addresses the contribution of the Old Testament prophets to the question of religious pluralism, the issue cannot be settled in the prophets. The content of faith for those living during this Church Age is more detailed and explicit than during the period of the Mosaic Law.[15] Although the New Testament prescribes saving faith in Jesus Christ, the Old Testament merely prescribes faith in Yahweh (as would be expected according to the principle of progressive revelation). Erickson argues that people can be saved by means of general revelation alone because of the experience of Old Testament believers.

> If Jews possessed salvation in the Old Testament era simply by virtue of having the form of the Christian gospel without its content, can this principle be extended? Could it be that those who ever since the time of Christ have had no opportunity to hear the gospel, as it has come through special revelation, participate in this salvation on the same basis? On what other grounds could they fairly be held responsible for having or not having salvation (or faith)?[16]

To Erickson's credit, he anticipates the objection that the reason Old Testament believers could be saved without Christ is that the Incarnation was yet future, but that now the Incarnation leaves people without excuse. Appealing to the eternality of God, Erickson rejects this objection, stating that "an eternal God does not necessarily view events sequentially."[17] However, by resorting to such an argument, Erickson denies the salvation-historical principle utilized by God. Further, Old Testament believers did have special revelation, not simply general revelation. They were introduced to the "Seed," the Messiah in Old Testament special revelation.[18]

The Testimony of the Old Testament Prophets

Some may suppose that the Old Testament displays disdain toward people of other cultures, focusing on the nation Israel alone. Exclusivists are sometimes viewed as those who see God as apathetic toward the majority of people groups. Such a view, however, certainly does not harmonize with the claims of the loving, compassionate, and concerned God. The Old Testament pictures God as caring for Gentiles as well as Jews. A number of statements in the Old Testament prophetic books relate to the promises given to Abraham in Genesis 12 and 15—promises that are international as well as national. God told the patriarch that blessing would radiate through him to all nations.

The Old Testament prophets did not engage in "dialogue" with those of other religions as if there were some redemptive value in their religious experiences. Instead the prophets spoke of the one true God in contrast to false deities of other religions.[19] Pinnock argues that there are "teaching passages in the Old Testament which confirm the point that God is in dialogue with the nations."[20] Based on Amos 9:7, he proceeds to present God as concerned for "pagan saints." Pinnock is correct in asserting God's concern for other nations besides Israel, for He does intervene in their affairs and histories. This concern for others outside Israel is a constant though not central theme in the Old Testament prophets.[21] Yet no Old Testament passage (including Ps. 87:6; Amos 9:7; the Book of Jonah; or Mal. 1:11) gives any hint that God works through other religions to redeem people. Pinnock speaks of "God's saving presence in the wider world and in other religions,"[22] but the prophets granted no legitimacy to pagan deities or religions, despite His love or concern for Gentiles. Meanwhile, the prophets explicitly denounced Israel's worship of any supposed deity other than the true God, Yahweh.

ISAIAH

In fact God brought judgment on the nations primarily because of their idolatry and their refusal to embrace the true God. God chose Assyria to judge Israel for her idolatry. Similarly God through Isaiah pronounced judgment on other nations that engaged in idolatry, including Babylon (13:1–14:23); Assyria (14:24–27); Philistia (14:28–32); and Moab (15:1–16:14). The Moabites went to their temple in Dibon, and to the high places to weep (15:2), clearly implying they were involved in idolatrous practices. Though sincere followers of various gods, the Moabites were condemned. And the idols of Egypt were inferior to Yahweh, for they "tremble at His presence" (19:1).

A central motif of the prophet Isaiah is that Yahweh alone is God; He alone is to be worshiped and feared (8:12–13).[23] Appealing to any other god brought God's judgment, and trusting in idols resulted in shame (42:17). In addition the punishment of the wicked is eternal (66:24).[24]

Isaiah stressed that there is only one God through whom salvation is made available to both Jews and Gentiles. Isaiah consistently contrasted the true God of Israel, Yahweh, with idols of neighboring nations. He is superior to idol gods (e.g., 41:21–29). Labeled as "no-gods" (2:20–21), they are worthless and powerless.[25] God provides salvation for Gentiles through faith in Him, using Israel as His agent or mediator. Yahweh's ability to predict the future validates Him as the true God (44:7–8; 45:21), in contrast to foreign deities.

The nation Israel was to mediate blessing to other nations (Isa. 19:24; 25:6–7).[26] Israel, in the person of God's uniquely endowed Servant, was to be the agent or mediator of salvation for various ethnic groups (42:5–9). The exclusivity of Yahweh as the God who provides salvation is indicated by the article with the generic word for God (הָאֵל, "*the* God," 42:5).[27] He is the true God.[28] Through Israel would come the Messiah, the light for nations (42:6),[29] bringing them justice (42:1).[30] Light symbolizes deliverance or salvation[31] (42:16; 45:7),[32] and darkness, by contrast, signifies difficulty or trial. Gentile nations, Isaiah prophesied, will confess Yahweh exclusively as God, acknowledging that their own deities are nonexistent (45:14, 22, 24).[33] These people will forsake their idols (45:16) to worship the God of Israel (45:14, 22–23), for their own idols "cannot save" (45:20). Further, Messiah as the embodiment of Israel, will be "light for the Gentiles" (49:6) with the result that the Lord's salvation will be universal in extent ("to the ends of the earth").

Gentile nations will look to the Lord for salvation and justice (51:5); they will "wait in hope" for deliverance from Him. Some have argued that יָחַל means "to wait in dread or fear" in the sense of anticipating judgment. But when the word is used of waiting for Yahweh, it consistently means to trust in Him (Pss. 31:25; 33:18; 119:43).[34] The context indicates that Isaiah's oracle was addressed to those who seek God's righteousness, not those who reject it (Isa. 51:1–3). In addition, His justice will be "a light to the nations" (51:4), again a picture of deliverance (cf. 9:1; 58:8).

In the eschaton, Israel will attract other nations to Zion, the center of divine blessing (2:2–4; cf. Mic. 4:1). Worship of Yahweh in Jerusalem is not presented as merely one among many legitimate expressions of faith. For Isaiah and other prophets, universal blessing[35] will come from Yahweh (e.g., Isa. 66:19–23; Jer. 3:17; 16:19; Hos. 14:6–7; Zech. 14:16–19). He will draw foreigners into His temple so that it becomes "a house of prayer for all the peoples" (Isa. 56:6–8; cf. 60:1–3).

The name Yahweh argues for the exclusivity of the offer of salvation.[36] Since this name distinguishes Him from all other so-called gods, the prophets proclaimed that there can be no salvation in any other. No other god is ever invoked for salvation. As Scullion notes, "Not only is Yahweh the One, he is the only One; other gods are not simply powerless, ineffective; they do not exist."[37]

JONAH

The Book of Jonah likewise supports the exclusive nature of salvation through Yahweh. When Jonah referred to Him as "the God of heaven," the Gentiles on the ship with him were aware of Yahweh (Jon. 1:9–10). He is not some local deity, but the One who is superior to all others.[38] In fact the non-Israelite sailors worshiped Yahweh and offered a sacrifice to Him (1:16). That the sailors "feared the Lord"[39] points to the fact that they placed their trust for deliverance in the God of the reluctant missionary rather than their own gods. The Book of Jonah also demonstrates God's concern for those outside the commonwealth of Israel.[40]

It is reasonable to infer that when the people of Nineveh believed in God (3:5), they were placing their faith in Yahweh. Salvation was only through believing (אָמַן[41]) the true God, not foreign idols. This clearly presents exclusivism, not pluralism.[42] The Hiphil form of אָמַן[43] means "to declare trustworthy."[44] And when this verb is followed by the preposition בְּ ("in") linked to יהוה ("Yahweh"), the idea of a response of genuine faith is indicated.[45]

The Hiphil form of the verb אָמַן occurs first in Genesis 15:6. Abraham's faith was reckoned to him as righteousness in the judicial or forensic sense. Based on this faith in God's promise, he entered into a trusting relationship with Yahweh. As Childs notes, this understanding of faith, which surfaced in Genesis 15:6, became a central motif in Isaiah.[46] The verb אָמַן linked with בְּ conveyed faith in the Lord, as stated in Isaiah 28:16 and 43:10.[47]

Conclusion

The Scriptures consistently present a simple, yet narrow way to God. Salvation is not available through sincerity or religious efforts. Rather, individuals are accorded a place of blessing and salvation with God for eternity solely through the "seed," the Branch, the Servant, the Messiah of the Old Testament. This way to salvation is not restricted to Israel; it is available to all nations. Thus religious relativism and pluralism do not square with the testimony of the Old Testament and must be rejected. Continuing the exclusive message of the antecedent special revelation, the Old Testament prophets also proclaimed the possibility of Gentiles enjoying salvation. However, just as with the people of Israel, for Gentiles deliverance was available only through explicit faith in Yahweh. God desires to extend His blessings to all peoples, with Israel having a special place as a mediator of blessing. Yahweh is not viewed as one of several ways of blessing, for the requirement is for explicit faith in Yahweh alone.

The Old Testament prophets give no sanction to the notion of religious pluralism. God's love and dealings are universal, but the message of salvation presented in the Old and New Testaments allows for only one God and one means of salvation. The church must not give up the centrality of Jesus Christ for the sake of accommodation.

CHAPTER 11

The Fate of Those Who Never Hear

Millard J. Erickson

At various times in the history of the church, different areas of doctrine have been disputed. The situations leading to these debates have varied considerably. In a sense Pelagius' desire that people live a good life led to the debate over human goodness and sinfulness in the late third and early fourth centuries, the debate known as the Augustinian-Pelagian controversy. Disagreement over the selling of indulgences in the sixteenth century led to the dispute between Martin Luther and the Roman Catholic Church over the nature and basis of salvation. One of the burning issues of the present day is the extent of salvation, occasioned by increasing cultural and religious pluralism in what have formerly been "Christian" nations, and by the discussion of the fate of those who never hear the gospel of Jesus Christ.

From its very beginning, Christianity has been evangelistic, holding its adherents responsible to share with others the good news of Jesus Christ and salvation through faith in Him. This in turn entails certain concepts. One is universal sinfulness, guilt, and condemnation. Another is the necessity of faith in Jesus Christ, involving a certain element of information that must be believed. While there never was exact agreement on the relative percentage of the human race that would be saved, there is consensus that not all who have lived will receive eternal life.

However, in recent years controversy has arisen about these concepts. The uniqueness, exclusiveness, and necessity of Jesus Christ and belief in Him for salvation are being questioned. In light of this and other considerations, it is important to investigate carefully the question of who will be saved, and on what basis. The study of this question is especially important at this time for several reasons.

Widespread Confusion

First, it is important to address this subject because confusion has arisen regarding salvation and Christ, even in circles where this has traditionally been given the highest value. The Barna organization's polling data published in 1992 indicated a rather high degree of correct understanding of the basis of salvation. When asked to describe their belief about life after death, 62 percent of the respondents agreed that "When you die, you will go to heaven because you have confessed your sins and have accepted Jesus Christ as your Savior." Only 6 percent said people go to heaven "because God loves all people and will not let them perish."[1] However, when asked to respond to the statement, "All good people, whether they consider Jesus Christ to be their Savior or not, will live in heaven after they die on earth," those who disagreed outnumbered those who agreed by less than a five to four ratio! Probably this means that the emotional factor has overwhelmed the rational. Perhaps this conflict results from a sympathy for others, a desire to see others receive the same benefits of salvation they themselves have received, rather than relating this belief to rational or doctrinal considerations.

Effect on Other Doctrines

A second reason for addressing this subject is that doctrinal considerations in this area affect other doctrines. Doctrine is organic, so that the position taken on one doctrine influences conclusions in other areas as well. Even when this is not consciously done, and a doctrinal scheme is internally inconsistent, sooner or later the logic of the matter prevails, producing a modification in the other beliefs.

THE INCARNATION

One obvious connection is between one's view of the extent of salvation and the doctrine of the Person of Christ, specifically, the Incarnation. If, as Christianity has traditionally claimed, Jesus is the unique Incarnation of God, then one's relationship to Him is potentially also unique and indispensable to a proper relationship to God. Hick has edited or coedited two books whose titles bear an interesting similarity: *The Myth of God Incarnate* and (with Paul Knitter) *The Myth of Christian Uniqueness*. The parallel in titles is not surprising, for if God has become incarnate in Jesus, then the Christian faith is unique. Hick puts it this way: "If Jesus was literally God incarnate, the second Person of the holy Trinity living a human life, so that the Christian religion was founded by God-on-earth in person, it is then very hard to escape from the traditional view that all mankind must be converted to the Christian faith."[2] The logical flow may of course move in either direction. If for some reason a person is convinced that all humanity need not necessarily be converted to belief in Jesus, then He was not the unique Incarnation of God.

THE TRINITY

Another doctrine closely and logically connected with this issue is the Trinity—a concept that causes the Christian view to stand out as unique among the world's religions. On the one hand, it contrasts with strictly monotheistic religions such as Judaism and Islam, and on the other hand with pantheistic Eastern religions such as Hinduism. Thus any attempt to say that people may be saved by any one of several religions because they are basically all the same would appear to founder on the unique doctrine of the Trinity, which cannot simply be assimilated to the doctrinal views of these other religions. As a result, some people challenge the legitimacy of the doctrine of the Trinity, claiming that the Bible does not really teach such a doctrine. Others call into question the uniqueness of the Christian doctrine of the Trinity, maintaining that parallels can be found in other religions.[3]

GOD'S CHARACTER

Other aspects of the doctrine of God relate to and are affected by this matter. Does God have the right to do whatever He chooses, or must He follow and be judged by some antecedent standard of right and wrong? Does He have a right to condemn those who by their circumstances are at a disadvantage in meeting the requisite conditions for salvation? Some consider that God's omniscience (i.e., His knowledge of what is good and right), and, even more, His justice need to be rethought.

Sometimes a related question is raised: Does God have the ability to condemn people? To say that He does, it is argued, would conflict with human freedom, which is considered indubitable. This calls into question His omnipotence.

BIBLICAL AUTHORITY

The nature of biblical authority, or the doctrine of Scripture, is also affected by this doctrine. Apparent tension arises when one examines certain Scripture passages that seem to teach that relatively few will be saved, such as Jesus' statement about the small gate and narrow road, which few find (Matt. 7:13–14). If on other grounds one is convinced that many, perhaps a majority, of the human race are to be saved, then one must interpret those passages differently. One ploy may be to assert that the Bible indeed teaches that relatively few will be saved, but that the Bible is wrong on that point. Another may be to say that there are varying, and even conflicting, motifs in the Bible. Either of these approaches calls for revision of the usual understanding of Scripture.

Another point in which the doctrine of Scripture is affected is in the uniqueness of biblical authority. The traditional understanding of the Bible is that it is the sole authority in matters of faith and practice. If this is the case, then what of those who have no access to the content of the specially revealed truth preserved in the Bible? Some believe that salvation may be possible through "implicit faith," or by responding to what can be known about God and the human predicament from general or natural revelation. If this is the case, then what is the unique status of special revelation? Is it really necessary?

A further point at which tension arises in this area is the complex of factors known as religious (or in this case specifically, Christian) authority. Some varieties of Protestantism, such as the scholastic orthodoxy of the seventeenth century and some streams of twentieth-century fundamentalism have emphasized the Bible exclusively. More classical Reformation thought speaks of a twofold authority, the external or objective authority, the Bible, and the internal or subjective authority, the internal witness of the Holy Spirit. Roman Catholicism and, to a lesser extent, Anglicanism and Eastern Orthodoxy emphasize tradition as a channel of divine authority. Other movements, usually on the fringe of Christianity, have emphasized a direct speaking by the Holy Spirit. In the 20th century, Pentecostalism, followed then by the charismatic movement and the so-called "Third Wave," has been of this variety of approach. Methodism, following the lead of John Wesley, speaks of a fourfold basis of authority: Bible, reason, tradition, and experience. In recent times the emphasis on personal experience has grown, both in extent and in intensity. However, if personal experience plays a major role, then logically the Bible's authority must be downgraded to some extent. Thus the controversy over the saved at least potentially creates controversy over the Bible and its authority.

Salvation

Another and more obvious point of effect of the discussion relates to the nature of salvation. What is the nature of salvation? What does it mean to be saved? This raises a whole complex of issues in contemporary thought. Whereas traditionally salvation was thought of as restoration of fellowship with God, canceling guilt and condemnation and bringing about positive favor with the Lord, this is now being challenged. The various nuances of liberation theology see salvation as at least in part a deliverance of a person or group from oppression, with this oppression being seen as racial (black theology), sexual (feminist theology), or economic (third-world liberation theologies).

Also in recent years some writers have emphasized salvation as holistic. Rather than simply a spiritual matter, affecting the spiritual standing of the person relative to God, salvation, it is argued, involves the whole person. For example, Clark Pinnock says Acts 4:12 ("There is salvation in no one else; for there is no other name under heaven that has been given among men, by which we must be saved") includes physical healing in the concept of salvation.

These definitions of salvation that include physical healing or freedom from oppression either as supplements to or substitutes for the older idea of salvation as primarily justification, regeneration, and the like, create or encounter broader problems. For if God's failure to provide salvation in the older sense to all persons is a difficulty, then the failure to provide these other dimensions must be an even more severe problem, since many who are devoutly religious and even devoutly Christian suffer ill health or injustice. The nature of salvation relates to divine justice, and thus the matter is in need of further discussion.

TRUTH AND LOGIC

This problem also bears on the nature of truth and of logic. An earlier view of truth held that the truth of a proposition also means the falsehood of its contradiction. One way to refute a statement was to verify its contradiction. Conversely, arguing for the truth of a proposition might require refuting what contradicted it. This was because logic was believed to apply.

This position encounters some difficulty in the current discussions on salvation. Traditionally Christianity and its competitors, the other major world religions, have been seen as contradicting each other in sufficiently significant ways so that both could not be simultaneously true in the same respect. If, however, contemporary pluralism is correct, these apparently contradictory views are actually the same thing. To say this, however, requires one of two tactics. One would require a criticism of one or both of the religions, concluding that they do not teach what they have been thought to teach, or if they do teach that, people are not bound to accept that teaching. The other tactic would be to revise logic, so that two statements can actually contradict each other, and yet both be true. On this basis, the locus of truth would not be objectively within the propositional statements, but subjective or in terms of the effect produced in the person exposed to them.

HERMENEUTICS

This teaching or this set of issues also affects hermeneutics. One solution to the problem of the apparent conflict of biblical teachings, either with the teachings of other religions or with the contentions of a theory such as pluralism or inclusivism, is to interpret exclusivist passages, such as Jesus' words, "I am the way, and the truth, and the life; no one comes to the Father, but through Me" (John 14:6), as metaphorical, rather than literal. When one takes this approach, however, there are other potential complications. Does one interpret all biblical teachings in this metaphorical fashion? If not, on what basis does one distinguish among them? Is there a consistent basis for this, or is it simply ad hoc in nature? One's hermeneutical theory and practice are put to the test by these issues.

THE NATURE OF RELIGION

This discussion also raises and sharpens the question of the nature of religion. In the past, religion has been considered largely a matter of doctrine or of ideas, so that what separated different religions from one another was their teachings. Faith was then also thought of in a corresponding fashion. Being a Christian, or being Christianly religious, involved what one believed, believing the doctrines of Christianity rather than those of some competing religion.

The nineteenth century opened this issue to debate, however. Immanuel Kant said human experience includes three areas: (a) pure reason, or the cognitive, the domain of rational "sciences"; (b) practical reason, or the volitional, the domain of ethics; and (c) judgment, or the emotional, the domain of esthetics. Whereas religion had usually been thought of largely as belief, Kant placed it in the second realm, ethics. Albrecht Ritschl largely followed him, but Friedrich Schleiermacher made religion a matter of feeling.

It is apparent that the ideological content of the various world religions differs considerably. If, however, religion is a matter of certain feelings and experiences, rather than ideological concepts, then the various religions may have a more generic quality than has been thought. Indeed, this seems to underlie the pluralism of John Hick, who describes at some length worship experiences of different religions, and who documents those descriptions with excerpts from religious literature of various sources.[4] This point is also found in the writing of Raimundo Panikkar, who claims that the Trinity is not distinctively Christian, and who interprets each of the Persons of the Trinity in terms of experience, showing how each of the three types of experience is found in several religions.[5] Thus the whole question of the nature of religion, whether it is an autonomous sphere of human experience, or whether it can be assimilated into some other type of experience, becomes part of the agenda generated by this discussion.

Global Changes

Another reason this subject or set of issues needs to be addressed is the changing world situation. One major phenomenon is "globalization," the fact that individuals living in one part of the world are in contact with and influenced by things transpiring elsewhere in the world. For much of the history of the world, most people lived their entire lives without coming into contact with individuals of drastically different persuasions or cultures. In such a setting it is easy to be ethnocentric, to think of one's own way as being the right way and indeed the only way. If there was contact with something different, it was immediately thought of as wrong by virtue of its being different.

But this is now changed. A large portion of the earth's population now has had contact with individuals in other religions. This happens through international travel or through refugees from other countries immigrating to one's own nation, bringing their customs, language, and religion with them. And, in fact, missions activity is not restricted to Christianity. Islam has become aggressively evangelistic and missionary on a worldwide scale.[6]

One can no longer assume that a person who stays at home will have no contact with followers of other religions. Other religions are now coming to one's own country and community.

Traditionally Christians have tended to be condescending toward other religions, regarding them either as idolatry, or as clouded or mistaken constructions of the revelation that has been given to all persons. However, as a result of a closer contact, Christians need to ask about the status of these individuals and their religions. What should be the Christian's attitude toward them? Should they be evangelized, or should they be regarded as "fellow travelers," who though they express themselves differently, are bound for the same place?

This question has become more urgent because of the missions crisis. Especially in mainline denominations, missions has retrenched. The number of missionaries under appointment by the mission boards of those denominations has steadily declined over the years. At the same time, evangelical missions has grown rapidly, compensating for the decline of these other organizations' missions programs.[7]

This prosperity of evangelical missions may soon come to an end, however, for changes are taking place within evangelicalism. One is the strong orientation of ministry toward the consumer. This has resulted in large numbers of people coming into the church, but the nature of their commitment differs somewhat from that of earlier generations of evangelicals. In particular, their support of missions differs. Rather than supporting a program, they prefer to support individual missionaries. More recently, evangelical baby boomers have shown reluctance to make long-term commitments to mission activities of which they have only secondhand information. They want personal, direct acquaintance with the work they are asked to support, and they are more inclined to give to limited, concrete projects rather than ongoing programs.[8]

As a result, missions giving is now declining. In fact, giving of all kinds is declining in many churches. This is due in part to the nature of the appeal. Rather than emphasizing responsibility or stewardship, many of these churches have been built on the idea of the church meeting the needs of those to whom it ministers. In this setting, receiving has not always moved on to giving. In one large contemporary ministry only about 15 percent of those who attend are givers. Some churches are attracting large numbers of "seekers" but are not succeeding in bringing them to the stage of being "finders" in sufficient numbers to sustain a ministry of the magnitude developed. Consequently the per capita giving of such ministries, especially when adjusted for changes in the cost of living, is not growing.

Even established churches are experiencing such a decline. While it has been popular to attribute this to a reaction against organized religion as a result of the televangelists' scandals of the late 1980s or to the economic recession and stagnation of the United States and of the entire world economy, the problems seem to go beyond this. With a shortage of financial support, ministries outside the local church are the first to be cut. Thus missions, even in conservative circles, is falling on hard times. As the traditional givers come to retirement age and then die, a financial crisis will confront the churches, and it will hit missions first.

All this challenges believers to rethink their stance toward missions. Some in mainline circles have attempted to be optimistic by concluding that perhaps their inability to send missionaries to evangelize those who have not heard is not such a great tragedy after all. Perhaps these persons, it is argued, possess the truth, so that they do not need to be told of Christ.

Some say the traditional analysis of the status of those who have never heard the gospel is not correct. Evangelism, they point out, is not only unnecessary; it may even be improper, for it is simply exporting one's own cultural quirks to others. It has not been uncommon to attach typically Western or Northern culture, customs, and tastes to the Christian message. For example some missionaries have taught indigenous persons to dress like Westerners or to build houses of worship that are Western in architectural style. Beyond that, some suggest that missionaries have been provincial or ethnocentric in calling on Buddhists, Hindus, Jews, and Muslims, and other non-Christians to abandon their religious beliefs and practices to become Christians.

Those who find in the various religious practices simply "variations on a theme" may have some basis for their interpretations. Some developments within American evangelical popular religion suggest that the uniqueness of Christian practice is more apparent than real. For example some see in certain varieties of contemporary evangelical worship, and especially its music, much that resembles the practices of other religions. A new faculty member at a seminary attended the all-school retreat before the fall quarter. After the first period of singing, he remarked to the academic dean, "We haven't sung anything that a Hindu could not have sung!" Some have seen in the countless repetitions of the words of a song, parallels to the mantras repeated in some Eastern religions. The changing culture of Christian churches and their changing worship practices make this inquiry and discussion all the more pertinent.

Growing Criticisms of Exclusivism

This study also merits attention because of the increasing crescendo of criticisms leveled at the traditional exclusivist approach. One of these, referred to earlier, criticizes the concept of God's justice. If He chooses to save some persons by giving them opportunity to hear the gospel and condemns others who because of their circumstances have not heard of Him, how can He be called just? Has not the term "just" become so elastic as to be virtually meaningless? How can one appeal to others to be just in their human relations when the meaning of justice is not clear? Similarly how can "love" be meaningfully predicated of a God who condemns persons to endless punishment because they have never believed, when they have actually never heard of Him in whom they are supposed to believe?

Another criticism directed toward the traditional view is that it has led to injustice within the human race. The missions enterprise and colonialization have proceeded together, or at least in parallel. The brown and black populations of the countries colonized were regarded by Europeans as inferior and therefore in need of a higher guardianship. This categorization was thought of as including their culture and their religions. Thus one moral justification of the imperial enterprise was that it helped raise the level of the people colonized. Political subjugation of a people was justified because, it was argued, it resulted in or accompanied their conversion to a superior religion, namely, Christianity. Hick says, "But without going into further detail it is, I think, clear that in the eighteenth and nineteenth centuries the conviction of the decisive superiority of Christianity infused the imperial expansion of the West with a powerful moral impetus and an effective religious validation without which the enterprise might well not have been psychologically viable."[9]

A further criticism of the traditional exclusivist position is that it represents a disregard for other humans, failing to respect other people's cultures and religions. To elevate one's own culture and religion above that of others is to elevate oneself. As such, some view Christianity's exclusivism as another version of Western imperialism, in which exclusivism is seen as an expression of hostility toward others.

Also some leaders accuse Christianity's exclusivist approach of setting up doctrines or ideas as idols. Its concepts limit what God can do or they stipulate what He must do. It is argued that this mistakes a human concept of what God is like for God Himself. As such, it is an illicit substitution, usurping commitment to God by commitment to particular doctrines.

Current Widespread Discussion

The discussion of the topics considered in this series of articles is also important because they have never received definitive treatment by the church. No official council has ever given them the concerted attention and authoritative ruling that was given to such doctrines as the Person of Christ and the Trinity, for example. Elements of the doctrine of salvation were certainly treated, but the question of how many will be saved, the ultimate destiny of the lost, or the duration of punishment for unbelievers, did not receive such attention.

There also is a need for this discussion because of the large amount of attention given to this topic in recent years. Not only liberal Protestants, but also Roman Catholics and even evangelical Protestants are wrestling with these issues. Groups as conservative as the Evangelical Theological Society are riven by debate regarding these matters, with Clark Pinnock, John Sanders, and others taking more inclusivist positions. Literature has sprung up in response to this.[10] The question of annihilation has proven especially troublesome in evangelicalism in recent years, with such staunch conservatives as John R. W. Stott, Philip Edgcumbe Hughes, and John Wenham declaring themselves believers in this view. In fact debate over the doctrine of annihilation broke out at a Consultation on Evangelical Affirmations, and no statement could be adopted by the assembled theologians.[11]

One measure of the level of interest in a subject on the scholarly level is the amount of material being published on the subject in journals. An examination of this topic in the *Religious Index One: Periodicals* shows that a virtual explosion of writing on this subject has occurred in recent years. Articles have been published in a number of different kinds of journals. Because this not only concerns theology but also deeply affects missions, the literature has come from a variety of sources.

Practical Implications for Ministry

The implications of these topics for ministry call for discussion. This is especially true of evangelism, whether domestic or foreign. Traditionally, evangelism was motivated at least in part by the conviction that all must be reached with the good news of the gospel, because all are lost and are under God's condemnation for their sins. Now, however, some view the status of the unevangelized differently. Perhaps those who have not heard the gospel are not lost, it is argued. They may be savingly related to God on the basis of the knowledge all humans can obtain from the study of nature and of themselves. Perhaps those who have not heard the gospel in this life will have opportunity to hear it after they die, and such a presentation might well be more convincing than that of an ordinary human evangelist. Thus, if not already "saved," they may well be in the future, even without human instrumentality. Rather than bringing about their salvation, efforts at evangelism and missions may serve only to bring about their condemnation. Further, if some *are* lost, perhaps they will not experience eternal suffering, but will simply cease to exist.

These discussions are spurring new debates regarding the necessity of evangelism. While the more inclusivist views do not eliminate the need for evangelism, they do suggest the need for rethinking its grounds. Whatever the church has believed in the past, it has always included the conviction that it must take the good news to others. This is no mere ivory-tower theoretical endeavor. It is of the utmost importance for it relates to the church's understanding of its reason for existence.

Conflicts in Values

The debate is important also because of much wider issues. To some extent, this interaction is part of a larger collision between traditional beliefs and values and those arising in the present day. As such, the struggle between two different cultures will be affected by this. One such belief, as already noted, is the view of God's authority and justice. Is He bound to follow an external standard of what is right and wrong? Does He have any inherent obligations to humans, other than to fulfill the promises and covenants He has made with them?

Another issue pertains to the nature of responsibility. To what extent are individuals responsible for their decisions and actions? This question does not apply to the matters of implicit faith and so-called postmortem evangelism, for there the question is the justice—or injustice—of condemning persons who have not really heard and thus have not really rejected the offer of salvation. Some of these discussions suggest degrees of punishment in proportion to the knowledge involved. This issue becomes especially provocative in respect to annihilation. Traditionally the sense of freedom and responsibility required the view that one is held responsible for the consequences of one's actions and that individuals should make such choices enlightened by awareness of those results. More recently, however, modern-day culture has tended to blunt the unfortunate results of poor choices. This is seen in the substitution of "no credit" for the grade of "F." It can also be seen in the type of rhetoric being expressed in connection with the "pro-choice" position on abortion, often insisting on the right to reverse an earlier decision, whether made consciously or by default. Insisting on being able to make this choice is really a case of "pro-*second* choice."

In many areas of life, one gets one chance, without a second opportunity. True, annihilationism does not give "lost" individuals a second chance. However, if the traditional position on this doctrine is correct—namely, that the Bible teaches eternal suffering as the consequence of rejection—annihilation is an attempt to nullify the full extent of the effects of one's choices.[12]

CHAPTER 12

Is There Opportunity for Salvation After Death?

Millard J. Erickson

This article discusses another aspect of the question of whether those who have never heard the gospel will be saved. Perhaps, some argue, those who have never heard the gospel explicitly will yet have opportunity to hear and believe in the future, after death. Might there be an opportunity beyond death, when the message will be presented? This view—which goes by various names but will here be called "postmortem evangelism"—has experienced something of a resurgence of interest.

This view has had a fairly long history, though only in recent years has it been popular. For much of its earlier history, it has existed virtually on the fringes of Christianity. Only recently have orthodox or evangelical Christians expressed interest in it. This view is an alternative not only to the orthodox position, but also to the implicit faith position. It agrees with the former in that faith must be explicit, that is, a person must consciously understand and accept Jesus Christ as his or her Savior. And postmortem evangelism agrees with the latter (that faith may be implicit) in that God is considered unjust and unloving to condemn anyone to eternal punishment who has had no opportunity to hear of Christ's redemptive work.

Doctrinal and Logical Inferences Given in Support of Postmortem Evangelism

According to Bloesch, hell is part of God's loving plan. It is exclusion from communion with God, but not from His presence. It is to be thought of as "a sanitorium of sick souls presided over by Jesus Christ."[1] Bloesch's concept of election, which draws on Karl Barth's doctrine, enters into the consideration, so that he contends that "even those who dwell in unbelief are elected by God in Jesus Christ, though not to salvation as such but to the exposure to salvation."[2] While hell is not seen as providing purification in the sense advocated by Nels Ferré, Bloesch does not exclude the idea that some might be transferred ultimately from hell to heaven.

> We do not wish to build fences around God's grace, however, and we do not preclude that some in hell might finally be translated into heaven. The gates of the holy city are depicted as being open day and night (Isa. 60:11; Rev. 21:25), and this means that access to the throne of grace is possible continuously. The gates of hell are locked, but they are locked only from within.[3]

Hell, according to Bloesch, is not outside the sphere of God's mercy or His kingdom. It is conceived of as the last refuge of the sinner. Bloesch professes something of an agnosticism about the future state of unbelievers: "Edward Pusey voices our own sentiments: 'We know absolutely nothing of the proportion of the saved to the lost or who will be lost; but this we *do* know, that none will be lost, who do not obstinately to the end and in the end refuse God.'"[4] This way of putting the matter and the insistence that "even the despised and reprobate are claimed for Jesus Christ in some way or other,"[5] leaves the impression that only eternally persistent rejection of the offer of grace excludes a person from heaven.

Probably the person who has exerted the strongest influence for this concept, even among conservative interpreters of Scripture is John Peter Lange, in his commentary on 1 Peter 3:18–20. He wrote, "Holy Scripture nowhere teaches the eternal damnation of those who died as heathens or non-Christians; it rather intimates in many passages that forgiveness may be possible beyond the grave, and refers the final decision not to death, but to the day of Christ."[6]

Sanders reports several of these passages. While not identifying these as supporting his own arguments, he elsewhere says, "I also see many strengths in the concept of eschatological evangelization, particularly theological plausibility of its account of universal evangelization."[7] Since he cites several supporting texts without naming any advocates, one may safely conjecture that the argument is his:

> Several texts are customarily cited in defense of this assertion: "He has fixed a day in which He will judge the world in righteousness through a man whom He has appointed [Jesus]" (Acts 17:31); "I know whom I have believed and I am convinced that He is able to guard what I have entrusted to him until that day" (2 Tim. 1:12); "in the future there is laid up for me the crown of righteousness, which the Lord, the righteous

> Judge, will award to me on that day; and not only to me, but also to all who have loved His appearing" (2 Tim. 4:8); and "we may have confidence in the day of judgment" (1 John 4:17; see also John 5:25–29). In addition, it is pointed out that Jesus said that "many shall come from east and west, and recline at table with Abraham, and Isaac, and Jacob, in the kingdom of heaven" (Matt. 8:11/Luke 13:29) and that the gates of the heavenly Jerusalem will never be closed (Rev. 21:25). These texts are taken to mean that God still invites sinners from all areas of the globe and all periods of history to repentance in the afterlife.[8]

Sanders notes the objection by many evangelicals to this concept of opportunity after death on the basis of the parable of Lazarus and the rich man, which they believe to be evidence that an individual's destiny is fixed at death. Sanders responds by stating that "so literalistic an interpretation is by no means generally accepted in the scholarly community, especially in light of the fact that the point of all three parables in Luke 16 is to instruct us about the use of wealth, not about eschatology."[9] He says the issue is which view "makes best sense of God's universal salvific will and the other guiding themes of Scripture." He says the verses typically cited in support of the view that human destiny is fixed at death can easily be answered by the advocates of postmortem evangelization, and that, at the very least, it can be argued that the biblical witness is not clear-cut in this matter.[10]

Pinnock contends that Scripture does not require the view that death closes the door of opportunity. He bases this at least in part on the idea that while the fate of some may be fixed at death, for others that is not the case. Babies who die in infancy are a major example, he says. The question then becomes whether others may qualify for special treatment. Yet having said that, he asserts that it is not so much a matter of qualification as of disposition:

> Humanity will appear in its entirety before God and God has not changed from love to hate. Anyone wanting to love God who has not loved him before is certainly welcome to do so. It has not suddenly become forbidden. No, the variable is the condition of the human souls appearing in God's presence.[11]

What Pinnock seems to assume is that if one responded to God with love at this point, it would be accepted and would therefore result in the person receiving eternal life. But is that the case? The question cannot be settled simply by asserting that it is not a question of qualification but of disposition. What is under dispute at this point is whether God gives opportunity after death for salvation.

Pinnock adds another point, this time from logic. He contends that the logic behind postmortem encounter "rests on the insight that God, since he loves humanity, would not send anyone to hell without first ascertaining what their response would have been to his grace. Since everyone eventually dies and comes face to face with the risen Lord, that would seem to be the obvious time to discover their answer to God's call."[12] This contention in turn rests on another feature of Pinnock's theology, namely, that God does not know in advance what human beings will do, how they will choose, or what they will believe. This in turn is an inference from Pinnock's view of freedom. Whereas Arminians customarily regard God as foreknowing what humankind will freely choose to do, Pinnock (rightly, in this writer's judgment) says that for God to be able to know individuals' actions, it must be certain what they will do. That, however, is incompatible with the usual Arminian understanding of freedom. Therefore Pinnock has abandoned belief in divine omniscience. Some theologians suggest the solution of "middle knowledge," whereby God knows what human decisions *would have been.* But Pinnock's view does not allow him to accept this as a resolution of the difficulty.[13]

The View That Christ Actually Offered Salvation to Some Dead Persons

Several passages, especially 1 Peter 3:18–20 and 4:6, that refer to Jesus' descent and preaching, play a crucial role in support of postmortem evangelism. Salvation after death is related to the belief that Jesus, between His death and resurrection, descended into hades and there proclaimed the gospel to individuals enslaved there from Old Testament times. This is supported by the statement in the Apostles' Creed, "He descended into hades," which in turn is supposedly suggested in Acts 2:31; Ephesians 4:9–10; 1 Peter 3:18–20; and 4:6. Two steps are required if one is to believe on biblical grounds that such an opportunity is given after death to all persons who have not believed during this life. First, it is necessary to demonstrate that 1 Peter 3:18–20 does indeed teach that Christ preached the gospel to individuals in hades between the first Good Friday and Easter, and that this was a genuine offer of salvation on the basis of belief. Second, one must demonstrate that the offer made to those Old Testament persons is also available to all persons who live and die after that time.

It is worth noting that the presence of the clause in the Apostles' Creed, which undoubtedly was a major factor in inducing belief in the doctrine during the medieval period, did not occur until relatively late. It is not found universally in the creed until the eighth century, though it was found in some versions as early as patristic times. It is included in the Athanasian Creed, composed about the middle of the fifth century and accepted by both the Eastern and Western wings of the church.[14]

The tradition of a descent of Christ into hades goes back to early church history. Interestingly, however, it was not associated with 1 Peter 3:18–20 for some time. Selwyn says that "the outstanding fact in the Patristic evidence before A.D. 190 is that, despite the popularity of the doctrine of Christ's 'harrowing of hell,' I Peter iii. 18ff. is never quoted as authority for it."[15] Loofs says Irenaeus "never quotes the passage at all, nor, in dealing specially with the *Descensus,* does he even allude to it,"[16] though Irenaeus regarded 1 Peter as an authentic epistle. Clement of Alexandria, Origen, and Hippolytus, however, did mention the descent in relation to 1 Peter 3. According to Augustine Christ's preaching was in His preexistent form to the people of Noah's day. Three of the major interpretations of the passage (i.e., Christ preaching in hades to men, or to angels, or to those living in the days of Noah) were held by some of the church fathers.

QUESTIONS ON 1 PETER 3:18–20

Several issues are involved in the interpretation of this passage. Those questions and the major answers given to them are as follows:

1. Who did the preaching?
    a. Jesus (most interpreters hold this view)
    b. Enoch[17]
    c. Noah, but Christ was actually preaching through him by the Holy Spirit[18]
2. To whom was the preaching given?
    a. Fallen angels[19]
    b. Humans, in hell[20]
    c. Humans, who repented just before they died in the Flood[21]
    d. People who lived in the time of Moses[22]

3. What was preached?
   a. The gospel, that is, the good news of the availability of salvation
   b. Christ's triumph over death
   c. Judgment of condemnation[23]

4. When was the preaching done?
   a. In the days of Noah[24]
   b. Between Jesus' death and resurrection
   c. After Jesus' resurrection but before His ascension[25]
   d. At the time of an "invisible ascension" of Christ on Easter Sunday morning, just after His appearance to Mary[26]
   e. Throughout history, being symbolic of the universality of salvation, rather than a single literal occurrence[27]

SIX MAJOR VIEWS ON 1 PETER 3:18–20

Taking into account all possible combinations of the above answers would theoretically allow for 180 different theories. Since, however, the position taken on one of these questions in many cases severely limits the available options, the actual number is considerably less. The number tends to reduce to the following six interpretations.

1. Christ "in spirit" preached through Noah when Noah was building the ark. This was a message of repentance and righteousness, given to unbelieving persons who were then on earth but are now "spirits in prison" (i.e., persons in hell).
2. Between His death and resurrection Christ preached to humans in hades, giving them a message of repentance and righteousness, thus giving them opportunity to believe and be saved, though they had not availed themselves of such an offer during their time on earth.
3. Between His death and resurrection Christ went to people in hades and announced that He had triumphed over them and that their condemnation was final.
4. Between His death and resurrection Christ proclaimed release to people who had repented just before the Flood. He led them from imprisonment in purgatory to heaven.
5. Between His death and resurrection or between His resurrection and ascension, Christ descended into hades and

proclaimed His triumph over the fallen angels who had sinned by mating with women before the Flood.

6. The reference to Jesus' preaching is not to be taken literally. It is symbolic, conveying in this graphic form the idea that redemption is universal in its extent or influence.

Examination of the passage requires much more attention than can be given in the space of this article. Several issues need to be addressed, however, which should narrow considerably the number of viable options.

A basic question pertains to what was preached, and that centers on the meaning of the word κηρύσσω in 1 Peter 3:19 and 4:6. According to views three and five above, this means preaching either judgment or a triumph over the hearers. In views one and two the preaching was the proclamation of the need to repent and the possibility of forgiveness. In view four it means a declaration of forgiveness and liberation. Thus in views one, two, and four the preaching was "good news," while in views three and five it was "bad news." Which meaning is to be understood here?

The word used here is simply the broad word for proclamation. It is not necessarily restricted to evangelization or declaration of good news, or the message of salvation. The idea of bad news here, however, seems to be problematic on one or two grounds. For one thing, it is not consistent with the rest of Jesus' preaching. While He certainly spoke words of harsh criticism and even condemnation of the Pharisees, it is difficult to find parallels to Jesus "lording it over" persons who were already in prison and incapable of harming or misleading others. Further, the context does not seem to fit this interpretation well. The argument of 1 Peter 3 seems to be concerned with the matter of bearing witness, or giving an account of one's faith. In fact verse 15 speaks of believers doing this witnessing "with gentleness and respect." This hardly seems consonant with a declaration of condemnation or victory by Christ. This, then, seems to favor interpretations one or two.

Who were the recipients of the message? Were they humans or angels? Much has been made of the idea of a parallel with the Book of Enoch, in which Enoch preached to the angels who were disobedient in the time of Noah. The claim is then made that this tradition would have been familiar to Peter's readers and that he merely modeled his argument along that line. Further, there is the claim that the "sons of God" in Genesis 6 were angels. Genesis 6 is then linked with 2 Peter 2:4 and Jude 6. Then 1 Peter 3:19 is associated with these several verses and with the idea of preaching to fallen angels.

There is much to commend this view, since there was considerable interest in angels at that time. Yet there are problems with it. For one thing, there is no assurance that the "sons of God" in Genesis 6 refers to angels. This is a highly disputed passage. Further, the idea of angels mating with humans to produce offspring seems to contradict Jesus' statement in Matthew 22:30. (Some say Matthew 22:30 indicates that though they do not marry, they do mate. That seems to be a remote interpretation, however.)

What of the view that this was a declaration of deliverance to those who repented in the time of the Flood, but who did so too late to avoid perishing? This view faces several difficulties as well. For one thing, there is no reference to such repentance in the account of the Flood. For another, this creates a special class for these persons, as compared with the rest of those who lived and died in Old Testament times. Why should this be? Presumably, if others in the Old Testament who repented were spared spiritually, these would be spared also, though they perished physically in the Flood. Why should this preaching then focus on them?

Pannenberg holds a rather different view, namely, that this passage is to be understood symbolically. In an exposition of the Apostles' Creed he discusses the tradition in the early church of Christ's preaching in hades and notes that this tradition is found in the New Testament only in 1 Peter 3:18–20 and 4:6. That Pannenberg does not take this descent and preaching literally is indicated by his comment that the controversy between Lutheran and Reformed theologians over whether it was the crucified or the risen Lord who descended into hell could come only to the kind of mind that confuses the image with the thing itself.[28] This is made clearer still in his book, *Jesus: God and Man,* in which he speaks of the "increasingly mythological conception of Jesus' preaching in the realm of the dead or in hell" which attached itself to the statements in 1 Peter. He says 1 Peter 3:18–20 and 4:6 should be thought of as referring to "the universal significance of Jesus' vicarious death under the curse."[29]

> The proclamation of the missionary message of primitive Christianity by Jesus himself in the realm of the dead is not, like the crucifixion, a historical event. The pictorial character of this concept is not simply a part of the

> mode of expression, as is the case with the resurrection which still is a specific, historically definable event. The symbolic language about Jesus' descent into hell and his proclamation in the realm of the dead is just what has been falsely asserted about Jesus' resurrection, namely, a statement about the real significance of another event, his death.[30]

It is difficult to ascertain the basis of Pannenberg's position. In his view neither biblical nor ecclesiastical tradition per se carries authority. Thus it is somewhat puzzling to know why he considers this a viable view. He seems to say that this idea in the Scriptures is acceptable only because of extrabiblical writings.

EVALUATION OF VIEWS ONE AND TWO

This leaves two major alternatives: views one and two. The second interpretation, that Christ preached a message of repentance to people in hades, seems to be the only one that could support the idea of postmortem evangelization. Yet it faces a problem: Was the preaching given only to people in Noah's time but not others? In other words this theory does not seem to explain the reference in the context to those in the time of Noah. In addition, this theory seeks to draw support from other references, but on closer examination those are even more ambiguous. They refer either to God not leaving Jesus' soul in hades or to Jesus descending to earth.

View one, that Christ preached through Noah, of course, has difficulties both with the "spirits" in prison and with the preaching. The latter does not seem to be without parallel, however. For example Luke wrote of the Holy Spirit speaking through the mouth of David (Acts 1:16; 4:25) and the expression "the word of the Lord came upon me, saying . . ." is virtually a paradigm for the Old Testament prophets. Regarding the spirits in prison, Selwyn argued that πνεῦμα is never used absolutely (i.e., without a "defining genitive phrase") to refer to human spirits, and thus it must refer to good or evil angelic spirits.[31] Grudem, however, has shown that this is not the case.[32] Grudem further argues that the question of time regarding the "spirits in prison" may be understood from the time perspective of the writer.

Probably the most important issue between views one and two is the context. As suggested earlier, the focus of 1 Peter 3 is on faithful, gentle, respectful witnessing, giving a reason for one's faith, even in the face of opposition. This, plus the references to those in the time of Noah, seems to favor the first view, even though it has not been greatly in favor of late. Careful defenses of this position, taking into account the usual objections to it and the weaknesses of the alternatives, have recently been advanced.[33]

Related Doctrinal Issues

The wider contextual issue, however, concerns the question of the harmony of this teaching with broader doctrinal issues taught in Scripture. Evangelicals generally have not held to the view that Christ descended into hades and preached there. In the late 1960s the chaplain of Wheaton College decided that a series of chapel messages on the Apostles Creed would be desirable. Members of the Bible department were asked to preach, each on a different phrase of the creed. No one, however, was willing to preach on "descended into hades," because no one believed in it. Therefore that phrase was omitted from the series.

The major reason for hesitancy about this concept stems from the conviction that the Bible teaches that death ends all opportunity for decision for Christ, so that one's eternal destiny is sealed at death. This is defended on the basis of several passages. One is Jesus' portrayal of Lazarus and the rich man (Luke 16:19–31). Scholars have debated whether this is a parable. If it is, it is the only parable in which one of the characters is named. Those who hold that it is a parable maintain that one cannot obtain doctrine from parables. However, even if events referred to in Jesus' parables may not have been historical occurrences, there was nothing in the details of those occurrences untrue to life. Thus in the events referred to in the parable of the prodigal son, though such an event may not actually have happened to three specific members of one family, there is nothing in the parable contrary to the circumstances of life. There is nothing in the parable that could not have happened, and nothing contrary to the culture of that time. The same is true of the other parables. If the story in Luke 16:19–31 is a parable, Lazarus and the rich man were not actual persons and this incident did not occur. However, if this is not an accurate picture of the state of individuals following death, this parable is strongly different from others.

Some writers object that the point of the passage is not to teach eschatology. Sanders, for example, states that "so literalistic an interpretation is by no means generally accepted in the scholarly community, especially in light of the fact that the point of all three parables in Luke 16 is to instruct us about the use of wealth, not about eschatology."[34] This seems, however, to be an example of the common fallacy of assuming that the only lesson that can be drawn from a parable is the central one. That assumption is seriously in need of justification. For if the basic teaching is like the conclusion of a syllogism, then for the conclusion to follow as true from the premises and the syllogism to be valid, those premises must also be true. Therefore one may draw from the passage the premises as well as the conclusion.

Other passages as well speak to the point that death brings opportunity for salvation to an end. The thrust of much of Psalm 49 is that the sinner will go to the grave and perish there, there being no indication of any possibility of release from that place. Revelation 20:11–15 records the scene at the Great White Throne Judgment at which each person who wanted to be judged on the basis of his or her works is judged, and all are accounted guilty. No offer of salvation will be made at that time. In addition, Hebrews 9:27, "It is appointed for men to die once and after this comes judgment," seems to assume an invariable transition from death to judgment, with no mention of any additional opportunities for acceptance. To be sure, this may be labeled an argument from silence, but it would seem that the burden of proof rests on those who maintain that opportunity for salvation follows death.

In the interpretation of 1 Peter 3:18–20 no one view is completely satisfactory. One must be content with finding the one with the fewest difficulties. The present writer finds least problematic the first of these, the idea that Christ by the Holy Spirit spoke through Noah to those of his day. In view of the context of 1 Peter 3:18–20 and when one attempts to bring all the biblical revelation together into a coherent whole, this view seems preferable.

It should be noted, however, that the argument for postmortem evangelism is not successful even on the interpretation that says that Christ descended into hades and offered salvation to the imprisoned sinners there. For even if that view is accepted, it takes care of only those few people. It says nothing about others who have lived since that time or will live in the future. To be sure, the principle of no salvation beyond the grave, or death being the end of all opportunity, has been breached, but that does not give any guarantee that others will be saved. It might have been a unique situation. It is necessary to establish an additional link in the argument, namely, that because Christ proclaimed and provided salvation for those imprisoned sinners, there will also be an opportunity for others. What is offered for this particular premise?

Here there is an amazing absence of argumentation or even of apparent awareness of the issue. Sanders, for example, does not seem to see the point, moving quickly from the former to the latter. Bloesch also seems to identify the two, stating, "What the descent doctrine affirms is the universality of a first chance, an opportunity for salvation for those who have never heard the gospel in its fullness."[35] That, however, does not seem to be the teaching of the doctrine of the descent. If interpreted in the way Bloesch interprets it, what the passage asserts is that Jesus preached to and offered salvation to those persons in hades at that time, not that everyone is guaranteed an opportunity for salvation after death. Nor does Pannenberg offer much help here. He sees 1 Peter 3:18–20 as primarily symbolic, so that the truth is not to be identified with a particular occurrence. This, however, requires a fairly serious revision of the way one handles Scripture.

Beasley-Murray takes a somewhat different approach. He evidently regards as key to interpreting the passage the fact that the generation referred to here is also regarded as the most wicked generation in history. Thus it becomes an example, since it is an extreme case, of the truth that there is hope for all generations. He says:

> The primary reference of both statements [3:19 and 4:6] is the same, and the primary lesson in the writer's mind is to exemplify the universal reach of Christ's redeeming work and the divine willingness that all should know it. The preaching of Christ between his cross and his Easter is intended to prove that the wickedest generation of history is not beyond the bounds of his pity and the scope of his redemption, hence there is hope for *this* generation, that has sinned even more greatly than the Flood generation in refusing the proclamation of a greater Messenger of God and that faces the *last* judgment (4.7).[36]

One could wish for a bit more evidence and support. How does Beasley-Murray know that this was the writer's primary intention? A plausible explanation has been transformed into a probable one, but with no further evidence than the theory itself.

For Pinnock, the argument rests on a certain logic, as he terms it. He sees scriptural warrant for the idea of a postmortem encounter in the preaching of Christ in Hades. He seems to be making an assertion similar to that of Beasley-Murray.

> Could the meaning of the descent into hell be that the people who never encountered the Gospel in their lifetimes can choose to receive it in the postmortem situation? Such a possibility would make good the universality of grace and God's willingness that all should know it. It would make

> clear that the most wicked of sinners are not beyond the scope of God's mercy, and that God is patient even with them.[37]

Could it be? Yes, most certainly that is a possibility. Is it the case, however? That is the question. Pinnock acknowledges that "the scriptural evidence for postmortem encounter is not abundant," but he contends that "its scantiness is relativized by the strength of the theological argument for it."[38]

Conclusion

Evangelicals are faced with whether to accept the notion of postmortem evangelism, a view for which there is no clear biblical teaching and which seems at points to contradict other, clearer biblical teachings. As Mounce observed, the major passage appealed to—1 Peter 3:18–20—is "widely recognized as perhaps the most difficult to understand in all of the New Testament."[39] It is strange to rest a doctrine about the eternal destiny of humans on such an obscure passage. The doctrine is based on a series of interpretations of Scriptures and philosophical and other assumptions which, by the admission of the proponents of this view, are in many cases at best possibilities, and which are scant in number. When, however, a theory is based on a series of statements and inferences, each of which has a rather low level of probability, the probability of the theory decreases. A four-step argument, each step of which was 75 percent probable, would have a probability for the conclusion of only 32 percent. The burden of proof for a view such as this, which at least on the surface conflicts with other teachings of Scripture, rests on those who advance it. And here, one must conclude, the proof falls far short of demonstration.

CHAPTER 13

Is Hell Forever?

Millard J. Erickson

The view known as annihilationism holds that at some point human beings cease to exist. Annihilationism takes one of three forms.[1]

1. Pure mortalism is the idea that human life is inseparably bound up with the human organism. Thus with the death and dissolution of that organism, the person also passes out of existence. This understanding that annihilation applies to all persons is not commonly found within Christian theologies.
2. Conditional immortality, a view considerably more common within Christian circles, agrees with the preceding view in that humans are naturally mortal, but this second view disagrees with the first view by saying that humans can, under certain circumstances, become immortal, or as Paul put it, "put on immortality" (1 Cor. 15:53–54). The essential point, however, is that human beings are not naturally immortal but must have immortality conferred by God.
3. Annihilationism proper says humans are naturally immortal, not mortal. Thus the soul, or more correctly, the person, does not pass out of existence simply because of death; he or she ceases to exist because of God's action. This action occurs either at death, at the general judgment, or at the end of a period of punishment based on each individual's guilt.

Warfield pointed out that these three views do not always appear in pure or unmixed form. Because their advocates are not always careful to keep strictly within the logical limits of one of the three theories, mixed versions of the views are often held.

The overall concept of annihilation has recently received renewed interest, exposition, and defense from somewhat surprising sources. In the past decade a number of rather prominent evangelical theologians and leaders have affirmed they are annihilationists. Among these are Philip Edgcumbe Hughes, Clark Pinnock, John R. W. Stott, Stephen Travis, and John Wenham. At the Consultation on Evangelical Affirmations, held at Trinity Evangelical Divinity School in May 1989, debate broke out on this topic and it proved impossible to formulate an article that would articulate the overall views of those present.[2]

Arguments Advanced in Favor of Annihilationism

A number of arguments are given by those who currently represent this position.

THE ISSUE OF MORTALITY VERSUS IMMORTALITY

One argument, which is both theologically and biblically broad, is to reject the idea that humans are somehow inherently immortal, thus moving the discussion toward the position of conditional immortality. The reason for concern about this, Edward Fudge argues, is that if the natural immortality of the soul is accepted, then the options are reduced to an unacceptable few.[3] He quotes Pusey, who wrote, "If man is admitted to be immortal, and punishment is not endless, there is no other conclusion but that he should be restored."[4] For those who reject this conclusion and who find either alternative unacceptable, rejection of natural immortality takes on significance.

Part of the argument against inherent immortality is that this idea of the soul is of Greek philosophical, rather than biblical, origin. It has found its way into Christian theology at a number of points. Some, especially those of the Reformed tradition, maintain that immortality is part of the image of God in man and God's life-giving by breathing into man the breath of life.[5] Critics, however, have claimed increasingly that this doctrine, which has had a rather long and in some periods unchallenged reign in the churches, is not biblical. They say this doctrine is of pagan origin and crept into Christian thinking through Platonic philosophy. When the Bible speaks of immortality, it refers to the future glorified body, rather than the present soul. Thus the basis of confidence in life after death is bodily resurrection, not immortality of the soul.[6]

While conceding that the early church fathers such as Origen and Augustine believed in the immortality of the soul, Fudge insists that their view differed from that of the Greek philosophers. Their view was not that the soul was inherently immortal. It had come into being at the creative hand of God. Though it survives death, its future existence also depends on God's will. Others, however, such as Justin Martyr and Tatian, openly opposed the pagan doctrine of immortality.[7]

Fudge maintains that the traditional biblical arguments that man is immortal must be rejected. Immortality, he says, does not follow from the fact that humans have been created in the image of God. This divine image in mankind obviously does not include God's omnipotence or omniscience, so why should it include immortality? If it did, it was certainly lost in the Fall, since Genesis 5:3 states that Adam "became the father of a son in his own likeness, according to his image."

Another argument used to support human immortality is from Jesus' statement, "I am the God of Abraham, and the God of Isaac, and the God of Jacob" (Matt. 22:32). Surely, some say, this must argue for the immortality of at least these three patriarchs. However, the context indicates that Jesus' point was to prove the resurrection, not immortality. The parallel passage in Luke 20:37 makes clear that Jesus was speaking of the resurrection of those who belong to God, not the immortality of every person. Further, expressions in the Bible such as "salvation of the soul" (e.g., 1 Peter 1:9; cf. Mark 8:35) do not argue for a separate immortal soul. These are merely quotations of passages such as Psalms 16:9–11; 49:15; and 73:24, which speak of the psalmist's hope for abiding fellowship with God, who will not let His own perish. The word "soul," for both Old and New Testament writers, is here simply referring to the person, not to some entity within him.[8]

Fudge then develops this view at some length through examining the biblical data from both Testaments. The Hebrew word נֶפֶשׁ is so rich and varied in its meaning that it is rendered in 45 different ways by the translators. The same terms are applied to both humans and animals. The conclusion to be drawn from such data is that the human person is an indivisible whole. When death occurs, it is the death of the soul, the whole person, not simply the death of the body, with the soul somehow surviving.[9] Similarly the word ψυχή usually denotes the life of a person, not some part of the individual. Sometimes the adjectival form of the word refers to the unspiritual or carnal person in contrast to the spiritual person (1 Cor. 2:14–16), or the natural body of this life, contrasted with the spiritual body of the life to come (15:44).[10]

ANNIHILATIONISM AND THE IDEA OF "DESTRUCTION"

A second argument used to support the doctrine of annihilation centers around the idea of destruction, together with the concept of its means, namely, the consuming fire. Stott notes that words for "destruction" are often used in relation to the final state of perdition, the most common Greek words being ἀπόλλυμι ("to destroy") and ἀπόλεια ("destruction"). When the verb is active and transitive it means to kill, as in the case of Herod's attempt to murder the baby Jesus and the plot of the Jewish leaders to have Him executed (Matt. 2:13; 12:14). Jesus told His hearers not to be afraid of those who kill the body but cannot kill the soul (Matt. 10:28; cf. James 4:12). If, then, to kill is to deprive the body of life, it would seem that hell is a deprivation of both physical and spiritual life, in other words, an extinction of being.

When the verb ἀπόλλυμι is in the middle voice it means to be destroyed and so to perish, whether physically, as by hunger or snake bite (Luke 15:17; 1 Cor. 10:9), or eternally in hell (John 3:16; 10:28; 17:12; Rom. 2:12; 1 Cor. 15:18; 2 Peter 3:9). Just as believers are those being saved, so unbelievers are οἵ ἀπολλύμενοι ("those who are perishing"). This term occurs in 1 Corinthians 1:18; 2 Corinthians 2:15; 4:3; and 2 Thessalonians 2:10. Jesus said that the broad road leads to destruction (Matt. 7:13). Other verses using this verb are Romans 9:22; Philippians 1:28; 3:19; Hebrews 10:39; 2 Peter 3:7; and Revelation 17:8, 11. It would seem strange, then, Stott says, if those who are said to suffer destruction are not actually destroyed. He agrees with Edwards that it is "difficult to image a perpetually inconclusive process of perishing."[11]

The biblical imagery of hell is also referred to by annihilationists in support of their view. The most prominent element in this imagery is, of course, fire. This is commonly understood as teaching that those who are lost will be submitted eternally to punishing flame and will never be consumed by it. Jesus used the expression "the fire of hell" (Matt. 5:22; 18:9) and spoke of "eternal fire" (18:8; 25:41). The Book of Revelation refers to "the lake of fire" (20:14–15). Stott suggests that fire is associated in people's minds with "conscious torment" because of their having experienced acute pain from being burned. He maintains, however, that the main function of fire is not to cause pain, but to bring about destruction, as incinerators bear witness. This also fits well with the biblical expression "a consuming fire" and with John the

Baptist's warning of the Judge's "burning up the chaff with unquenchable fire" (Matt. 3:12; cf. Luke 3:17). From this data Stott draws this conclusion:

> The fire itself is termed "eternal" and "unquenchable," but it would be very odd if what is thrown into it proves indestructible. Our expectation would be the opposite: it would be consumed for ever, not tormented for ever. Hence it is the smoke (evidence that the fire has done its work) which "rises for ever and ever" (Rev. 14:11; cf. 19:3).[12]

Stott responds to four objections to his understanding of the lake of fire. The first is the vivid picture of hell as a place where "their worm does not die, and the fire is not quenched" (Mark 9:48). He points out that Jesus' quotation is from the last verse of Isaiah (66:24), which refers to the dead bodies of God's enemies being consigned to the city's rubbish dump, to be eaten by maggots and burned. While the apocryphal Judith 16:17 applied this to everlasting pain for the nations hostile to God, Jesus, in quoting this verse from Isaiah, did not mention everlasting pain. The worm will not die and the fire will not be quenched—at least not until their work of destruction is done, Stott says. The worm and the fire are everlasting, not the persons subject to them.

A second objection to annihilationism is Jesus' reference to "eternal punishment" in contrast to "eternal life" in Matthew 25:46. If eternal life means that the righteous shall live forever in conscious bliss in the presence of God, does not the parallelism require that wicked unbelievers will forever experience conscious punishment in hell? Stott replies that this interpretation reads into the text what is not necessarily there. Though Jesus said that both life and punishment will be eternal, He did not, at least in this passage, define the nature of either of these. Elsewhere (John 17:3), He spoke of eternal life as conscious enjoyment of God, but it does not follow, Stott argues, that eternal punishment must be a conscious experience of pain at God's hand. "On the contrary, although declaring both to be eternal, Jesus is *contrasting* the two destinies: the more unlike they are, the better."[13] Pinnock responds in a slightly different way. Like Stott, he says Jesus did not define the nature of either eternal life or eternal punishment in Matthew 25:46. But Pinnock adds that Jesus simply stated that there will be two destinies and leaves it there, so that one is free to interpret this verse as meaning either everlasting conscious torment or irreversible destruction. The text allows both possibilities. All it teaches explicitly, he says, is the *finality* of the judgment itself, not its *nature.*[14]

A third objection raised against annihilationism is based on the parable, if that is what it was, of the rich man and Lazarus, as found in Luke 16:19–31. Did not the rich man (called Dives, after the Latin word for rich man) declare that he was "in agony in this flame" (vv. 23–24, 28)? However, one must be cautious in interpreting a parable (if it was a parable) that speaks of "Abraham's bosom" as well as hell fire. Also, since the experiences of the rich man and Lazarus occurred immediately after their death, the most natural interpretation of the passage would be that it refers to the intermediate state between death and resurrection. Stott, in fact, believes this is when the lost come to the horrible realization of their fate. And such an interpretation, he says, is surely not incompatible with annihilation. Similarly, since the "torment" mentioned in Revelation 14:10 will be experienced "in the presence of the holy angels and in the presence of the Lamb," that seems to refer to the moment of judgment, not to the eternal state. The smoke, symbolizing the completed burning, and not the torment, will be forever.

ANNIHILATIONISM AND JUSTICE

A fourth objection against annihilationism is the concept of justice, the belief that God will judge people "according to their deeds," as stated in such passages as Revelation 20:12. This implies that each person's penalty will be commensurate with the evil he or she did. This principle was of course followed in the Jewish law courts, in which the lex talionis limited punishments to retributions corresponding to the offenses. However, Stott argues that if eternal conscious torment is administered as punishment for sins done in time, is there not a serious disproportion between the wrongdoing and the penalty? Is not God guilty of the same sort of inequity that His law prohibited? While not minimizing the seriousness of sin as rebellion against the Creator, Stott wonders if "eternal conscious torment" is compatible with divine justice as revealed in the Bible. The only possible exception to this, Stott says, would be if somehow one's impenitence also continues throughout eternity.[15]

Pinnock also argues this point. This would be infinite punishment for finite sin, for a finite being cannot commit an infinite sin, even if it is against an infinite Being. The major point, however, as he sees it, is that such unending torture of the wicked would serve no conceivable purpose of God except sheer vengeance and vindictiveness. It would spell endless and total unredemptive suffering, punishment for its own sake. There is no question here of reformation or reeducation of the wicked. There could never be any resulting good beyond the suffering itself. He cites with approval Hans Küng's observation that (quite apart from the point that a merciless God contradicts Jesus' teachings about the Father) this concept is strangely out of harmony with present-day practice. In education and in criminology in many states, retributive punishments without an opportunity for probation are being abandoned. It is thus most inappropriate, and to most persons it is monstrous, that God should administer not only lifelong but also eternal punishment of body and soul.[16]

Stott also argues for his view on the basis of verses that have traditionally been used as the basis for universalism. These include John 12:32; 1 Corinthians 15:28; Ephesians 1:10; Philippians 2:10–11; Colossians 1:20. He is not led to universalism because of these verses, but he raises the question of how the impenitents' eternal existence in hell could be reconciled with the biblical teaching of God's apparent reconciling of all things to Himself in His final victory over evil. How can God in any meaningful sense be said to be all things to all people if a certain number of people continue in rebellion against Him and under His judgment? Stott feels that "it would be easier to hold together the awful reality of hell and universal reign of God if hell means destruction and the impenitent are no more."[17]

Pinnock presents at least two more reasons for his belief in annihilationism. One is the doctrine of God. A God who would torment even the rebellious eternally is cruel and merciless. How can one worship and imitate such a Being? Further, everlasting suffering, especially if linked to soteriological predestination, according to which God predestined persons to that fate, raises the apologetic task connected with the problem of evil to an impossible and hopeless level.[18]

Pinnock also argues that a metaphysical problem is involved in the teaching of eternal conscious torment. An unending hell involves a similarly unending cosmological dualism. Heaven and hell just go on existing together forever. Pinnock feels that it would make better sense metaphysically, as well as biblically, morally, and justice-wise, if hell meant destruction and the wicked simply were no more. Otherwise, the "disloyal opposition would eternally exist alongside God in a corner of unredeemed reality in the new creation."[19]

An Evaluation of Annihilationism

The traditional evangelical view is that those who are not saved will suffer endless punishment in hell. The following response to annihilationism includes criticism of arguments advanced by the annihilationists, and a positive argumentation for the traditional view.

THE PHILOSOPHICAL BASIS OF ANNIHILATIONISM

It is necessary first to examine the philosophical concept present within the usual form of annihilationism. As stated earlier, annihilationists contend that the idea that the human soul is immortal, and hence cannot cease to be, or cannot be destroyed, even by God Himself, does not derive from biblical sources, but from Greek philosophy, especially Plato. This argument is built on two false assumptions. One is that similarity of two ideas demonstrates a common origin or cause, or that one of these originates from or is caused by the other. The other assumption is the claim that a causal explanation of something adequately accounts for it, or settles the question of its truth.

These two assumptions must now be scrutinized. The overall difficulty with this argument is the lack of specificity and precision in the description of the Greek view. Greek thought had a variety of concepts on any given issue, rather than one monolithic idea. In Platonism, the view most frequently cited, the idea of immortality is related to the concept of the preexistence of the soul. Thus the soul is eternal or immortal in both directions, past and future, having neither beginning nor end. However, this is not true of the Christian view of man. What is usually described as the doctrine of immortality in Christian theology is that the soul is immortal into the future but not into the past. It will never cease to be at any point in the future, but came into existence at some point in the past.

Also the Greeks viewed the soul as having natural or inherent immortality. The biblical view, on the other hand, is of a derived or dependent, and contingent or conditional, immortality. A person's ability to survive forever derives from God. The soul was potentially immortal when created, but it could have become truly immortal only if the requisite conditions were fulfilled, in other words, if the first parents of the human race had obeyed God's command completely. Therefore a causal connection between Greek philosophy and the Bible on the subject of immortality has not been established. There simply must be more specific resemblance to establish any sort of derivation or common origin of the Christian view from the "Greek" view.

Even if there were some sort of derivation or causation, however, it would not account for the Christian view of immortality. It might give a causal explanation of how this belief came into being, but not the actual reason for it. It would not settle the question of the truth of the idea. One who holds that this does suffice would seem to be guilty of the genetic fallacy, of assuming that explaining the existence of an idea also accounts for its truth.

THEOLOGICAL ISSUES AND ANNIHILATIONISM

God's love. The Scriptures often refer to God's love. But what is its nature? As Pinnock, Stott, and others depict it, His love seems to be a sentimentalized version, in which God would not do anything to cause pain, displeasure, or discomfort to anyone. Thus endless suffering would be incompatible with divine love.

Is this really the picture of God's love given in Scripture? May it not be that God chooses some actions that cause pain to some persons for the sake of a higher good, namely, the greater joy or welfare of the whole of humanity, or more significantly, the good of the whole of reality, especially, the glory of God Himself?

God's will. Annihilationists also seem to have a truncated understanding of God's will. Pinnock complains that if God does not want anyone to perish, then the idea of eternal conscious suffering for anyone is incredible. One must ask, however, whether there may not be more than one sense of God's will. Are there not situations in Scripture in which God willed to permit persons to do what He really did not wish or did not like? A clear case is Jesus' statement in Matthew 19:8 about divorce in the Old Testament era. God's "wish" and God's "will" are to be distinguished.[20] Certainly all moral beings periodically make decisions contrary to their wishes. People choose to do things that they do not really like and choose not to do things that they would very much like to do. This distinction, however, does not seem to be part of Pinnock's thinking. If God wants something to happen, and has the power to bring it about, then, Pinnock says, it must surely occur.

God's justice. As already noted, annihilationists argue against eternal conscious suffering on the basis that it is a punishment grossly disproportionate to the offense. How can a just God punish eternally or for an infinite period of time someone who has committed only a finite sin? How can a finite person be guilty of an infinite wrong?

These questions, however, assume that God and man are basically equal partners, and therefore are able to negotiate a mutually acceptable agreement between them. In such a situation, the human might protest against what is to him a disagreeable outcome. Here, however, one person is finite and owes everything to God, the infinite Person, including even life itself. To fail, then, to honor God, obey Him, and accept what He says is indeed an infinite act of ingratitude and of rejection.

Some contend that no sin or combination of sins could be infinite. What must be measured, however, is the effect, which may seem out of all proportion to the act. Thus one person might make just a tiny pinprick in the body of another, so slight as to be scarcely noticeable. Yet if it is made in a crucial spot or with a contaminated instrument, the effects may prove fatal. The act is then an absolute one, slight though it seems. Annihilationists, in protesting what they see as the injustice of everlasting suffering as punishment, assume that sin does not have a great effect on God, and so it should not be punished infinitely. But this overlooks the full extent of sin's effect on a perfectly holy God, for whom sin must be exceedingly offensive, since it is a contradiction of His very nature.

Annihilationists also assume that punishment in hell is something God administers by His own deliberate, voluntary, and vindictive action, when He really would not need to do so. May it not be, however, that it is primarily the human person who chooses the eternal punishment, or at least chooses the action that leads to that punishment? Indeed, this is the very point C. S. Lewis proposed as a possibility.[21] He wrote that what is most characteristic of hell is not physical flame and attendant suffering. Instead what really makes it hell is the absence of God, with the consequent loneliness, anguish, and longing (whereas God's presence is what makes heaven heaven). Thus sin is a human being saying, "God, go away and leave me alone," and hell is God finally saying, in effect, "All right, you shall have what you wish." In the final analysis it is not God who sends individuals to hell, but those persons themselves.

May it not be that for persons to be what they are, so that salvation may be what it is, they must be so constituted as to have the potential of living forever? Perhaps this is one of those necessary matters, such as God's incapability of making triangles without three sides or circles in which all points on the circumference are not equidistant from the center of the circle.

Of course Pinnock objects to this and similar attempts to minimize in some fashion the severity of hell. One may ask, however, why hell must be understood in the most offensive way possible. It almost seems as if annihilationists are stating the eternal punishment option as unfavorably as possible in order to give rhetorical appeal to their alternate view. This seems, however, to be a less than ideal way of handling a difference. (One of Socrates' opponents or dialogue partners once complained that Socrates stated the opponent's view in the worst possible way.) If true, that is a serious charge, since it suggests an attempt to gain an unfair advantage.

The doctrine of eternal punishment is not well accepted in American society. The idea of individual responsibility is not popular. Though individuals take unwise actions, they are not regarded as having contributed to the outcome of those actions. To suggest that the agent of the action is responsible may seem cold or hardhearted. Reality, as God defines it, is not that way, however. Certain actions bear certain consequences, and justice means that those consequences have to be experienced. God provides for the removal of those eternal consequences for those who repent and accept His provision—and that is grace. Justice, however, does not require that He cancel the inevitable results for those who continue to live independently of Him.

OTHER ASPECTS OF ANNIHILATIONISM

As already noted, both Pinnock and Stott have appealed to Bible passages that are generally used by universalists. They feel, for example, that these verses speak of God's victory over all things, of His reconciling all things to Himself. Yet universalists contend that this is not accomplished without the actual restoration of everything, which would preclude the disposal of anyone, as in annihilation. According to annihilationists, eternal punishment would seem to be a matter of God's giving up on some of His children as incorrigible. They say this would certainly not be the triumph of love. However, it would be the surrender of God's love to the fact of failure.

The same problem applies to the question of God's love and justice. Pinnock has argued that such precludes endless punishment. For a universalist such as Nels Ferré, however, the problem is not solved quite so easily. In his thinking, God's love and justice preclude annihilationism. He argues for universal salvation and against annihilation, using terminology and arguments strikingly similar to those of Pinnock. (Actually, to avoid an anachronism, one should say instead that Pinnock's arguments resemble Ferré's.) Ferré contends that if God gives eternal life to some or most, He would then be unjust in allowing or causing some persons to pass out of existence.[22] That would be a failure of sovereign love. Ferré would probably suggest that an expedient such as annihilation is a case of "taking the hell out of hell." Thus on both these points the annihilationists may be dealing with a two-edged sword.

BIBLICAL EVIDENCE AGAINST ANNIHILATIONISM

The significant passage in support of eternal conscious punishment is Matthew 25:41–46. The usual argument is that just as Jesus was promising believers everlasting life, unending bliss with Him, He was also threatening unbelievers with everlasting punishment. In an extensive argument Fudge attempts to show that when applied to nouns that speak of a resulting condition (such as punishment), αἰώνιος does not denote eternity as it does when modifying nouns that refer to activities (such as punish*ing*). Yet he does not discuss the matter of parallelism in verse 46, namely, that if in the one case (life) the adjective αἰώνιον means eternal, it must also mean eternal in the other phrase (punishment). The parallelism requires that if life for believers is of everlasting duration, punishment for unbelievers must be also.[23] Perhaps most impressive, because of its source, is this statement by John A. T. Robinson, a universalist:

> The genuine universalist will base nothing on the fact (which is a fact) that the New Testament word for eternal *(aionios)* does not necessarily mean everlasting, but enduring only for an indefinitely long period. For he can apply this signification to "eternal punishment" in Matt. 25:46 only if he is willing to give exactly the same sense to "eternal life" in the same verse. As F. D. Maurice said many years ago now, writing to F. J. A. Hort: "I did not see how *aionios* could mean one thing when it was joined with *kolasis* and another when it was joined with *zoe*" (quoted, J. O. F. Murray, *The Goodness and Severity of God,* p. 195). To admit that the two phrases are not parallel is at once to treat them with unequal seriousness. And that a true universalism must refuse to do.[24]

Another issue in this passage may provide some guidance. The place to which the "goats" are consigned in the judgment of the sheep and goats is "the eternal fire which has been prepared for the devil and his angels" (v. 41). Revelation gives more information on this future condition of the devil. The beast and the false prophet will be "thrown alive into the lake of fire which burns with brimstone" (19:20). Then the devil will be cast into the same lake (20:10), and they "will be tormented day and night forever and ever" (v. 10). Then verse 15 states that "if anyone's name was not found written in the book of life, he was thrown into the lake of fire." While these verses only say explicitly that the devil, the beast, and the false prophet will be tormented forever and ever, no statement suggests that the persons whose names are not written in the book of life have any different fate in the lake of fire. This supports the view that the punishment spoken of in Matthew 25:41, 46 is also everlasting in nature.

Is this fire everlasting, however? According to Revelation 14:11 the smoke from this fire of torment of the beast and the false prophet will be forever. Fudge and others contend that the smoke, not the punishment, is everlasting. However, how can there be smoke without something being burned? If these bodies are burned up, consumed, destroyed, how can there still be smoke? What would produce smoke, unless something was burning? For that matter, why would the lake of fire continue to exist, with nothing left to burn?

Another point needing evaluation is Stott's contention that the contrast between life and punishment requires maximum difference. That means that if the former is eternal, the latter is not. One must ask, however, whether this is really so. On what evidence is that contention based? And if it is valid, what does it really require? It would seem that the greater contrast would be between the eternality of "life" and the eternality of "punishment." Overall, this argument for annihilationism is not overly impressive.

Pinnock's argument from metaphysical dualism is not impressive either. He argues, as noted earlier, that hell cannot be eternal because that would require an ongoing dualism in which opposition to God would exist forever alongside God. However, this dualism as such is not ultimate; it is a derived dualism in which continuation of evil depends on Him. Yet its continuation is not a true dualism in the sense of being an active opposition. It presents no challenge or threat to God. It has been brought into complete and permanent subjugation. Thus equilibrium has been attained or achieved in the universe. This would seem, therefore, not to be a genuine tension for theology.

Luke 16:19–31, on the rich man and Lazarus, is frequently presented in arguing against annihilation. Actually, its application is somewhat narrower. This story actually refutes only the idea that unbelieving humans cease to exist at death. There is no explicit basis for believing in a later annihilation. In fact the opposite would seem to be the case.

The idea of the wicked being obliterated rather than suffering endlessly will continue to appeal to sensitive Christians. Yet emotion cannot be the primary consideration in settling theological issues. In this case the biblical and theological data weigh strongly on the side of eternal conscious punishment of the wicked.

CHAPTER 14

Does the Bible Teach Annihilationism?

Robert A. Peterson

In recent years a number of leading evangelicals have stated in writing that they believe in annihilationism—the view that ultimately the resurrected wicked will be obliterated and no longer exist. Michael Green, for example, wrote, "But it [Scripture] does not teach the conscious unending torment of those who are eternally separated from God."[1]

In 1989 Philip Edgcumbe Hughes said, "The conception of the endlessness of the suffering of torment and of the endurance of 'living' death in hell stands in contradiction to this [biblical] teaching."[2]

John Stott affirmed, "I also believe that the ultimate annihilation of the wicked should at least be accepted as a legitimate, biblically founded alternative to their eternal conscious torment."[3] And according to John Wenham, "I believe that endless torment is a hideous and unscriptural doctrine which has been a terrible burden on the mind of the church for many centuries and a terrible blot on her presentation of the gospel. I should indeed be happy if, before I die, I could help in sweeping it away."[4]

Michael Green, Philip Hughes, John Stott, and John Wenham are four stalwarts of evangelical Christianity (in its Anglican expression), and four proponents of annihilationism (though with varying degrees of conviction, as the quotations suggest).

What arguments do these respected evangelical thinkers adduce in support of this view? Are there good answers to these arguments? And what difference does it make whether Christians believe in annihilationism or eternal conscious punishment? This article seeks to address these questions, examining both biblical and theological arguments that are given in support of a view traditionally considered false.

Biblical Arguments

For more than fifty years John Wenham privately believed in annihilationism but hesitated to state it in print. In 1992, however, he was no longer hesitant when he penned "The Case for Conditional Immortality." Conditional immortality, or "conditionalism," for short, is the view that human beings are not innately immortal, but are only potentially so. God gives the gifts of eternal life and immortality to believers, and the unsaved, not having received immortality, ultimately go out of existence. Today the term "conditionalism" is frequently used as a synonym for annihilationism.

Wenham argues for conditionalism by writing that the words used to describe hell in the New Testament "in their natural connotation are words of destruction rather than words suggesting continuance in torment or misery."[5] He said he found 264 New Testament references to the destiny of the unsaved, and he assigns these references to various categories, four of which he believes teach annihilationism. These are references to fire, destruction, separation from God, and death.

FIRE

Gehenna, Wenham points out, refers to the garbage dump in the Hinnom Valley outside Jerusalem, where maggots and fire consumed the refuse (Matt. 5:22, 29, 30; 10:28; 18:9; 23:33; Mark 9:43, 45, 47; Luke 12:5). In Wenham's estimation, when Jesus called hell "the Gehenna of fire," He meant that those cast into it will be annihilated.

Wenham also asserts that Scripture's hellfire imagery (he lists twenty-six references) conveys annihilation. "Fire naturally suggests destruction and is much used for the destruction of what is worthless or evil."[6] He admits that fire in the Bible sometimes causes pain, as in the case of Dives (the name traditionally given to the rich man in the parable of the rich man and Lazarus in Luke 16:19–31). But, he says, this is "a secondary use." Fire chiefly signifies consumption, and therefore hellfire imagery conveys the idea of annihilation rather than endless torment.[7]

However, when Jesus warned of being "cast into the eternal fire . . . the fiery hell" (Gehenna, Matt. 18:8–9), this fate is awful because, unlike fires on earth, hell is where "the fire is not quenched" (Mark 9:44, 48). This is a picture of everlasting suffering, not of destruction.

Jesus' explanation of the parable of the weeds bears out the fact that biblical hellfire imagery signifies pain: "Therefore just as the tares are gathered up and burned with fire, so shall it be at the end of the age. The Son of Man will send forth His angels, and they will gather out of His kingdom all stumbling blocks, and those who commit lawlessness, and will cast them into the furnace of fire; in that place there shall be weeping and gnashing of teeth" (Matt. 13:40–42).

Although Jesus referred in the parable to weeds being burned (v. 30), He did not use it to teach annihilationism. Instead, when He interpreted the weeds being thrown into the furnace, He spoke of suffering. The "furnace of fire" is a place characterized by "weeping and gnashing of teeth" (v. 42), that is, by great anguish.[8]

In Jesus' message about the sheep and the goats, He said the ungodly will be banished to "the eternal fire which has been prepared for the devil and his angels" (25:41). John wrote that "the devil . . . was thrown into the lake of fire and brimstone, where the beast and the false prophet are also; and they will be tormented day and night forever and ever" (Rev. 20:10). Here fire denotes unending torment. This is the fate that awaits the devil, his angels, and unbelieving human beings alike.

How can Wenham claim that hellfire pictures consumption and only secondarily pain, when Revelation 14:10–11 states that the wicked "will be tormented with fire and brimstone. . . . And the smoke of their torment goes up forever and ever; and they have no rest day and night"?

The lake of fire is where the devil will be tormented endlessly (20:10), and where sinners will be cast (vv. 14–15); the lake of fire is said to be their place (21:8). Condemned human beings, therefore, will suffer forever in hell.

Contrary to Wenham's contention, the biblical pictures of fire and burning signify the endless suffering of the unrighteous in hell and not their annihilation.

DESTRUCTION

Wenham argues for conditionalism based on fifty-nine New Testament references to destruction, ruin, and the like. In particular he cites (a) Jesus' contrast between the broad "gate that leads to destruction" and the narrow "gate that leads to life" (Matt. 7:13), (b) Paul's warning that the enemies of Christ's cross will suffer "destruction" (Phil. 3:19), (c) Peter's words about "destructive heresies . . . bringing swift destruction" (2 Peter 2:1), and John's statement that the beast will "go to destruction" (Rev. 17:8, 11). Wenham says these references to eternal ruin, destruction, and loss signify the literal destruction of the unsaved, that is, their annihilation.[9]

Considered in isolation, these verses might seem, at first glance, to teach conditionalism. But they should not be considered in isolation from the rest of the Bible's teaching. Verses such as Matthew 25:41, 46; Mark 9:42–48; Revelation 14:9–10; 20:10, 14–15 have led church leaders throughout the centuries to believe, teach, and confess the never-ending suffering of the lost.

Moreover, not all the passages Wenham cites are even compatible with annihilationism. He calls attention to Revelation 17:8, 11, which states that the beast will go to his destruction. True, this passage does say that, but not in the sense that Wenham understands the word "destruction."[10] He insists that the word "destruction" and its synonyms denote the extinction of the wicked. But the description of the beast's "destruction" that unfolds in the Book of Revelation does not mean he will cease to exist. Two chapters after the prophecy of the beast's "destruction" (17:8, 11) the beast and false prophet are "thrown alive into the lake of fire which burns with brimstone" (19:20). They will still be there "one thousand years" later (20:7, 10). Furthermore, John wrote, as already noted, that the beast, the false prophet, and Satan "will be tormented day and night forever and ever" (20:10). The beast's "destruction," therefore, is not annihilation; it is eternal punishment. This proves that at least two references to "destruction" signify endless torment, not extinction. It also opens the door for us to understand the remaining references in the same way, in light of all of Scripture.

SEPARATION FROM GOD

Wenham bases his case for conditionalism on twenty New Testament references to separation from God, asserting that these references carry "no connotation of endlessness unless one presupposes immortality."[11] Examples include Jesus' words, "Depart from Me" (Matt. 7:23), "cast him into the outer darkness" (22:13), and "he is thrown away as a branch" (John 15:6). Wenham asserts that this separation means "being utterly cut off from the source and sustainer of life. It is another way of describing destruction."[12]

Wenham's argument is not convincing. Although some of the passages he cites could be construed as teaching annihilationism, at least three of the verses clash with it: Matthew 25:41, 46 and 2 Thessalonians 1:9. In Matthew 25:41 the returned Son of Man will consign the "goats" to hell, and will say, "Depart from me, accursed ones, into the eternal fire which has been prepared for the devil and his angels." Jesus banished the wicked from His presence of blessing into eternal fire. And as seen previously, that fate is plainly depicted in Revelation 20:10 as involving endless torment. So separation from Jesus' presence in Matthew 25:41 means suffering forever in hell, not annihilation.

Surprisingly Wenham uses Matthew 25:46 to support the idea that separation should be understood as annihilation. This verse, the most often cited biblical declaration concerning hell, does not support his view. In this verse—"And these will go away into eternal punishment, but the righteous into eternal life"—"punishment" and "life" are both qualified by the same adjective "eternal." It is difficult therefore to hold that the bliss of believers will last forever, but that punishment of the wicked will come to an end. Instead, one should conclude that conscious existence in heaven and hell is never-ending.

Wenham also claims that 2 Thessalonians 1:9–10 presents separation from God as extinction. There Paul taught that the ungodly "will pay the penalty of eternal destruction, away from the presence of the Lord and from the glory of His power when He comes to be glorified . . . and to be marveled at." "Eternal destruction" will entail the wicked being forever excluded from the gracious presence of the Lord. This cannot be annihilation, for their separation presupposes their existence. Some conditionalists contend that being shut out from Christ's presence means obliteration. Their argument goes like this: "(1) God's presence will fill all that is, in every place; (2) the wicked will not be in his presence; (3) therefore, the wicked will no longer exist."[13]

This argument, however, is based on a faulty understanding of God's presence in 2 Thessalonians 1:9. Here the presence of God is not His general omnipresence, with the idea that separation from His presence would mean nonexistence. Rather, the verse refers to Christ's revealing His special presence as King to His people. That is why Paul said that the unsaved are "shut out from the presence of the Lord and from the majesty of his power" (NIV).

DEATH

Wenham argues that twenty-five New Testament references to "death in its finality, sometimes called the second death," teach annihilationism.[14] But for the New Testament to refer to the final fate of the lost as "death" does not prove that they will be annihilated. These references are also compatible with the view that involves endless torment. In fact, annihilationism is false, because at least some of Wenham's proof texts contradict the notion that hell means extinction. These are the references to "the second death" in Revelation 20:6, 14; and 21:8. These last two verses equate the second death with "the lake of fire." And 20:10 states that in the lake of fire the devil, the beast, and the false prophet "will be tormented day and night forever and ever."

The "lake of fire" signifies eternal torment for the devil, beast, and the false prophet, and four and five verses later (20:14–15) human beings are cast into the same lake of fire. Surely it means eternal torment for them too, in the absence of any indication of change of meaning. The words, "the lake of fire is the second death," disprove Wenham's contention that the language of death indicates extinction.

CONCLUSION

Wenham's strong conclusion, therefore, is unwarranted: "So both Old and New Testaments taken in their natural sense seem to be almost entirely, if not entirely, on the conditionalist side."[15] This is simply untrue. Verses in each of Wenham's four categories are irreconcilable with annihilationism: fire—Mark 9:44, 48; Matthew 25:41, 46; Revelation 14:10–11; 20:14–15; destruction—17:8, 11; 20:10; separation—Matthew 25:41, 46; 2 Thessalonians 1:9; and death—Revelation 20:6, 10, 14; 21:8. These verses support the traditional view that the suffering of the unsaved in hell will know no end.

Theological Arguments

Evangelical annihilationists use theological arguments as well as biblical arguments in seeking to defend their position. Four of their most prominent theological arguments are based on God's love, on immortality, on God's justice, and on God's triumph.

THE ARGUMENT FROM GOD'S LOVE

In 1992 well-known pastor and scholar Michael Green penned a helpful book, *Evangelism through the Local Church,* in which he asked, "What becomes of those who have never heard the gospel?" Green lists three "positively unchristian" answers.[16] These answers are universalism, the view that everyone will be saved; the view that all who do not hear the gospel are consigned to eternal conscious torment; and the view that the heathen will be saved by their good works.[17]

In reference to the second of these three answers, Green holds that the New Testament "does not teach the conscious unending torment of those who are eternally separated from God."[18] Instead, according to Green, it teaches annihilationism. He marshals biblical arguments for his view, the same ones given by John Wenham above.

In addition, Green argues for annihilationism from the concept of God. He asks rhetorically, "What sort of God would He be who could rejoice eternally in heaven with the saved while downstairs the cries of the lost make an agonizing cacophony?"[19] Green answers his own question: "Such a God is not the person revealed in Scripture as utterly just and utterly loving." Green labels the traditional view of hell, "a doctrine of savagery."[20]

Admittedly this argument exerts a powerful influence on the minds of many. It is difficult for modern people to believe in both a loving God and eternal punishment. In fact it is difficult for moderns to believe in hell at all. Liberal Anglican John Robinson speaks for many when he says, "Christ, in Origen's old words, remains on the Cross so long as one sinner remains in hell. That is not speculation; it is a statement grounded in the very necessity of God's nature. In a universe of love there can be no heaven which tolerates a chamber of horrors, no hell for any which does not at the same time make it hell for God."[21]

This quotation and the mindset it discloses expose the weakness of Green's argument. It is unreliable to base views of the afterlife on what human beings think God should be like. Humans are simply not qualified to say what a loving God would or would not do. Instead, they are limited to what God Himself has declared in His Word. Scripture must tell humankind about God's nature and the world to come. And Scripture declares that the loving God who made the universe created heaven and hell, for saint and sinner, respectively.

Jesus will say to "the sheep" (believers), "Come, you who are blessed of My Father, inherit the kingdom prepared for you from the foundation of the world" (Matt. 25:34). And to "the goats" (the unsaved), He will say, "Depart from Me, accursed ones, into the eternal fire which has been prepared for the devil and his angels" (v. 41). The Savior and Judge of the world declared that heaven and hell were prepared by God. Furthermore, as noted, Jesus said both destinies are "eternal" (v. 46).

The idea of God's rejoicing in heaven with His people while the wicked suffer endless punishment in hell is a distortion of Scripture. The Bible teaches that God is present everywhere, including heaven and hell. The unsaved "will be tormented with fire and brimstone in the presence of the holy angels and *in the presence of the Lamb*" (Rev. 14:10, italics added).[22] Of course, Christ is not present in hell in the same way He is in heaven. He is present in heaven in grace and blessing, but He is present in hell in justice and wrath.

Green's portrayal of God rejoicing in heaven while the lost suffer in hell also fails to appreciate the fact that God will be glorified by every person's fate. The glory of God's grace will be eternally magnified in His people on the new earth, and the glory of God's justice will be eternally magnified in the punishment of the wicked in hell. Praise is due God for His holy hatred of sin. Revelation 15:1 speaks of the completion of God's wrath in seven final plagues. The redeemed in heaven sing God's praise: "Great and marvelous are Thy works, O Lord God, the Almighty; Righteous and true are Thy ways, Thou King of the nations. Who will not fear, O Lord, and glorify Thy name? For Thou alone art holy; for all the nations will come and worship before Thee, for Thy righteous acts have been revealed" (15:3–4). These great and marvelous deeds for which His people will praise God include the outpouring of His wrath mentioned in 15:1, 7.[23]

Although Green's argument has great popular appeal, it must yield to the testimony of Scripture. The loving and holy God has created heaven for those who believe in His Son and hell for those who reject Him. Believers must allow His Word to govern their thinking and emotions. Admittedly, these are difficult tasks, but faithfulness to God and His truth requires nothing less.

THE ARGUMENT FROM IMMORTALITY

Near the end of his book *The True Image* Philip Hughes asks, "Is the soul immortal?"[24] He answers this question in the negative:

> Immortality, or deathlessness . . . is not inherent in the constitution of man as a corporeal-spiritual creature, though, formed in the image of

> God, the potential was there. That potential, which was forfeited through sin, has been restored and actualized by Christ, the incarnate Son, who has "abolished death and brought life and immortality to light through the gospel" (2 Tim 1:10). Since inherent immortality is uniquely the possession and prerogative of God (1 Tim 6:16), it will be by virtue of his grace and power that when Christ is manifested in glory our mortality, if we are then alive, will be superinvested with immortality and our corruption, if we are then in the grave, will be clothed with incorruption, so that death will at last be swallowed up in victory (1 Cor 15:51–57; 2 Cor. 5:1–5). And thus at last we shall become truly and fully human as the destiny for which we were created becomes an everlasting reality in him who is the True Image and the True Life. At the same time those who have persisted in ungodliness will discover for themselves the dreadful truth of Christ's warning about fearing God, "who can destroy both body and soul in hell" (Mt. 10:28).[25]

According to Hughes, although most Christian thinkers have assumed the inherent immortality of the soul (and its corollaries, everlasting life and everlasting punishment), this is a false assumption. Only God, he says, is inherently immortal, and human beings, by contrast, were created only potentially immortal. By sinning, Adam lost immortality for himself and the entire human race. Immortality is regained only by those in Christ. Since the unsaved were never given the gift of immortality, they will be annihilated after receiving punishment for their sins, Hughes alleges.

This argument, a common one among annihilationists, has been overrated for at least three reasons. First, it is a mistake to say that those who hold the traditional view of hell do so chiefly because they believe in the immortality of the soul. On the contrary, they hold to eternal punishment because of what they believe is fidelity to biblical teaching. This is true, for example, of Tertullian, Augustine, Thomas Aquinas, Martin Luther, John Calvin, Jonathan Edwards, and Charles Shedd, to name some stalwarts of orthodoxy.

Second, these theologians agree with Hughes in rejecting the Platonic doctrine that the souls of humans are inherently immortal. Instead, they hold, again with Hughes, that God alone is immortal (1 Tim. 6:16). Nevertheless against Hughes, they have taught that the immortal God grants immortality to all human beings, not just to believers.

Third, and most importantly, persons ought not believe in the traditional view of hell because they accept immortality. It should be the other way around. They should believe in the immortality of human beings because the Bible clearly teaches everlasting damnation for the wicked.

THE ARGUMENT FROM GOD'S JUSTICE

In 1988 John Stott shocked the evangelical world when he tentatively defended annihilationism. Among the arguments he used was an argument from God's justice. The Bible, he wrote, teaches that God will judge justly, "which implies that the penalty inflicted will be commensurate with the evil done."[26] But, he said, eternal conscious torment is seriously disproportionate to sins consciously committed in time. It clashes with the biblical revelation of divine justice.

This argument loses some of its impact when it is examined carefully. First, it must be pointed out that few people take sin seriously. As evidence of this, consider five of God's judgments against what might be called "little sins."

Because Lot's wife looked back at Sodom and Gomorrah "she became a pillar of salt" (Gen. 19:26). The death penalty was exacted because of a glance. Because of irregularities in their priestly service in the tabernacle, Nadab and Abihu "fell dead before the LORD" (Num. 3:4; cf. Lev. 10:1–2). This was capital punishment for "only" faulty worship.

Because Achan coveted and stole a robe, silver, and gold, he and his family were stoned and burned (Josh. 7:25). A whole family was destroyed because of one person's greed. Because Uzzah steadied the ark with his hand, the Lord was angry and took his life (2 Sam. 6:6–7). Because Ananias and Sapphira lied to the apostles, God struck them dead (Acts 5:1–10). Lying led to capital punishment.

On hearing these things our first response is to think that justice has not been served; repeatedly, it seems, God has been overly severe. God's assessment, however, is far different.

Lot's wife disobeyed God's command and failed to heed his warning, "Escape for your life! Do not look behind you, and do not stay anywhere in the valley; escape to the mountains, lest you be swept away" (Gen. 19:17). Is God unjust to repay disobedience with a previously announced penalty? Evidently Jesus didn't think so, for He admonished His hearers, "Remember Lot's wife" (Luke 17:32).

Leviticus informs us that Nadab and Abihu "offered strange fire before the LORD, which He had not commanded them" (Lev. 10:1). God viewed their disobedient priestly service as dishonoring to Himself, as is evident from His evaluation of it, "By those who come near Me I will be treated as holy, and before all the people I will be honored" (v. 3). Can anyone question God's right to keep His worship pure?

Achan "acted unfaithfully" (Josh. 7:1), and when he was confronted, he confessed, "I have sinned against the LORD, the God of Israel" (7:20). Was it unfair for God to inflict capital punishment on him?

Uzzah was guilty of what Scripture calls "his irreverence" (2 Sam. 6:7). God is to be worshiped in spirit and truth (John 4:24). Israel, however, had followed the Philistines' example instead of obeying God's instructions for transporting the ark (cf. 2 Sam. 6:3; Exod. 25:12–14; Num. 4:5–6, 15). Should God be criticized for giving only one person what David and many others deserved?

If someone is offended by God's bringing capital punishment on Ananias and Sapphira because they merely lied to the apostles, we are missing Luke's whole point. The husband and wife were ultimately guilty of lying not to men but to God (Acts 5:3–4). People have difficulty in recognizing God's justice in His punishment of so-called little sins because they adopt a human-centered perspective, rather than a God-centered one. If a person today lied to someone else, disobeyed another, or spoke against someone, that individual would not be worthy of death. If a person does these things against God, however, he or she deserves capital punishment. The Bible views sin as an attack on God's character, and therefore it is deserving of great punishment.

Readers may agree in principle, but perhaps they protest that these examples illustrate temporal not eternal punishment. This criticism is fair. The most scandalous example, however, has been saved for last. Because Adam ate the forbidden fruit, he plunged the human race into sin and misery. "By the transgression of the one the many died. . . . the judgment arose from one transgression resulting in condemnation. . . . by the transgression of the one, death reigned through the one. . . . through the one man's disobedience the many were made sinners" (Rom. 5:15–19).

Is this penalty proportionate to the crime committed? Because of Adam's sin physical and spiritual death, even eternal condemnation, came to the entire human race. "Through one transgression there resulted condemnation to all men" (5:18). Condemnation of the entire human race came because of one man's eating a piece of fruit.

Pride, disobedience, and unfaithfulness summarize the

significance of Adam's primal sin, when it is viewed from a God-centered perspective. Adam proudly wanted to be like his Maker. He disobeyed God's prohibition. And he was unfaithful to the Lord (Gen. 3:1–6). Can anyone charge God with injustice since He warned Adam, "from the tree of the knowledge of good and evil you shall not eat, for in the day that you eat from it you shall surely die" (2:17)? Of the Fall God said "judgment arose from one transgression resulting in condemnation" (Rom. 5:16).

If believers submit to the authority of God's Word, they must accept the fact that He was not unjust in punishing the human race with condemnation for Adam's sin. And He condemned the world not only because of Adam's sin, but because of individual sins as well, as Paul emphasized in Romans 1:18, 32; 2:5, 12; 3:10–12, 23.

It will not do to protest against God's judgments on the basis of what seems fair or unfair. Instead, people must adjust their thinking—including their view of God's justice—to God's truth.

Aquinas was right: Sin is an attack on the infinite and holy character of God.[27] God therefore sets the penalties for sin in this world and the next. He justly condemns sinners for Adam's sin and for their own. And He plainly teaches that He punishes the wicked forever. Certainly God is just in doing so.

THE ARGUMENT FROM GOD'S TRIUMPH

Another argument has played a major role in the annihilationist literature—that of the implications of God's triumph over sin. Hughes summarizes it well.

> The everlasting existence side by side, so to speak, of heaven and hell would seem to be incompatible with the purpose and effect of the redemption achieved by Christ's coming. . . . The renewal of creation demands the elimination of sin and suffering and death. . . . The conception of the endlessness of the suffering of torment . . . in hell stands in contradiction to this teaching. . . . When Christ fills all in all and God is everything to everyone (Eph 1:23; 1 Cor 15:28), how is it conceivable that there can be a section or realm of creation that does not belong to this fulness and by its very presence contradicts it?[28]

Hughes is correct when he asserts that Scripture envisions God as ultimately victorious. The crucial question is, What does God deem compatible with His being "all in all"? This question is answered by the Bible's final three chapters: God's victory does not involve the eradication of evil beings from His universe.

At the Great White Throne judgment "the dead, the great and

the small," will stand before God's throne (Rev. 20:11–19). Immediately before presenting this judgment, John had written that the devil, the beast, and the false prophet will be thrown into the lake of fire and brimstone to suffer everlasting torment (v. 10). Four verses later, he stated that wicked human beings share their fate (v. 15).

Revelation 21:1–8 then confirms this conclusion. Believers will enjoy the new heavens and the new earth, whereas the final destination of the unrepentant will be "the lake that burns with fire and brimstone" (v. 8). Evidently God does not view unbelievers' being eternally alive in the lake of fire as incompatible with His being "all in all."

That God's ultimate victory does not include the annihilation of the unsaved is substantiated by the picture of the New Jerusalem in Revelation 21–22. John spoke of the bliss of those privileged to live in this city. God will be in their midst to "wipe every tear from their eyes." For them "there shall no longer be any death; there shall no longer be any mourning, or crying, or pain" (21:3–4). Yet four verses later he wrote of the wicked being in the lake that burns with fire and brimstone (v. 8).

Furthermore, in chapter 22 John contrasted the joy of those who "may enter by the gates into the city" of God with the godless who are "outside" the city (22:14–15). Here the wicked are not annihilated. Instead, they are alive, but are cut off from the happiness of eternal fellowship with God.

The traditional view of hell fits the scriptural vision of the end better than does annihilationism. The Bible's concluding chapters reveal that God's being "all in all" means that He reigns over the just and the unjust; it does not mean that only the former remain.

CONCLUSION

The contemporary case for annihilationism has been set forth from the writings of four respected evangelicals, Michael Green, Philip Hughes, John Stott, and John Wenham. Their arguments have been weighed on the scales of Scripture and are found wanting. The conviction that the church's traditional doctrine of hell is correct has been strengthened.

Some important implications follow. "One key difference between [Jonathan] Edwards and our contemporary spokesmen who abandon the historic Biblical view of hell is that Edwards was radically committed to deriving his views of God's justice and love *from God.* But more and more it seems contemporary evangelicals are submitting to what 'makes sense' to their own moral sentiments. This will not strengthen the church or its mission. What is needed is a radical commitment to the supremacy of God in determining what is real and what is not."[29]

John Piper's observation is accurate. Since annihilationism contradicts the teaching of the Bible, it is an error. Although some evangelical Christians hold this doctrine, they should be encouraged to abandon it because error dishonors God and His truth.

In fact annihilationism is a serious error because it leads unrepentant sinners to underestimate their fate. Annihilationists insist that the obliteration of the wicked is a terrible destiny when measured against the bliss of the righteous.[30] However, it is simply not that bad to cease to exist, especially in comparison to suffering in hell forever. The ungodly could live selfishly their entire lives, without any thought of God, and after death face ultimate extinction rather than eternal punishment. No doubt the unsaved in hell would *like* annihilationism to be true, as Jonathan Edwards noted: "Wicked men will hereafter earnestly wish to be turned to nothing and forever cease to be that they might escape the wrath of God."[31] But annihilationism is not true, and believers who love the lost must tell them the truth—all who fail to trust Christ as their Savior face eternal conscious torment at the hands of the living God.

This leads to the final implication. If annihilationism is widely accepted by Christians, the missionary enterprise may well be hindered. True, some evangelicals such as John Stott and Michael Green have consistently shown a zeal for evangelism while holding to annihilationism. Nevertheless what would be the effect on churches and denominations that once held to eternal conscious torment, if they were to shift to annihilationism? Their missionary zeal might well wane.

D. A. Carson speaks a hard but necessary truth: "Despite the sincerity of their motives, one wonders more than a little to what extent the growing popularity of various forms of annihilationism and conditional immortality are a reflection of this age of pluralism. It is getting harder and harder to be faithful to the 'hard lines' of Scripture. And in this way, evangelicalism itself may contribute to the gagging of God by silencing the severity of his warnings and by minimizing the awfulness of the punishment that justly waits those untouched by his redeeming grace."[32]

CHAPTER 15

Major Flaws in Liberation Theology

J. Ronald Blue

Liberation theology is one of the most significant movements springing from contemporary Latin America. What began among a few Latin theologians has grown into a recognized movement with influence all over the world. From the earliest expressions of the liberation theme by missionary Richard Schaull in 1955,[1] the liberation motif appeared with increasing frequency in a number of progressive Roman Catholic councils and ecumenical conferences in the 1960s. It gained widespread recognition at the second Latin American Episcopal Council (CELAM II) in Medell'n, Colombia in 1968.

Liberation theology is a "new way of 'doing theology' that radically challenges traditional concepts and practices."[2] Liberationists propose to free man from all that enslaves him socially, economically, and politically through peaceful protest or, if necessary, through revolutionary violence. While the social conditions that prompted the birth of liberation theology can be verified, the liberationist solutions need to be challenged. There are several major flaws in the proposed liberation cures.

Conditions in Latin America

The social frame of reference for liberation theology lies in the reality of poverty. Liberationism is rooted in the struggle to free people oppressed by unjust economic structures. As Carlos Fuentes has declared: "South of your border, my North American friends, lies a continent in revolutionary ferment—a continent that possesses immense wealth and nevertheless lives in misery and a desolation you have never known and barely imagined."[3] The poverty, illiteracy, and hunger in Latin America are undisputed facts.

POVERTY

Of Latin America's 400 million people, 60 percent are reported to have incomes of less than $50 a year, and another 30 percent earn between $50 and $190 a year. This means 90 percent of the people have incomes below the subsistence level.[4]

An evident tension exists between these poor masses struggling for survival and the privileged elite who control the power structure comprised of large landowners, industrialists, professionals, bureaucrats, and the military and religious leaders. It is the power elite who primarily benefit from any economic advance in Latin America. The top 10 percent eat 41 percent of the meat and get 44 percent of the clothes, half the electric appliances, 74 percent of the furniture, and 85 percent of the motor vehicles.[5]

These statistics, however, do not adequately portray the overwhelming burden that poverty inflicts on the individuals caught in its grasp. Mooneyham turns from abstract statistical analysis to specific reality in the case of Juan D'az, a coffee worker in El Salvador.

> He and three of his five daughters spend long, hard days in the coffee fields of Montenango. On a good day, Juan picks enough coffee to earn $1.44; his daughters make a total of $3.35. With $1.24 of these wages, Juan and his wife, Paula, are able to feed their family for one day. In bad times, Juan and his daughters make as little as $.56 a day—less than half the money they need just to eat.
>
> At the end of the six-week coffee season, Juan does odd jobs around the hacienda—provided there is work to be done. He can earn about $.90 there for an eight-hour day. Paula de D'az supplements her husband's earnings by working in the market. When people have enough money to purchase the tomatoes, cabbages and other home-grown vegetables she sells, Paula can make about $.40 a day.
>
> The hacienda provides a simple dwelling for the D'az family, but no modern facilities. Candles are used for light, water has to be hauled from a well, and furnishings consist of little more than a table and some chairs. Aside from a dress and shoes for each of the girls during the coffee season, the family has not been able to buy much else in the last five years. Whatever money doesn't go for food is spent for visits to the health clinic ($.40 each time), the high interest on bills at the company store, expenses for the children in school, and for the burial of Juan's father, who died last year.
>
> "You know, I look forward to a better life for my children," Juan says. "I dream that if it is possible—if I can possibly afford it—my children will not follow in my footsteps, that they will break out of this terrible way of life. But the money problems we face every day blot out those dreams. I feel bad, nervous, I don't sleep nights worrying about how I'll get something for them to eat. I think and think but don't find any answers. I work hard; my wife and daughters do, too. We all do. But still we suffer. Why?"[6]

The nagging question, why, demands an answer. This is not a case of poverty from indolence. In spite of all the hard work, this family remains trapped in a seemingly hopeless state of poverty. The case of Juan D'az is the case of millions all over Latin America.

ILLITERACY

Related to poverty is illiteracy. The problem of illiteracy contributes to the problems of underdevelopment. It accompanies and has a bearing on undernourishment, disease, and all kinds of economic and cultural problems.

In Guatemala almost two-thirds of the people are unable to read and write.[7] In most of Latin America, the number of illiterates is rising more rapidly than schools can be built and staffed with teachers. Millions of children move toward adulthood without any instruction at all. Others enroll in the primary grades and drop out without ever learning to read or write. In rural Latin America and in the mushrooming slum areas of Latin America's cities, it is a rare child who is privileged to complete the sixth grade. In many countries it is the sixth-grade graduate who then becomes the teacher in the faltering educational system.

Poverty and population factors contribute to the problem. The countries with the least to spend on education and literacy usually have the highest birth rates. Funds are in short supply. In a rapidly growing population the ratio of trained teachers to school-age children often decreases. As a result, many governments once committed to universal education have quietly abandoned this objective.

The lack of minimal educational opportunities only adds to the inequalities between the wealthy and poorer sections of society. In many cases Latin America's so-called "elite" are in power simply because only the "elite" are educated. A nation that is largely illiterate can hardly be strong. Literacy is essential for those who would improve their quality of life, achieve social mobility and dignity, and participate in community affairs. Economic poverty is clearly related to educational poverty, and Latin America suffers from both maladies. Poverty and illiteracy yield a third and perhaps even more distressing problem: inadequate nutrition.

HUNGER

Poverty and illiteracy produce hungry people, and hunger is widespread and persistent in Latin America. It affects a vast majority of the population and continues to plague increasing numbers. McGovern reports, "Most of the people in Latin America go hungry. An estimated two-thirds of the population are undernourished."[8]

With so many of the people of Latin America suffering malnutrition, it is difficult to make any progress. A vicious cycle puts the continent into a tailspin. Undernourished people are not usually healthy people; weak, ailing people are not usually productive people; and unproductive people are not usually prosperous people. The result is more poor people suffering greater malnutrition. And the cycle continues to abysmal proportions. Hunger produces poverty, poverty produces hunger, and in many cases poverty and hunger conspire in the tragic finality of death.

In Latin America, malnutrition is said to be the primary or contributing cause in more than half of all deaths of children.[9] In 1988 the infant mortality rate of Latin America was about six times that of North America. While only ten babies out of a thousand died before they reached one year of age in North America, fifty-seven out of a thousand infants died in Latin America.[10]

In spite of these disturbing statistics of infant mortality, the population of Latin America continues to explode, often adding to the problems of poverty and malnutrition. The number of mouths to feed increases while the resources necessary to feed them do not increase. While the population of North America, at its present rate of growth, would take ninety-nine years to double, Latin America's population would double in only thirty-two years. The 429 million people in Latin America in 1988 have been projected to swell to more than 711 million by the year 2020.[11] Latin America is adding four times as many people to its population each year as North America. Mexico alone is adding more people than are the United States and Canada together.[12]

This rapid population growth only aggravates the situation in Latin America. The quality of life continues to decline for the majority of people who are caught in the throes of poverty, illiteracy, and hunger.

Liberation Theology

Liberation theologians of Latin America address the pressing problems that plague their continent. The prevailing poverty, widespread illiteracy, and increasing malnutrition are realities that must be challenged. Little wonder Gutiérrez exclaims, "To characterize Latin America as a dominated and oppressed continent naturally leads one to speak of liberation and above all to participate in the process."[13]

There is no question about Latin America's severe economic problems. The situation in which the continent finds itself is fact. No one can deny it or dispute it. The point of inquiry revolves around the cause and cure for Latin America's economic crisis. Liberation theologians are in general agreement both on the underlying reasons for the prevailing economic inequities in Latin America and on what they propose as the most viable solution to those problems. Both in their analysis and in their answers, liberation theologians are deeply indebted to Marxism.

Salvadoran theologian Núñez writes,

> No one can fail to notice that Marxist thought exerts a powerful influence on liberation theology. And the exponents of liberation theology do not try to hide that influence. On the contrary they seem to pride themselves on the use they make of Marxism both for social analysis and for the action they propose to transform the structures of Latin American society.[14]

The stark reality of need in Latin America provides the setting for the Marxist solutions advocated by liberation theology. The rich are few but powerful, while the poor are plentiful and in most cases pitiably exploited. As DeKoster so poignantly expresses it, "The wealthy live in unimaginable splendor, and the poor in unimaginable squalor."[15] It does not take exceptional intelligence or special emotional sensitivity to recognize something is wrong.

Proposed Solutions

From the undeniable crisis that Latin America is experiencing socially, economically, politically, and religiously, one must turn to the proposed solutions. It is only right to commend liberation theologians for their deep concern for the people of their continent and for their strong commitment to provide a cure for the ills of their society, but it is equally right to question their diagnosis of the ailments and their proposed cure. To administer the wrong treatment might make the patient only worse. If the diagnosis is wrong, the prescription could be erroneous. And if the prescription is faulty, the cure could be deadly.

There are four grave problems in the health of Latin America that liberation theology proposes to cure. In some cases the liberationist prescription needs to be withdrawn and an entirely new one written. In other cases an alteration or addition is needed. In all cases, however, there seems to be something lacking. There are major flaws in each of the prescriptions liberationists have written.

INJUSTICE

What is to be done about never-ending injustices that deny the most basic rights of people and negate the dignity of human beings?

Every person deserves the respect and honor due him. Vatican II expresses it well, "Coming down to practical and particularly urgent consequences, this Council lays stress on reverence for man." The Vatican framers go on to clarify their position:

> Whatever is opposed to life itself, such as any type of murder, genocide, euthanasia, or willful self-destruction, whatever violates the integrity of the human person, such as mutilation, torments inflicted on body or mind, attempts to coerce the will itself; whatever insults human dignity, such as subhuman living conditions, arbitrary imprisonment, deportation, slavery, prostitution, the selling of women and children; as well as disgraceful working conditions, where men are treated as mere tools for profit, rather than as free and responsible persons; all these things and others of their like are infamies indeed.[16]

The infamies so eloquently denounced above are the very injustices that continue to plague Latin America. Certainly it is only fair to say that people caught in the throes of such bondage deserve better.

Liberation theology came into being primarily to address these ills. As Sanders put it, "Liberation theology is an ethical theology that grew out of social awareness and the desire to act."[17] It is a clear attempt to relate theological perspectives to ethical responsibility for the complex problems in Latin America.

Gutiérrez concurs that the "task of contemporary theology is to elucidate the current state of these problems, drawing with sharper lines the terms in which they are expressed." He then places man at the center of the solution for these problems.[18] Liberation theologians advance a revived humanism in the cure for the continued problems of injustice. They conclude that since man caused the problems of injustice man must provide the solutions.

They seem to ignore the thought of any kind of divine intervention in the curative process. The divinity developed in liberation theology is the "divinity" to be found in all mankind. The stress is clearly if not almost exclusively on a horizontal plane.

Through social revolution driven by love, albeit at times violent love, man is to attack injustice and establish a new society and become a new man. Liberation theology begins with man and ends with man. The strong core of humanism is undeniable.

Herein lies a grave danger in the proposed solution to injustice. Liberation theology has overlooked the creative force of the transcendent Deity. Without God and His transforming power it is doubtful that any lasting change can be realized in society. The alienation between human beings reflects their alienation from God. Humanistic attempts at reform fall short of the mark. Man needs more than a change of clothes; he needs a change of heart.

Most liberationists conclude that God is in every man. It is curious to note that in Gutiérrez's three-step argument to support this conclusion, he uses biblical references to underline two steps—that God was in Christ and is in the Christian—but he has no reference for the third and final step—that God is in *all* men.[19] The reason is simple. There is no such biblical reference.

The liberationists' concern for the injustices in society is admirable, but to contend that society can be transformed solely through naturalistic forces is at best misguided if not naive. Social sin is, after all, simply a conglomerate of personal sin. Society does not commit acts of torture, murder, and rape. People do. Therefore society can only be changed when people are changed.

Liberationists would do well to infuse a little more theology of redemption into their theology of liberation. In the focus on man, the theologian need not lock out God. In placing man at the center of the stage, there is no need to turn out the lights. The spotlights from the upper gallery may be the only way anyone will be able to see his way around the obstacles and put order to the action on stage. Better yet, the light from above needs to become a light within. This will be done only by divine intervention not by humanistic efforts.

In the attempt to seek new answers for the injustices of Latin America, liberationists would do well to turn back to some of the old themes found in the Bible. The good news of the Lord Jesus Christ, who came to suffer the ultimate injustice of death on the cross to pay the penalty for man's sin and to thereby offer new life, eternal life, is still the best news of all. Through supernaturally redeemed men and women, perhaps society can be relieved from so much injustice.

INEQUITY

For liberationists there is no injustice so devastating and debilitating as the injustice of poverty. The gross inequity between the rich and the poor is of major concern. The focal point in most liberation theology writings is the cause of the poor. Julio de Santa Ana declares: "Whenever theology takes a prophetic stance, it has to take cognizance of sociological reflection. Similarly, the biblical proclamation leads us to a basic option for the poor."[20] Everyone agrees that poverty is a severe problem. Vatican II sounded a clear call:

> Some nations with a majority of citizens who are counted as Christians have an abundance of this world's goods, while others are deprived of the necessities of life and are tormented with hunger, disease, and every kind of misery. This situation must not be allowed to continue.[21]

Not all agree, however, on the cause of poverty. Fewer still agree on the cure.

Liberationists have chosen to follow the theories espoused by Karl Marx. Poverty is the result of a class society, they say, and people are poor because others are rich. Or to put it more bluntly, the liberation theologians to the south contend that Latin America is poor because the United States is rich. Capitalism is the culprit. Gutiérrez says, "There can be authentic development for Latin America only if there is liberation from the domination exercised by the great capitalist countries, and especially by the most powerful, the United States of America."[22]

The Marxist solution follows the Marxist diagnosis. If the poor are poor because the rich are rich (the dependency theory), and the poor are getting poorer while the rich are getting richer (the gap theory), it is clear that the poor are good and the rich are evil (the dualism theory). The solution is to revolt against the evil rich, take what they have, and give it to the poor. It is a glorified Robin Hood approach to economics.

It is far too simplistic to blame capitalism for poverty, and specifically to blame the United States for the poverty in Latin America. Marxist theories lead people to some irrational conclusions. There are multiple factors responsible for the tragic poverty that exists in Latin America. Latin America was built on a weak foundation of conquest and feudalism. By contrast, the United States was built on a foundation of colonizers and free enterprise. The structures that have emerged and the inequities between them are far more likely the result of the contrasting foundations than they are of subsequent exploitation.

This is not to excuse the exploitation that has occurred. It is the greed and graft, the exploitation that must be attacked, not the so-called "evil system of capitalism." Greed, graft, and exploitation are as evident in socialistic countries as they are in capitalistic countries. The greatest flaw in Marxist theory is that it stops with the system and never reaches the heart of the matter—individual ethics.

Marx rejected the authoritative source that can provide the needed ethical standards to make any system work—the Bible. He declared that he would take a "scientific" approach to the inequities evident in society. By "scientific" Marx meant "naturalistic." Darwin, Freud, and Dewey all used the term in the same way. "Scientific" does not mean that the hypothesis will be verified by empirical facts. On the contrary, the theories are proposed without any tests or evidence and are declared "scientific" only because they are "naturalistic." They are stripped of any supernatural influence.

Liberationists would do well to interpret Marx in light of the Bible rather than interpret the Bible through the teachings of Marx. One of the few places where the high ideals of Marx have been achieved was in the early church. Class and racial barriers were broken down (Rom. 10:12) and believers shared all things (Acts 2:44). But this was not achieved through a revolution in which the empire was destroyed, the rich landholders of Rome were exterminated, and a dictatorship of the proletariat was established instead. The only violence recorded was that of authorities against the growing band of Christians. Marx had an admirable goal, but the process he proposed is neither scientific nor scriptural, and therefore will fail.

Instead of condemning biblical exegesis as an "exegesis of the dominant class" and calling for a "reinterpretation of the Bible from the viewpoint of the poor,"[23] liberationists need to realize the Bible speaks with equal force to rich and poor. Instead of isolating its attack to economic systems, as does Marx, the Bible gets down to the source of the problems—personal ethics and human character. For example the Bible neither condones nor condemns slavery (though by inference it opposes slavery). Rather than attack the system of slavery, the Bible attacks the sins in slavery—the sins of brutality, disrespect, and mistreatment on the part of the owner and the sins of hatred, dishonor, and indolence on the part of the slave. Better yet, the Bible instructs the owner to treat the slave with care and concern as though he were a son, and it encourages the slave to work with dignity and diligence as unto the Lord (see the Book of Philemon).

The solution for Latin America's poverty is not to be found in capitalism or socialism. The solution is to be found in a growing number of productive citizens who treat one another with dignity and respect. Instead of championing capitalism or, as does liberation theology, a Marxist-inspired socialism, one should champion increased production and equitable distribution.

> It is clear that absolute economic freedom fails to establish sufficient justice to make it morally viable. It is also clear that consistent socialization or even regulation of property unduly maximizes political power, replaces self-regulating tendencies in the market with bureaucratic decisions, and tends to destroy the initiative which helped to create modern technical efficiency.[24]

The solution is simply "liberty and justice for all." There must be freedom to produce and justice to constrain inordinate greed and economic power.

In their sincere attempt to help the poor, liberationists are making the situation in Latin America worse. Liberationists have given legitimacy to guerrilla movements that have caused many Latin American countries to be further destabilized (part of the Marxist process) and their economies further eroded.

Liberationists' adherence to Marxist theories as a solution to the economic inequities that plague Latin America has led them to a position that is imbalanced and therefore ineffective. They should not so quickly have abandoned biblical authority. While the Bible condemns ill-gotten gain and the exploitation of the poor, it highly commends those who are generous and promises material blessing to the righteous. God is Creator of both rich and poor and He desires for all a lifestyle that is "neither mired in poverty nor choked in wealth."[25] The Bible provides a balance that Marxism cannot achieve.

INSECURITY

An essential element in liberation theology is hope. While it is a theology born out of a critical reflection on the present, it is directed almost exclusively toward the future. It is proposed as the best answer to the identity crisis that prevails in Latin America. It supposedly gives purpose and meaning to life through political aspirations for a new society in which people can develop to their fullest potential. They will at last be free from uncertainty and insecurity. Gutiérrez stresses the hope factor: "Hope thus emerges as the key to human existence oriented towards the future, because it transforms the present. This ontology of what 'is not yet' is dynamic, in contrast to the static ontology of being, which is incapable of planning history."[26] This dynamic of hope "assumes a concrete utopic function," says Gutiérrez, "mobilizing human action in history."[27]

There is a strong element of utopianism in liberation theology. The focus on man and his great potential (humanism) through the Marxist lens of socialist theory (Marxism) has led liberation theologians to project a society governed with justice and perfect harmony (utopianism). Liberationists challenge their readers to remove the shackles of uncertainty and insecurity and to forge ahead to build a new society, to establish the kingdom of God on earth.

By adhering so strongly to an earthly, man-wrought, political utopia to be achieved through "historical praxis," liberationists neglect or even deny the eternal, God-wrought heavenly kingdom to be established through divine intervention. While liberationists may feel that talk of heaven or some future messianic kingdom is illusive and "unscientific," their proposals for a utopia in which all men will share their possessions freely and where justice will prevail seems even more illusive and unrealistic. What Thomas More has written in parody,[28] liberationists have proposed as fact. The "no place" ("utopia" stems from Greek words for "no place") island created in the imagination of More has become the "new place" goal of liberation theology. Idealism can provide direction but it can also project catastrophic, unattainable goals.

In the strong pursuit of historic utopianism, liberationists have turned their backs on eternal reality. The insecurity and the search for identity among the masses in Latin America may be stirred into political action by the promise of utopia, but their hopes will be shattered when their utopia turns out to be a repressive dictatorship or an unrestricted anarchy. Dreams can often turn into nightmares.

Liberation theology has again emerged with an imbalance. The strong dose of human hope in a political utopia needs to be tempered and thus enhanced by the divine hope of an everlasting kingdom, the biblical hope that extends beyond time and the limitations of "historical praxis" and human frailty.

INIQUITY

Only in the realm of religious experience and theological constructs do cultural, economic, and political proposals find ultimate meaning. Liberation theology is, above all, theology. Liberationists are not attempting to propose a new *ideology* for liberation; they present a *theology* of liberation. With sincere pastoral concern, most liberation theologians try to lead the church to see the relevance of religion in a society that is all too often filled with injustice, oppression, and corruption.

Actually the problems of injustice, inequity, and insecurity are by-products of a deeper social problem called sin. Iniquity abounds, and where iniquity abounds other destructive elements run rampant. The problem is clear: "Theologically, this situation of injustice and oppression is characterized as a 'sinful situation' because 'where this social peace does not exist, there we will find social, political, economic, and cultural inequalities.'"[29] At the heart of the inequalities and injustices of society is the theological question of ethics.

While they recognize the problem of personal as well as social sin, almost all liberationists focus on social sin. Miranda decries the sin incarnated in social structures "which by no means is reducible to the sum of individual sins."[30] Liberationists develop what Scott concludes is the "thoroughly biblical notion that sin is not only individual and private but also institutional and public."[31]

In the strong attack on social sin, there has been a concomitant tendency to excuse personal sin. In the attempt to draw all men into a common cause against societal injustice and to create an ecumenical climate to unite diverse religious groups, liberation theologians advocate a universalistic approach in their solutions. All men are called to join in the battle. Even atheists are included in the universal family, a "family of God" that is said to help curb social sin and to bring about perfect harmony.[32] Liberationists claim that iniquity must be purged from society through the joint effort of mankind.

The proposal sounds admirable, but in the pursuit of social equality through holistic universalism, individual iniquity seems to go unnoticed. Universalism is an attractive whitewash treatment, but the rust of sin keeps seeping through. Liberation based on universalism and ecumenicalism is cosmetic and temporal. It does not provide a lasting freedom from iniquity. Society will be changed as men are changed and the change needed is internal, not external. By adhering so strongly to universalism, liberation theology neglects the uniqueness of the church and the redemptive liberty granted to each individual who is a part of the true church. The revolution so earnestly sought in society and the renewal desired in the church might best be accomplished as greater numbers of people in the society and church experience the revolution of new birth and the renewal of a new life.

Instead of condemning systems, liberationists need to denounce sin—hatred, greed, graft, alienation, exploitation, prejudice, domination, fraud, dishonesty, violence, murder, rape, and theft. These evil acts are wrong no matter who commits them. The place where an inclusive universalism fits is in the condemnation of evil and in the commendation of righteousness. To declare that all men are a part of the family of God, even those who practice iniquity, is confusing and contradictory. Worse yet, to advocate violence to defeat violence is irrational. Organized violence to attack "institutionalized violence" only creates more violence. Sin is sin no matter who commits it, and at the very core of the cultural, economic, and political problems of Latin America, and indeed anywhere in the world, is the theological problem called "sin."

Sin is universal. Sin is destructive and disruptive to human progress and the health of societies. And sin must be denounced. This world is in desperate need of liberation from sin and the heartache and chaos it brings.

The universalism of liberationism only muddies the waters and in many cases allows people who claim to be Christians to engage in reprehensible atrocities. And it welcomes those who deny God's existence to participate if not lead in the so-called "liberating process." All too often this liberation leads to enslavement.

Conclusion

Liberation theology is a sincere attempt to answer real needs. Its critique of the Latin American crisis is both penetrating and convicting. Nonetheless liberation theology and its "critical reflection" bears some critical reflection. By restricting their analyses and cures so stringently to historical time and earthly reality, liberationists have neglected the eternal dimension and divine intervention.

To humanism must be added transcendent deity. Marxism needs to be subjected to the light of biblical authority. Earthly utopianism needs the added dimension of eternal reality. Holistic universalism will never bring the unity and renewal that redemptive liberty affords. The theology of liberation needs a stronger touch of a theology of redemption. As the dialectic process continues among liberationists who are rightfully admired for their ingenuity and even more so for their concern, perhaps liberation theology will be drawn toward a more balanced position and thereby more effectively minister to the pressing needs of Latin America.

In the meantime it behooves everyone to do all they can to eliminate oppression and provide liberation. Gutiérrez's closing comment in his monumental *A Theology of Liberation* is a classic:

> All the political theologies, the theologies of hope, of revolution, and of liberation, are not worth one act of genuine solidarity with exploited social classes. They are not worth one act of faith, love, and hope, committed—in one way or another—in active participation to liberate man from everything that dehumanizes him and prevents him from living according to the will of the Father.[33]

Whatever the analysis one makes and irrespective of the solutions one proposes, every person must heed Gutiérrez's challenge to act on behalf of those in need. This is the will of the Father. True liberation, however, can only come through the touch of the Father. It behooves every believer to follow the Master's example and "preach good news to the poor" and "proclaim freedom for the prisoners" and "the oppressed" (Luke 4:18–19). God's good news will always do more than man's good works. Redemptive theology is the answer to the flaws of liberation theology.

Chapter 16

Defending God Before Buddhist Emptiness

Russell H. Bowers Jr.

In the past, apologetic work was considered complete when engaging only Western philosophies and objections. Wilbur Smith's *Therefore, Stand* opens with 102 pages outlining "The Forces and Agencies Engaged in the Modern Attack upon Evangelical Christianity,"[1] and yet it makes but passing reference to non-Western thought. Today, however, such an approach is clearly inadequate. The world is shrinking so fast that Westerners often rub shoulders with people from dramatically different backgrounds. And many Westerners are increasingly viewing life through Eastern spectacles. Sermon and catechism give way before mantra and meditation; guru and avatar displace pastor and savior; resurrection and judgment founder before reincarnation and karma. From *Star Wars* to Shirley MacLaine to Tina Turner to *The Tao of Physics* Hindu and Buddhist presuppositions are encountered. The State of the World Forum in 1995, attended by such notables as George Bush, Margaret Thatcher, and Mikhail Gorbachev, included a half day of practicing "mindfulness," the heart of Buddhist meditation. What all this means is that if the church is to defend Christianity adequately, apologists must answer Muhammad and the Buddha as well as Aristotle and Hegel.

For centuries the East and the West—and specifically the religions of Buddhism and Christianity—maintained only superficial relations and tended to view each other as oddities. But Western interest in Oriental thought was stimulated through the 1893 World Parliament of Religions in Chicago. Dialogue developed following World War II and accelerated after Vatican II. In 1980 the first International Conference on Buddhist-Christian Encounter was held in Honolulu. Fifty persons attended that conference; more than 150, the second conference in 1984; and more than 750 from nineteen countries and thirty-four states attended the third conference in Berkeley in 1987. Journals devoted to interreligious dialogue thrive; books are published and seminars are convened on this subject. Consequently an unprecedented desire stirs today to determine what Christianity and non-Christian religions have to say to each other and what relations should exist between them. Evangelicals need to address the issues raised by this dialogue.

The pace of interaction is accelerating, and the agenda is deepening. Only two decades ago Dumoulin asserted,

> Unity is not the goal of the dialogue between Christianity and Buddhism, neither syncretistically as an integration of one religion into another, nor as a sublimation of both religions into a higher unity. The goals of the dialogue . . . are to gain and deepen mutual understanding and cooperation, on the personal level, for the common welfare of mankind.[2]

But that has changed. In 1982 John Cobb published *Beyond Dialogue: Toward a Mutual Transformation of Christianity and Buddhism.* Two years later Masao Abe picked up Cobb's theme and wrote,

> Over the past few decades the dialogue between Buddhism and Christianity has evolved considerably. It has gone beyond the stage of promoting mutual understanding between the two religions [i.e., Dumoulin's goal], and is now entering a new stage in which the *mutual transformation* of Buddhism and Christianity is being seriously explored.[3]

To effect this desired "mutual transformation," thinkers probe foundational Christian doctrines. John Hick and Paul F. Knitter are rewriting Christology in order to promote their pluralist agenda, and Christological issues come under scrutiny by both Buddhists and Christians. To put it briefly, many are promoting an essential transformation of Christianity and its key doctrines.

Christian apologetics, therefore, must address Eastern as well as classical Western thought. Eastern thinkers and religions must not be relegated to a theological sideshow where the curious can plunk down an extra nickel if they wish to gape. Rather they must be seriously studied and answered if the work of apologetics is to be done effectively.

Keiji Nishitani is the late dean of the Kyoto School of philosophy, a movement that seeks to bring about "unity beyond differences" between East and West. He has been viewed as "a thinker who stands at the very cutting edge of the manifold spiritual tendencies of our times."[4] One writer has called Nishitani's book *Religion and Nothingness*[5] an "extraordinarily important work."[6]

> This is, I think, one of the outstanding volumes in philosophical reflection on religion in our century. In originality and depth it takes its place, so it seems to me, alongside the major works of Western religious reflection on which most of us have long since been dependent—of Barth, Niebuhr, Farrar, Tillich, Buber, Lonergan—except that unlike these classics, its horizons include both Western and Eastern traditions.[7]

Odin sees *Religion and Nothingness* as a foundation for Christian-Buddhist dialogue[8] and Van Bragt hopes it "may be an instrument for the two worlds of East and West to come to a real dialogue, to a real understanding of how their respective ways of thinking and feeling relate to one another, and from there to form a new synthesis."[9] In a world where East and West do meet (despite Rudyard Kipling), evangelical Christians need to interact with Nishitani's views.

The present article introduces *śūnyatā,* which Nishitani says represents ultimate reality; compares *śūnyatā* with the transcendent-personal God, who is the Christian's "first fundamental"; and proposes an apologetic for the latter in the light of the former.

ŚŪNYATĀ—Ultimate Reality in Buddhism

Whereas Western philosophy is built on *being,* Eastern thought centers on *nothingness.*[10] This is particularly the case in Buddhism.[11] The word *śūnyatā* or "nothingness" may be related to the root *svi,* "to swell." The word "suggests therefore that although things in the phenomenal world appear to be real and substantial outside, they are actually tenuous and empty within. They are not real but only appear to be real. . . . All things are empty in that they lack a subsisting entity or self-being."[12] *Śūnyatā* is not a "thing" which is nothingness, set up in opposition to that which "is." Rather, form and emptiness are identical or coextensive; "form is emptiness, emptiness is form." Since all is essentially *śūnyatā,* all things are interrelated.

To Nishitani, this construct solves the modern philosophic and societal dilemma that blossoms from Cartesian subject-object dualism. Such dualism, Nishitani believes, degenerates either to Marxist materialism or Hegelian idealism, both of which are untenable and underlie all that ails contemporary Western society.

In a universe where all is one because all is nothingness, no room remains for a personal Creator-God. Rather, all the things-which-are-at-heart-truly-nothingness come into existence through *pratītya-samutpāda* or codependent origination. *Pratītya-samutpāda* is symbolized in Buddhist art as a twelve-spoked wheel conveying the idea that "because of this, that becomes; because of that, something else becomes." Reality is thus "a boundless web of interrelations whose momentary nodes make up the 'things' of experience. It is pure relation without substance."[13] The related concept of *anātman* denies selfhood to human beings—there is no permanent "self" or "ego" that remains self-identical through time. Obviously, in a system where each entity comes about only because of the interactions of previously existing things, no room remains for a transcendent God who originates or controls the whole. At best that "god" is one of the "things" within the whole and is but one component involved in bringing about other things and is essentially *śūnyatā*. Nor can there be a transcendentally induced beginning or end to history.

Isolated statements in *Religion and Nothingness* might seem to contradict this assessment; Nishitani does refer to "God." "How can man look for God, and how can he recognize when he has found him? How can man become conscious of sin? How can man hear when God calls out to him?"[14] "The love of God is . . . seen as the love of one who emptied himself (the *kenōsis* of God revealed in the *ekkenōsis* of Christ, who 'emptied himself, taking the form of a servant') to save a sinful mankind."[15] But when Nishitani writes like this he seems to be engaged in an exercise in *upāya*.

Upāya is "skillful means" in bringing non-Buddhists, through their own "flawed" or "inadequate" religions and philosophies to Buddhist enlightenment.

> [B]ecause Theravada teaching claims the only way to "salvation," *nibbāna,* was through *its* system of meditative discipline guided by doctrine, the Theravada Buddhist Way was forced to develop an articulate understanding of its relationship with non-Buddhist Ways. The central notion under which this understanding evolved was the doctrine of *upaya [sic]* or "skillful means."
>
> Essentially, *upāya* refers to any method skillfully applied for the purpose of leading human beings to the experience of enlightenment. Therefore, any method of meditation, religious ritual, ethical discipline, or doctrinal formulation can be used to help persons spiritually advance beyond where they are as unenlightened beings toward the final truth of enlightenment. In short, *all* religious teachings and practices . . . that help advance the seeker towards enlightenment are forms of *upaya [sic]*.[16]

In other words by skillful use of the neophyte's flawed beliefs the Buddhist sage gradually leads the neophyte through and beyond these to enlightenment. "Buddhism does not attempt to tackle alternative religions head-on. Rather it prefers to tame them, by accepting some of the forms and then emptying them. . . . People can be seduced gradually into the true path."[17] Buddhism "has been patient of gods and brahmins, emasculating them along the way. It has not felt divine beings to be a threat."[18] Therefore

> if the Jew, Christian, Muslim, or Hindu finds that it is necessary to believe in a God to reach salvation, that is quite acceptable. . . . If such theistic beliefs do not get in the way, then there is no objection. Indeed . . . *Mahāyāna* Buddhism itself employs just such "spiritual devices" as aids to release.[19]

So references to "God" are found in the early pages of *Religion and Nothingness.* But this is not because Nishitani believes in Him, nor because his system allows room for Him. Although "the standpoint of *śūnyatā* is not an atheism in the usual sense of the word, even less should it be classed as a form of what is normally called theism."[20] Indeed, modern atheism itself must somehow be incorporated into Christianity "as a mediation to a new development" of that faith.[21]

Nishitani vigorously denies two attributes of the Christian God: His transcendence and His personality. Since for Nishitani all is one in a profound monism, neither creation nor providence nor judgment nor termination can break in from without. If there is a god, he/it must simply be part of the system.[22]

Further, Christianity, Nishitani says, must advance beyond its view of God as a *personal* being. This is not to say that belief in God's personality has until now proved unhelpful. "There is no denying that the image of a personal God, a God of judgment or justice, or a God of love has, by bringing human beings before the 'sacred' as a living subject, before a God no doubt beyond compare in the sacredness of his majesty and grace, drawn the conscience and love of man to special depths and thereby elevated the human personality to remarkable heights."[23]

According to the Kyoto School, Christians must mature to where they can drop this childish notion, adapt and adopt the insights of modern atheism, and advance to transpersonality. Two reasons call for this change. First, modern science has rendered untenable the old concepts of teleology and divine order in the natural world. Most educated people view the universe as "governed by laws of mechanical necessity."[24] Consequently a "religion based merely on the old teleological view of nature is, to say the least, inadequate for our day and age."[25] Second, modern historical consciousness disallows a transhistorical God who initiates, interacts with, and terminates history. Thus people must picture God as personally impersonal or impersonally personal, or, better still, accept *śūnyatā* as a field of force. Nishitani is seeking to use the idea of the Christian God as a starting point to bring his readers to the viewpoint of *śūnyatā*.

For the Christian the "first fundamental" of faith is the existence of the transcendent yet personal God.[26] As Berkhof stated, He is "personal in the highest sense of the word."[27] "God is represented throughout [Scripture] as a personal God, with whom men can and may converse, whom they can trust, who sustains them in their trials, and fills their hearts with the joy of deliverance and victory. And, finally, the highest revelation of God to which the Bible testifies [viz., Jesus Christ] is a personal revelation."[28]

Yet this personal God is transcendent; He stands above and exists independent of the material universe. "Before the mountains were born or you brought forth the earth and the world, from everlasting to everlasting you are God" (Ps. 90:2 NIV). "In the beginning you laid the foundations of the earth, and the heavens are the work of your hands. They will perish, but you remain; they will all wear out like a garment. Like clothing you will change them and they will be discarded. But you remain the same, and your years will never end" (Ps. 102:25–27 NIV).

One focal issue between Christians and Buddhists which touches on personality and transcendence and on which different answers are given by the two sides, is the kenosis of Christ, His "emptying" Himself (Phil. 2:7). Representatives from three generations of the Kyoto School write that God is *of necessity* kenotic. Kitarō's position in this regard is taken up by Nishitani and expanded by Abe. The latter writes,

> [T]his doctrine of Christ's kenosis should not be understood to mean that Christ was *originally* the Son of God and *then* emptied himself and became identical with humans. . . . Instead we should understand the doctrine of Christ's kenosis to mean that Christ as the Son of God is *essentially* and *fundamentally* self-emptying or self-negating.[29]

Such a view is opposed by many Christian theologians. Barth, for example, championed the idea that God acts freely out of love.

> Only when we are clear about this can we estimate what it means that God has actually, though not necessarily, created a world and us, that His love actually, though not necessarily, applies to us, that His Word has actually, though not necessarily, been spoken to us. The purposiveness

> we find in proclamation, the Bible and revelation is thus a free and actual purposiveness by no means essential to God Himself.[30]

Evangelical theologians say much the same.

> Not only do God's decisions not stem from any sort of external determination, they are not a matter of internal compulsion either. That is to say, although God's decisions and actions are quite consistent with his nature, they are not constrained by his nature. He is not like the gods of pantheism, which are virtually constrained by their own nature to will what they will and do what they do.[31]

In John 10:17–18 Jesus spoke not of the Incarnation phase of His kenosis but of the freedom and choice by which He acts: "The reason my Father loves me is that I lay down my life—only to take it up again. No one takes it from me, but I lay it down of my own accord. I have authority to lay it down and authority to take it up again. This command I received from my Father" (NIV). This difference between constraint and freedom is related to the question of personality. Whereas a force acts of necessity, a personal being has the capacity to choose.

Further, Nishitani's god is not transcendent, but is a part of the web of relationships that make up the universe, and he/it is as much nothingness as is everything else.

An Apologetic for Christianity

Thus one must choose, on the one hand, between personally impersonal self-emptying nothingness, which, compelled by its nature, expresses itself as form, and, on the other hand, a personal and transcendent God who acts freely out of His will. Which of the two is in fact the most basic of all realities in the universe? On what bases can the Christian apologist argue for God and Christ in the face of *śūnyatā* and *pratītya-samutpāta?*

First, it should be noted that just as the Christian worldview is based on faith, so is Kyoto philosophy. No one has either "seen" *śūnyatā* or disproven the personal God. Thus Christianity cannot be faulted for being built on unseen realities.

In deciding between these two faith positions, logic falls clearly on the side of Christianity. The Zen in which Nishitani's Buddhism is rooted is "characterized by a suspicion of logical, conceptual thinking."[32] But perhaps that puts it too mildly. According to Wiebe, Buddhism follows a system of three truths: "ordinary propositional truth, a kind of propositional truth about sacred realities . . . ; and 'pure religious truth' which transcends not only the scientific truths about the world but also the religious truths contained in the testimony of the seers."[33] The problem is that in Buddhist thought

> the superiority of the higher level of truth is so vast that it, in the final analysis, reveals the lower level of truth to be wholly insignificant; it is but a ladder to be discarded after use. . . . [A] claim is made for the sui generis nature of the higher level of truth—making it self-justifying for him who possesses (experiences) it and beyond the pale of comprehension or criticism of him who does not. And this, it seems to me, involves an abrogation of the "reason" that establishes the lower-level truths and hence stands in contrast to them rather than complementing them.[34]

According to the Kyoto School logic is not only unnecessary but at times an enemy that keeps humankind from enlightenment.

Because mind and logic oppose the seeker of truth, he counts his breath while sitting in *zazen* (cross-legged Zen meditation) so that "the discriminating mind has nothing to feed on, nor is there anything for reasoning to get hold of."[35] He or she also contemplates the *koans* (Zen paradoxes used as aids to meditation and enlightenment), which ask about such questions as one's original face before birth or the sound of one hand clapping. The purpose of the *koans* is "to build pressure on the conceptual mind like flood tides rising behind an earthen dam. As tension and frustration build, the structural integrity of the dam of logical thinking begins to break down."[36] Only when the dam bursts can one grasp *śūnyatā* and experience *satori* (enlightenment).

This kind of nonlogical (and sometimes illogical)—but intuitive or experiential—"knowledge" is what Nishitani promotes. For example he acknowledges that "infinite finitude" is impossible conceptually but true existentially.[37] Existential "truth" surpasses logical truth because, contrary to what has been believed for centuries, reason is not humanity's real "natural light."[38] Consequently *śūnyatā* "is not possible as a nothingness that is thought but only as a nothingness that is lived."[39]

Christianity, by contrast, while holding to truth which is not discovered by reason, nevertheless values and depends on reason. "By revealing Himself through the written Word, God has committed Himself to using rational concepts as a tool for revelation, thereby making human reason absolutely necessary."[40] Because of Christianity's "inherently rational character"[41] it may be that there is "no worldview in the history of the human race that has a higher regard for the laws of logic."[42]

Reason is one important factor that distinguishes humanity from animals.[43] Is it wise to discard that distinguishing characteristic as the means to arrive at ultimate truth? It may be that in *śūnyatā* Nishitani found a philosophy that enabled him to rise above his existential *angst*. But that does not make his thinking *true*. By contrast, "the attractiveness of a belief is all too often inversely proportional to its truth."[44] If there is a God who made humankind and to whom individuals must give an account, then a "comforting" worldview may turn out to be not so comforting after all. And by preferring intuition to logic Nishitani places himself among those Buddhists "who [employ] a highly metaphysical vocabulary and [insist] on the need for correct thinking while at the same time suspecting all metaphysical and, at the limit, all language."[45] Thus

> when he appears to say that we cannot understand *śūnyatā* at all intellectually (e.g., 124–25), or that "understanding" depends upon contradictory attributions, I wonder why he is writing. Despite his considerable contribution to a Buddhist metaphysics, he seems to share the confusion of many "spiritual philosophers"—both Eastern and Western—about the merit of comprehensibility.[46]

For Christians, rationality, while not sufficient, must not be discarded. Why not accept what one can learn through reason and logic rather than spend years in *zazen* and the contemplation of *koans* to help jettison humankind's most basic intuitions regarding the reality of the self, God, and the world?

The need to recognize personality in ultimate reality is suggested by Nishitani himself. After vigorously opposing the personality of God, he proceeds to personify nature. He does this so frequently and significantly that he is forced to attempt a disclaimer: "We are not thinking of things anthropomorphically."[47] Christianity offers a much more satisfactory solution by recognizing personality in the Creator and impersonality in many of the things He has made.

By pointedly ignoring or denying the personal Creator-God, Nishitani and the Buddhists deal only superficially with the suffering they propose to eliminate. In their thinking humanity's basic problem is ignorance of the fact that everything including themselves is emptiness. The solution to this problem is first the *satori* (or enlightenment), which comes through great effort and discipline, and ultimately the "blowing out" of all passions in nirvana. But Christians see suffering, both physical and psychological, as having deeper (or other) roots. Genesis 1–3 relates the story of humanity's creation in God's image for fellowship with the Creator. The Book of Genesis then describes the sin that marred that image and shattered that fellowship. Present-day anxiety stems from people longing to return to Eden and its true heritage of moral and immortal likeness to their Maker, to say nothing of personal communion with Him. Sin and separation from God constitute humanity's essential dysfunctionality and loneliness. True, a person can deny God, close his or her ears to His voice, and attempt to allay problems and anxieties in that way. One can forcibly deny passions and nearly "blow out" all desire. But doing so does not excise the cancer within. A person may take enough aspirin so that the cancer presently does not bother him, or he may hit his finger with a hammer often and hard enough that so he no longer heeds the pain. But this does not truly eliminate the cause of suffering.

A further conundrum for Nishitani lies in how to propose an ethic. On the one hand, since he denies the existence of a transcendent God, no standard exists by which to evaluate the state of the universe or people's moral choices. Everything is thus essentially as it should be.

> The existence of all phenomena and the changes they undergo are in accord with some definite rational order: phenomena *being* what they ought to be and *becoming* what they ought to become. In other words, all things are in the "ontological" order and under the control of *logos:* they are a "dharmic naturalness." Even what is seen as irrational or lawless from the viewpoint of human interests never departs so much as a single step from the dharma as far as its existence or change is concerned. In this sense, all things just as they are, are dharma-like.[48]

Consequently "in the mode of being of things as they are in themselves in emptiness, both 'as they are' and 'as they ought to be' are . . . entirely one and the same."[49]

If everything *is* as it *ought to be,* then there can be no such thing as natural evil or human sin. The earth's "thorns and thistles" and "subjection to frustration" and "bondage to decay" are neither unnatural, nor the result of a curse, nor someday to be removed. They are as they should be. Human sin likewise would seem to be as it ought to be; there is neither good nor bad. Even the unenlightened individual is properly unenlightened.

Such a philosophy can lead to ethical inertia. Why change self or society if all is as it should be? Abe admits that "the idea of justice is very weak and unclear in Buddhism."[50] Why not adopt the philosophy of Dōgen (which Nishitani approvingly cites): "I now while away my time, accepting whatever may come."[51] We should take things "as they come—as they are fated to come—consigning oneself to the destiny of circumstances."[52] Why try to change things, since they are both fated and as they ought to be?

On the other hand Nishitani both recognizes the fact of evil and argues for change. His closing sentence talks about "the problems that beset humanity."[53] But it is difficult to understand how to believe simultaneously that "are" equals "ought" and that humanity has problems. Thus grasping Nishitani's argument regarding ethics "turns out to be a difficult task" and may lead to "deep uncertainty about what Nishitani is saying and why he is saying it."[54]

> While I understand what Nishitani is saying (the formulations are intelligible in one sense), *I do not understand what they mean for action, and especially for the web of dutiful relations.* In having these deeply altered dispositions, does one *act* differently? How? In what way? Does one still honor one's commitments? Does one honor them in a different way? How? Does one still refrain from cruelty? How? Why? Does one still protect the innocent from arbitrary abuse by others? How? Why?[55]

Sharpening this line of argument, Phillips says that Nishitani

> insists that *śūnyatā* is a grand "life-affirmation" (124, 131, 138, 191–93, etc.), but he does not explain at all very well how it is life-affirmative nor [does he] make the claim precise. Does *śūnyatā* affirm all desires and goals equally, the murderer's and extortioner's as well as the Zen seeker's? . . .
>
> An easy rebuttal appears available in an appeal to social conscience . . . since "play" and "just sitting" are what the transformation is to amount to in a positive way. Are we to play and just sit while people are oppressed and nations with unenlightened leaders move closer to nuclear war? Are we to "just sit" while people in Africa, or anywhere, starve?[56]

Thus, though Nishitani himself was an ethical individual, his philosophy sounds an uncertain note in helping his disciples formulate a code of ethics. "Either it affirms too little, only 'play' and 'just sitting,' or too much, all the evils of existence."[57] It is even possible to go so far as to criticize his thought "as a neo-romantic and even escapist naturalism."[58]

A further advantage of the Christian worldview relates to history. Christianity offers a reasonable explanation of the origin of the universe and history; Nishitani suggests an infinite cycle of history which is somehow never repeated. Christianity announces and explains the amazing acts of God in history, particularly the resurrection of Jesus of Nazareth; Nishitani and Buddhism ignore these. A history of those families and nations that have followed biblical principles demonstrates the great good these principles have provided for their people.[59]

Conclusion

Eastern thought is increasingly accepted in Western society. Works of the Kyoto School philosophers, and Keiji Nishitani in particular, represent serious attempts to integrate East and West, or at least to explain the East in terms understandable to the West. The topics touched on in this article suggest issues that should be more extensively discussed. In the late nineteenth and early twentieth centuries Christians were asked, "How can you defend your faith in the light of modern scientific theories? How can you defend your conservative theology in the light of recent liberal thought and a growing sense of historical consciousness?" These questions still need to be answered. But in the late twentieth and early twenty-first centuries the query will increasingly be posed, "How can you insist on the normativeness of your faith in the light of other world religions and the many good people who practice them? How is your Christ unique when compared with other religious leaders?"

These are questions Christians must answer articulately and in a way that demonstrates understanding of those who ask them. Based, then, on an attentive listening to them, Christians should present reasoned objections to their positions. Much as Paul ascended Mars Hill and quoted the Greek writers Epimenides, Aratus, and Cleanthes as a preface to proclaiming Jesus and the resurrection (Acts 17:28), Christian apologists today need to show they understand the worldviews of those to whom they seek to present the gospel. This is an essential part of the responsibility of believers to "contend for the faith which was once for all delivered to the saints" (Jude 3).[60]

Chapter 17

Islamic Values and the Gospel

Patrick O. Cate

Today it is popular to state one's values, to think them through, write them out, post them in one's company, school, or institution. Values fire the imagination and drive actions and decisions. In his book *The Seven Habits of Highly Effective People,* Stephen R. Covey says, "The ability to subordinate an impulse to a value is the essence of the pro-active person. Reactive people are driven by feelings, by circumstances, by conditions, by their environment. Proactive people are driven by values—carefully thought about, selected, and internalized values."[1]

Everyone is driven by his or her values, whether they are carefully thought out or not, and whether that person is conscious of them or not. Though people may not state their values, they do live by them. Some individuals also may state one set of values, but in reality live by another set.

Understanding one's own true values and then understanding another person's values can promote appreciation. If another person's values are not understood, he or she may seem strange, odd, or wrong. Understanding values of others helps make sense of their actions and decisions and can often help remove misunderstandings. If a person always wore yellow-tinted sunglasses, eventually he might begin to think everything was yellow. But by understanding someone else's values, the sunglasses are removed and fewer misunderstandings exist.

People's values come from living within their own culture all or most of their lives. It is therefore easy to think that everyone shares those values, or to think that if people do not have those values they are wrong. Therefore it is important to seek to understand others.

Westerners, for example, value individualism and liberty. By self-effort they produce achievement. They appreciate the rights of individuals. They separate their public and private worlds; they value the accumulation of private wealth; they focus on the material and the human. But in the Muslim world opposite virtues are valued.

Christians need to seek to understand Islam from within. This does not mean becoming a Muslim. It does not mean diluting the gospel or accepting theology that goes against Scripture. It does mean learning what Muslims value and discovering what Muslims and Christians have in common and how they are different. Many Islamic values are much closer to biblical values than they are to Western values. Studying Islam and the Middle East can help Christians understand and appreciate the Bible better. And understanding Islamic values can help believers see how to build bridges to the souls of Muslims, how to develop deeper friendships with Muslim neighbors, and how the wonderful news of Jesus Christ can be brought to some of the one billion people within the household of Islam.

Theological Values in Islam

The Muslim world is extremely theocentric. Its focus is on God. In Islamic communities the phrases, "Lord willing," "Praise God," "In the name of God," "There is no God but God," are heard daily. However, in the Western world, with its materialistic, secular, and humanistic viewpoints, God is left out of almost every area of life.

UNDERSTANDING THEOLOGICAL VALUES IN ISLAM

The unity of God. Five times a day, every day of the year, from minarets piercing the sky, from neighborhood loudspeakers with volume controls turned to their highest, and from the low voices of the faithful at prayer, can be heard the creed, "There is no God but God, and Muhammed is his apostle."[2] When a baby is born, these words are whispered in his or her ear. In a dying person's ear are whispered the same words. By this brief creed, Muslims have done a superb job of simplifying their theology and driving it home. Normally when the creed is heard, the phrase, "Allahlau Akbar" also penetrates the air. It declares "God is the greatest." Nothing whatsoever competes with God.

The Muslim world is permeated with the concept that there is no God but God and therefore God is one. Possibly the greatest theological core value of Islam is *tawheed,* the unity of God. He is not a tri-unity. Muhammed, Islam's founder, encountered polytheism in some aberrant Christian circles in Arabia. Some professing Christians apparently believed in three gods. The oneness of God is considered by many to be Islam's central theological value. Therefore the concept of the Trinity is repulsive to Muslims.

The sovereign free will of God. Two major groups in the history of Islamic theology were the Asharites and the Mutazalites. The Mutazalites lost and the Asharites won, and so in a sense all Muslims are Asharites today. The two basic tenets of Asharite theology are the sovereign free will of God and the uncreated Qur'an. The sovereign free will of God affects every day of a person's life in the Muslim world. It includes the concept that God has complete power and can do whatever He wants to do. He has predestined every day of each person's life. He is transcendent and tends to be impersonal. Someday He will judge everyone.

At the beginning of every Surah (or chapter) of the Qur'an, all 114, with the exception of Surah 9, are the words, "In the name of God, the gracious, the merciful." To many Muslims, the concept of *rahim* (merciful) is not God's refusing to give people the punishment they deserve, but His beneficence, such as His giving rain and food. Because God is distant and impersonal, He does not have a covenant relationship with humans. He is omnipotent, and people cannot get close to Him. God in His will makes decisions and does what He wants and no one can question this. God wills one to go to heaven and another to go to hell. God wills one to live and another to die. God wills who in the womb will live and who will die. The words "Allahlau Akbar" (God is the greatest) herald the omnipotence and sovereignty of God. This clause is a common cry from a minaret's loudspeaker, the worshiper's mouth, and a frenzied mob.

Muslims recite ninety-nine names of God, going three times through a prayer strand with thirty-three beads on it. Christians can agree with Muslims on almost every one of these attributes of God. The fourth attribute is that He is the holy one, and the forty-seventh is that He is the loving one, but holiness and love are not driving passions in many Muslims' understanding of God. Three times the Qur'an teaches that God deceives. These same three verses say that God is the best deceiver (Surah 3:54; 8:30; 10:21). English translations of these verses use words like "plot," "plan," or "the best planner." But these translations do not reflect the full meaning of the original *makara.* Hans Wehr's standard Arabic dictionary says that *makara* means "deceive, delude, cheat, dupe, gull, or double-cross" and *makir* is defined as "sly, cunning, or wily."[3]

Submission and man's response to God. The Arabic word Islam means "submission." Thus Muslims are those who submit to the will of God. This can be seen most clearly in a mosque when a handful or thousands are kneeling in straight lines with their foreheads touching the ground, submitting themselves to Allah. Their concern before God is not to find forgiveness, but to submit to whatever He has decided. Submission to God is a crucial core value of Islam. A person is to submit to his Kismet, his predestination from God. Associated with the concept of submission to God is that of submission to Islamic authority. Muslims are to agree with what Islamic teachers say.

The concept of submission permeates Muslim culture as well as theology. Related to this is the concept of memorizing the Qur'an. Muslims and many people of the East are far better memorizers than people in the West. From this comes what could be called "vertical thinking." One accepts what the sheik in the mosque says, who accepts it from his teachers, who accept it from the Hadith (tradition), which accepts it from the Qur'an, which accepts it from Muhammed, who accepted it from God. Since authority is not to be questioned, many Muslims lack freedom of thought and of creativity. This concept makes life most difficult for Christian missionaries because Muslims are never to ask, "Could we be wrong?" Even though Muslims believe the Bible was originally revealed by God and given by Him for everyone, it has been replaced by the Qur'an. Therefore Muslims feel they need not read the Bible.

Of course there are some beautiful exceptions to this lack of freedom of thought and of creativity. While Europe was in the slumber of the Dark Ages, Islamic culture was blooming. The golden age of Islam under the Abbasids (A.D. 749–1258) gave rise to a renaissance of beautiful creativity whose rich culture, translations, and inventions in the fields of science, medicine, literature, and art are still evident today.

The Qur'an. The Asharites' basic doctrine—that "the Qur'an is the uncreated speech of God existing in the mind of God from eternity past"—has become the standard Muslim doctrine of the Qur'an. This is based on the fact that there could never be a time in which God could not speak, and since the Qur'an is the speech of God it must be eternal and uncreated. This doctrine is based on the defense of the eternality of the attributes of God. So the Qur'an is the eternal uncreated speech of God.

Protestants tend to think Muslims view the Qur'an as their supreme authority under God. However, Muslims are much more like Roman Catholics, who have the Bible, the church, the pope, and tradition as authorities. Muslims have four acknowledged sources of authority and two that are not acknowledged. The Qur'an is the first one; as already mentioned, it is the uncreated speech of God. *Hadith,* or the traditions of the prophet, is a second authority. *Qiyas,* a third authority, is analogy taught by Muslim scholars and based on the Qur'an and *Hadith. Qiyas* deduces how new laws should apply today in areas the Qur'an and *Hadith* do not address directly. The fourth source of authority is *Ijma,* the consensus of the community and especially of Islamic scholars. These four areas of authority possess almost equal weight. Frequently a Muslim will quote the Qur'an, saying that the Qur'an gives a certain piece of information. But the quotation comes from *Hadith,* not the Qur'an. However, this makes little difference to Muslims because they are a people under authority.

Muslims have two other sources of authority, ones they frequently do not acknowledge but that significantly influence their lives. *Adat* is the custom of the community, and from this has come animism. The fear of the evil eye, the power of saints' graves to get prayers answered, good luck brought by an unread copy of the Qur'an—these are all powerful non-Qur'anic, animistic authorities throughout the Muslim world. The second seldom-acknowledged authority is *Qanun,* international law. Muslim countries have adopted laws and legal systems from non-Muslim countries.

Muhammed. In the Muslims' five-times-a-day prayers, they recite, "There is no god but God, and Muhammed is his apostle." Christians agree with Muslims that "there is no God but God." (Arab Christians use the same word for God that Muslims do, namely, "Allah.") However, Christians cannot agree with Muslims in their belief that Muhammed is the apostle of God. Muslims believe that Jews and Christians, the people of the Book, were first called by God. However, because they changed their Scriptures and left the original religion God gave to mankind, God stepped into time and space and said about Muhammed, "This is his final apostle and there are no apostles to come after him." Thus he has virtually replaced those who came before and the door has closed on any who might want to come after.

Muslims are quick to say that Muhammed was just a man and not God, and yet they view him as much higher than a man. In almost every mosque two words are written in Arabic at equal height above the ground. One is "Allah" and the other is "Muhammed." In some mosques these are written in huge beautiful calligraphic letters with "Allah" always on the right. The Qur'an says, "We make no distinction between the prophets." However, other prophets have just a few stories in the Qur'an. Though all Muslims acknowledge other prophets, in reality Muhammed is the one who has central—or single—authority in their lives. Muslims would say, "We must believe in all the prophets, but we must obey the prophet Muhammed." To speak against the prophet Muhammed or the Qur'an is blasphemy, and is justification for capital punishment in many Muslim countries.

BUILDING BRIDGES BETWEEN CHRIST AND LOGICAL VALUES IN ISLAM

Are there any bridges by which Christians can build a pathway of communication to Muslims? Are there any windows or doors believers can open in the theological wall that separates one billion Muslims from Jesus Christ?

The unity of God. Unfortunately Christians often teach, live, think, and sing as if they worship three Gods. This is wrong. More focus needs to be given to the biblical truth that there is one God, who exists as three persons. Christians need to agree resolutely with Muslims that there is no God but God, that God is one. Believers should believe more firmly the truth in 1 Timothy 2:5 that there is one God and one Mediator between God and humankind. In conversing with Muslims it is usually not wise to begin discussing the Trinity, the Son of God, or the deity of Christ. This may unnecessarily close their minds to Christ before they have had an opportunity to get to know Him and fall in love with Him. Christ did not reveal everything about Himself in His first conversations with His disciples; He let them get to know Him gradually over three and a half years. The Synoptic Gospels record a gradual revelation of Christ through His teachings, life, miracles, and ministry. Eventually the disciples realized who Christ was. Thus it may be wise to encourage Muslims to read the gospel of Luke, which gradually unveils who Christ is.

The sovereign free will of God. Christians heartily agree that

God has sovereign free will. Puny little humans, who are here today and gone tomorrow, cannot tell God what He can and cannot do. Since God is all-powerful, He chose to reveal Himself through the Prophet Jesus for the salvation of those who will believe in Him. When a Muslim denies the deity of Christ, he is therefore limiting God's ability.

Christians need to stress God's holiness, the truth that He is not a God of deception, but is completely without sin. He is a personal, loving God, who provides the assurance of forgiveness of sin and the assurance of eternal life. These traits—God's holiness, a personal relationship, and love—are not part of the Islamic concept of God; they are vacuums within the Muslim soul.

Submission and man's response to God. Christians need to encourage Muslims to ask, "Is my faith based merely on tradition passed down through my parents and culture? Could truth relevant to God and my salvation exist, which I have not read and have not been exposed to?"

Muslims need help in realizing that everyone is a sinner, that all are separated from God, and that forgiveness is the crucial issue between God and humans. God is angry with people because of sin, although He is the friend of sinners. If one were to convince a Muslim that Christ is God and the Son of God, that the Trinity exists, and that the Bible is inerrant, this still would not make the Muslim a Christian. He must realize he is a sinner, confess his sin, and believe that Christ died for him. Muslims need help in realizing that God loves them, but that He hates sin. For a Muslim to go to heaven, he or she must have forgiveness of sin. Adding good works does not get rid of sin, which separates humanity from God. Adam did many things right but only one wrong, and thus he became separated from God and in need of forgiveness.

The Qur'an. When a Muslim says the Qur'an is "the uncreated speech of God existing in the mind of God from eternity past," he is saying that the Qur'an and God are two eternal and uncreated things. Yet he says there is only one God. Christians can point out that in a somewhat similar way Christianity holds to three eternal and uncreated persons but one God (John 1:1).

Muhammed. The Qur'an says God told Muhammed, "When in doubt ask those who read the previous scriptures" (Surah 10:95; 16:43). If Muhammed was told to read the Bible, the "previous Scriptures," should not Muslims read this same authority which God commanded Muhammed to read?

Animistic Values in Islam

UNDERSTANDING ANIMISTIC VALUES IN ISLAM

As stated earlier, popular animistic views have come through *adat,* or customs of the community. Most of this is not found in the Qur'an, though it has some roots there and certainly is rooted in *Hadith.* Popular Islam has a deep animistic value system. Animism is the belief that supernatural powers reside in animals, nature, and objects. Underneath are two driving values. One is fear and the other is power, or the desire to have power over what causes fear. Many Muslims will not readily talk about animistic areas of their lives. If the subject is brought up, they may say, "Some Muslims hold to this but it is not true; it is not Qur'anic Islam."

Since God is neither personal nor loving, and since He is far removed and transcendent, Muslims feel a need for power over certain fears in their lives. They desire an equilibrium or balance with the spirit world. Muslims strongly believe in a personal Satan and demons, called jinn. From the jinn come the powers of the evil eye. The fear of the evil eye, the jinn, and curses given by those with special power can lay a heavy toll on Muslims. In *zar* ceremonies women who are afflicted by a jinn can find a more stable relationship with the jinn inside of them. It does not mean that the evil spirit is cast out, but that equilibrium or balance comes through the *zar* ceremony.

Handmade rugs are almost always intentionally made with imperfections in them, because if they were perfect, they could attract and keep the evil eye. In children's first years they are frequently kept very dirty, even in clean houses by clean parents, because a clean child could attract the evil eye. No one is to compliment a baby or a young child, because this could open the child up to being zapped by the evil eye. If a compliment is given, then *Masha Allah* ("Praise God") is said in order to block the power of the evil eye from harming the child. Verses of the Qur'an are pinned to children's clothing to ward off the evil eye. And a kerosene light might be kept on all night in a village home in order to keep jinn away.

Muslims may pray to have a son, pass an exam, become healed, prevent their husband from divorcing them, or obtain a job. Throughout the Muslim world, in order to have prayers answered, Muslims flock to the tombs of saints, believing in the powers at the tomb of the dead bones of that saint to intercede or to answer their prayers. Muslims may walk around the tomb, touch it with their hands, and then put their hands on their face to pass the blessing from the saint onto themselves. A Muslim may hold an infant in one arm, put his or her free hand on the grave, and then place that hand on the face of the child to pass the blessing onto the child.

I have a friend who is a sheik in a five-hundred-year-old mystic order of Muslims. The grave of the founder of the order is to the right of the niche pointing toward Mecca, Muhammed's birthplace in Arabia. Throughout the day worshipers can be seen coming and praying in front of the grave. The sheik, who has a Ph.D. in chemistry from Cambridge University, said he did not believe there was any power whatsoever in praying at the grave of the founder of his Sufi order. However, he added, "But it doesn't hurt anything to pray through our founder." So with one sentence he denied the effectiveness of the animistic power of the dead bones, and in the next sentence he accepted its effectiveness.

Some say only illiterate village women, far from Mecca, are animistic. Some say animistic Islam exists only in a country like Indonesia. However, I believe all Muslims accept animism to some degree. All Muslims, when they pray, face toward a rock in the Kaaba in Mecca. In their pilgrimage to Mecca at least once in their lifetime, they go to that Kaaba, circle it seven times, and kiss it, believing there is power in it. The Kaaba was an idolatrous temple that existed before Muhammed, and the black stone within it was an idol.[4] There were 360 idols in Mecca and Muhammed got rid of 359 of them—all except the Kaaba. After their pilgrimage to Mecca, Muslims normally go to Medina, also in Arabia, to touch the grave of Muhammed to receive power.

The Qur'an itself sometimes is used in divination. Muslims also believe in intermediaries, who can cast spells of blessing or cursing. These intermediaries are considered more authoritative than the local sheik or the Qur'an. Though most women do not attend mosques, many of them go to a *zar,* where a woman with special powers can cast curses or give blessings. Many amulets are worn to ward off the power of the evil eye and the jinn. Many Muslims believe that some form of magical power helps them maintain equilibrium or balance with the spirit world. Interestingly, animism and fear of the evil eye stretches across Asia in Hindu and Buddhist countries as well as Islamic nations.

BUILDING BRIDGES BETWEEN CHRIST AND ANIMISTIC VALUES IN ISLAM

What bridges can ambassadors of Christ share with animistic Muslims? The Word of God addresses these issues. "God has not given us a spirit of timidity, but of power and love and self-discipline [or self-control, σωφρονισμοῦ]" (2 Tim. 1:7). The Word of God has power to change lives, for the gospel is "the power of God for salvation to everyone who believes" (Rom. 1:16). Christians should help Muslims see how meditating on Scripture can relieve fear, once they have believed in Christ. Christians can point to answers to prayer and share promises from God's Word.

Prayer from the heart touches Muslims. Most Muslims have never had anyone pray for them personally by name and for their problems. When I have prayed with a Muslim for a problem he is facing, frequently, as I have finished praying, I have seen tears in the Muslim's eyes. Many Muslims are looking for power over fears in their lives. The Word of God states they can have this power through salvation, through talking to God in prayer, through seeing God answer prayer and heal. The power of Christ is far greater than any other power. Christ can touch those who feel vulnerable and fearful.

Christians should never forget that they worship a personal God, who hears and answers prayer, who has created the world, who has all power, who has defeated Satan on the cross, who will ultimately defeat Satan, and who can solve the problems with which any Muslim is wrestling.

Cultural Values in Islam

UNDERSTANDING CULTURAL VALUES IN ISLAM

Th Umma (Muslim community). In hiring employees, a Muslim employer usually gives a job first to a family member. In the West this is known as nepotism or favoritism. To Westerners this seems wrong, but to Muslims this is a way of showing proper respect and loyalty. Muslims are obligated to care for their families and they tend to trust their family members more than others. As Bill Musk observes, "The Westerner wants to be objective and treat people fairly and equally. The Middle Easterner is immersed in a complex web of potential human connections, both positive and negative."[5]

The *Umma,* or Muslim community, is a foundation for unity

within the Muslim world. This is probably the strongest force that prevents Muslims from coming to Christ. Rather than thinking of individual rights and making decisions as individuals, the consensus of the community makes decisions for its members. In mosques, as Muslims pray while kneeling shoulder to shoulder with others in straight lines with their foreheads touching the ground, they sense a physical and emotional bonding with each other that many Christians have not experienced. Christians lack that unity of cultural oneness where they all pray in the same fashion together. They pray at home alone, or they go to their individual churches and pray in diverse ways.

Fasting in Islam is not something a person does by himself. Instead all Muslims fast at the same time during the day; together they feel hunger, thirst, and fatigue growing as the day progresses. Then when the cannon booms or the TV spokesman announces the time to break the fast, most Muslims are seated with family members around a table, or perhaps on a cloth spread on the ground with food prepared. All break the fast at the same time and enjoy eating and drinking together. There is a sense of unity as they realize that Muslims all over the world are fasting at the same time and breaking the fast at the same time.

When Muslims go on a pilgrimage to Mecca, about two million Muslims from almost every country of the world are doing the same thing, rich and poor dressed alike. When Muslims make the sacrifice at the end of the pilgrimage, they know Muslims from all over the world are also sacrificing. This provides a tremendous sense of unity.

Frequently when a Christian goes from a small town to a big city, he loses his walk with God. But a Muslim arriving in a city finds his identity in going to the local mosque, praying with strangers whether they are rich or poor. He kneels in prayer next to whoever comes in just before him. In this way he can quickly meet the faithful in his neighborhood. Normally those from a given village will settle in the same neighborhood of a city, praying in the same mosque.

In Islamic law Muslims are told they are their brother's keeper, and they are responsible to use whatever is necessary to keep other Muslims from doing wrong. In the West, Christians say each person must individually choose to follow Christ. But in Islam, individual thinking is not valued. Group pressure is exerted against those who would consider anything other than Islam.

Pressure from one's community and family encourages each Muslim to think and act in accord with Islamic values.

Family. One of the most powerful facets of Islamic community is the extended family. It is a warm, tight family, even though there may be arguments and disagreements. Arabs have a proverb which says, "I and my brothers against my cousins, I and my cousins against my tribe, I and my tribe against the world." Vocabulary in a language can teach a lot about culture and values. In Arabic only one word is used for time, clock, watch, and hour; this suggests that time is not so important. On the other hand Arabic has eight words used for cousin, depending on whether the cousin is a son or daughter of a mother or father's brother or sister. Family is of extreme importance.

When my family and I were missionaries in Iran, we asked our landlord's son if he could marry his first cousin. His answer was no, because they were *hamsheer* ("same milk"). As babies, they had drunk from the same milk of one of their mothers when the other mother had to go to the bazaar. There is a closeness in families that split, nuclear, or blended families in the West do not understand. This tight family exerts tremendous pressure against those who may be considering Christ.

Marriage is frequently within the extended family because of the desire to keep money, possessions, or power within the family. Parents instruct their children throughout their adult lives. A husband will listen to his illiterate mother more than to his college-educated wife. It is his responsibility. The sexes are segregated, each having their own specific roles, responsibilities, privileges, and requirements. A woman's place is in the home.

In the home of our landlord in Iran, the landlord's parents, his brothers and their wives, and all of their children lived in the same large home. Each had separate bedrooms and living rooms, but they shared the same kitchen, patio, and bathrooms. Except when our landlord served in the military service of his country, he spent every night of his life in this home. Many children live in the same house with their cousins every day of their lives. So if one family member came back to this warm, tight, extended family and said, "I believe Jesus Christ is the Son of God," all his cousins, uncles, aunts, brothers, sisters, parents, and grandparents would turn against him. For a Muslim to come to Christ, family pressure is undoubtedly far more challenging than theological issues.

Hospitality. One of the most wonderful benefits of living in the

Muslim world is enjoying and sharing its hospitality and kindness. This is true not merely in homes, but also in offices. There is a spirit of relaxation that Westerners do not have. If a person is going in for a signature from an administrator in an office, he must first sit, drink tea, and talk. Other people may come into the room and talk about other things during this time of waiting. A person never goes into a Muslim home without being asked to eat or drink something. Most Muslim cultures have their own unwritten codes of hospitality. Through questions, reading, and observation these unwritten codes can be deciphered. When Christians show and receive hospitality and kindness they are using an important means of communication.

Much in Islamic literature can be traced to its roots in the desert, where a bedouin encampment would warmly welcome a traveler. In the desert there are no motels for travelers. So he should be given hospitality. He in turn brings news from the outside world and possibly brings items to trade or sell. Just as Abraham showed hospitality for unknown guests, so to this day Muslims may offer a guest tea, followed by buttermilk and freshly baked bread. Then a goat is killed and a full meal is prepared. This was done for our party in a bedouin encampment deep in the mountains of Iran where there were no telephones to inform residents our group was coming.

A guest is a gift from God, says a Persian proverb. If someone admires a rug or something on a wall of the host, he needs to be careful what he says because it is very likely that the host will roll the rug up or take the object off the wall and insist that the guest take it home.

One time when I was completely filled with a delicious Egyptian meal, my host put a knife to my throat and a large pile of meat on my plate and with a smile on his face, told me to "keep eating." In the West, people are to clean their plates. In the East, if a person eats all the food on his plate, that says the host and hostess have done a poor job and that he must still be hungry. They will keep piling food on the plate until the guest has to leave some of it.

Honor and shame. One of the highest values in the Muslim world is honor. The opposite is shame. Persians refer to saving face as preventing the "water of the face"—embarrassment which causes the face to perspire. Saving one's own face and helping another person save face are deeply felt values, values that are more important than telling the truth. In the West, truth is valuable, but helping someone keep his or her honor and save face is not so important.

One of the highest points of honor in the Muslim world is that one's daughters are virgins when they marry. My language teacher in Iran said he would kill his daughters if they got pregnant before marriage. This is the normal Muslim response. Immorality does exist in the Muslim world but it is hidden. Women from puberty on are kept closely guarded in their homes.

On the other hand deception is encouraged. So lying can be a common part of communication. This contrast with the West is clear. Many Westerners are upset with their politicians if they lie, but not if they commit adultery. They might remove them from office if they lie under oath, but not if they commit adultery. When Gary Hart dropped out of the race for the United States presidency in 1988 over an adulterous affair, 85 percent of the people were against him because he lied about it. Only 15 percent were against him because he committed adultery. First Lieutenant Kelly J. Flinn was dismissed from the Air Force in 1997 primarily because she lied about an adulterous relationship, not because of the adultery itself. In the Muslim world the opposite is true. Lying is not a major problem, but fornication, especially fornication of one's unmarried daughters, can be unforgivable.

Fights take place over honor, not over who is right and wrong. In arguments, as insults grow, the worst insult (which I heard in Egypt) is to ask for someone's mother's house to fall in on her. As these insults build up, so does the tension, and the effort to bring shame.

On the other hand helping someone who is valued save face at all costs, to look good, to be respected, is of utmost importance. Good relations are more important than telling the truth. Muslims do not wrestle with the concept of guilt, of a legal sin, of doing something that is wrong before God. Instead they wrestle with the concept of shame, of bringing dishonor to one's family or to oneself. They are concerned with what people would say or what people would think. The preservation of self-respect is of the highest value. Value comes as much from the attitudes and actions of others as it does from internal motivation.

BUILDING BRIDGES BETWEEN CHRIST AND CULTURAL VALUES WITHIN ISLAM

Islamic cultural values contain many windows Christians should seek to open to let in the wonderful news of Jesus Christ. Many of their values are more biblical than are Western values, and these should be affirmed. The missionary accepts a dual responsibility to understand, appreciate, and value the good within Islam and at the same time to ask what bridges can be built through their value system into the Muslim soul.

The Umma (Muslim community). To help Muslims come to Christ, Christians must provide a community for them that is as strong or stronger than the community from which they come—one that will love them, help them find employment when they lose their job, care for them when their family has deserted them, visit them in prison, help meet the needs that their extended community would have provided.

Thankfully many missionaries are now targeting Muslim communities as a whole. If the entire community gradually believes, each believer remains an insider. This is easier to say than to do, and it carries with it a few potential pitfalls, but it is certainly worth the creative effort.

Christians emphasize going to meetings and having Bible studies, but they tend to minimize living and working together or having fun together. With Muslims, Christians need to plan time for games, tea, and doing things together in addition to attending church meetings.

The family. When a Muslim comes to Christ and is rejected by his family, Christians need to provide counsel, housing, jobs, mentoring, and encouragement that the original family would have provided. Our Savior spoke to this when He said, "And everyone who has left houses or brothers or sisters or father or mother or children or farms for My name's sake, shall receive many times as much, and shall inherit eternal life" (Matt. 19:29). Christians need, as best they are able, to be part of that. They need to concentrate on the needs that the converts' family of physical birth would have met.

Many Muslim converts say it is best for individuals who are living under the roof of their parents when they first come to Christ not to verbalize their witness but to witness by a changed life. They say it is wise to let their parents and relatives be attracted to their life, to the change Jesus Christ has made in the way they live, respond, and relate to their parents and extended family members. Later, when that change is deeply appreciated and sometimes when they have their own family under their own roof, they can share more openly their testimony about the one who has brought about the change.

We tend to think of the matchmaker in *Fiddler on the Roof* as an odd person from another culture. We tend to think that every person should have the right to choose his or her own spouse. However, in planting a church of Muslim converts, if a Muslim convert does not know and marry a Christian, a Christian home is usually not founded. Matchmaking is a biblical concept, with the patriarchs as examples. The Muslim culture normally uses matchmakers through family members. Missionaries need to seek to help Muslim converts marry other Muslims who have been led to Christ. When two believers of Muslim background are married, there is a beautiful opportunity for a new Christian community to be formed with that family.

Hospitality. In the West people do not often call on each other or visit with neighbors. As a result of busyness, air conditioning, electric garage door openers, and television, people live in their own "castles" and pull the bridges up once they enter their homes. They seldom sit on their front porches or visit with neighbors as was customary fifty years ago.

However, Christians are exhorted to entertain strangers as Abraham did (Heb. 13:2). Believers are to be given to hospitality (Rom. 12:13), and hospitality is one of the prerequisites of church leaders (1 Tim. 3:2). Giving and receiving hospitality is one of the joys of serving the Lord in the Muslim world. Hospitality is a language most Muslims fully understand and appreciate.

Honor and shame. Westerners tend to think that saving face and keeping one's honor is just an Eastern cultural concept. In reality it is a strong biblical concept. The words "shame," "ashamed," "honor," and "honored" occur often in the Bible. Paul commanded believers to give honor to whom honor is due (Rom. 13:7). Jesus endured the cross and despised its shame (Heb. 12:2). Christians are to honor others above themselves (Rom. 12:10). Elders who rule well are to be counted worthy of double honor, especially those who labor in the Word and doctrine (1 Tim. 5:17). After Peter and other apostles were beaten, they rejoiced that they were counted worthy to suffer shame for Christ's name (Acts 5:41). Honoring people and helping them keep face is a biblical concept seldom taught in the West.

Conclusion

One billion Muslims are separated from Jesus Christ. One of the reasons they are separated is that Christians do not understand or appreciate them and their values. Someone has said that missionaries will not be effective until they so appreciate the people they are seeking to reach that they are tempted to want to become part of their community. When they have that degree of appreciation, of understanding, of valuing Islamic positive values, then believers can begin to build bridges of witness to Muslims. Though Christians will always be outsiders to Muslims, they can continually try to understand Islam from within. The more they understand Islamic values, the better they can love Muslims. Then the more they love Muslims, the better they will be used by the Holy Spirit to draw Muslims to eternal salvation by faith in Jesus Christ.

CHAPTER 18

Principles and Methods of Household Evangelism

Ronald D. Runyon

In the early church, evangelism usually took place in three settings: public evangelism, personal evangelism (one-on-one witnessing situations), and household evangelism.[1] For most believers the latter two were their primary avenues of sharing their faith.

Most believers in the United States are not intensively involved in evangelism in any of these three areas. They have isolated themselves from the non-Christian world. As a result, they are not having an impact for Christ on people who are the closest to them.

This chapter focuses on the third type of evangelism: household evangelism. In this author's view this is still the most important method or strategy available to laymen today.

The Biblical Basis of Household Evangelism

The term "household" comes from the Greek word οἶκος. The word οἶκος and its related word οἰκία have several meanings. They communicate the meaning of both "house" and "family" since Greek has no word for the small social unit called the family. It can also mean a clan or larger tribal unit.[2]

In the New Testament οἰκία usually means a physical building (a house) as in Luke 4:38, "and He arose and left the synagogue, and entered Simon's home." But by metonymy it can sometimes mean the people or family living in the house (e.g., Luke 19:9, "Today salvation has come to this house"). Other examples in Paul's writings are in 2 Timothy 4:19 ("Greet Prisca and Aquila, and the *household* of Onesiphorus") and 1 Timothy 3:4 ("He must be one who manages his own *household* well").

In the Book of Acts, several times the word οἶκος means the members of one's household. Many of these instances relate to a situation where evangelism is being carried out. The following are verses in Acts where οἶκος means family. "And when she [Lydia] and her *household* had been baptized" (16:15); "And they said, 'Believe in the Lord Jesus, and you shall be saved, you and your *household*'" (16:31); "He was baptized, he and all his *household*" (16:33); "having believed in God with his whole *household*" (16:34); "And Crispus, the leader of the synagogue, believed in the Lord with all his *household*" (18:8).

In Acts οἶκος is also used to refer to more than one's own family members. Cornelius was "a devout man, and one who feared God with all his *household*" (10:2). He "had called together his relatives and close friends" (10:24). And Peter told Cornelius that God had told him to "speak words to you [Cornelius] by which you will be saved, you and all your *household*" (11:14).

The inference of the combination of these three verses related to Cornelius' household is that οἶκος referred not only to his immediate family unit but also to his other relatives and friends.

Thus the concept of "household evangelism" means the sharing of the gospel with the people with whom a believer has some kind of personal relationship, whether family members, relatives, friends, or associates. These are people in one's *sphere of influence*.

A study of the New Testament passages referring to laymen involved in evangelism demonstrates an important observation. With only two exceptions (Philip and Stephen), the primary target of New Testament laymen was their οἶκος(people in their sphere of influence). As a result of an ever-increasing network of Christians reaching others in their sphere of influence, the gospel spread rapidly throughout the many different regions in which the believers lived.

This concept of laymen presenting the gospel to people in their spheres of influence seems to be the primary target of lay-evangelism not only in Acts, but also in the Gospels and the Epistles, as evidenced by the following events. Andrew brought his brother Simon Peter to Jesus (John 1:41). Philip brought his friend Nathaniel to Jesus (John 1:45). Matthew held a banquet for his fellow tax collectors and other friends to meet Jesus (Matt. 9:10). Jesus instructed the former demoniac to go home and tell his family what happened (Luke 8:39). Jesus went to Zaccheus' house and his whole "house" was saved (Luke 19:9). The woman from Sychar who met Jesus at the well went back to Sychar to tell people in the town about Jesus (John 4:28). After the man born blind was healed by Jesus, he told his neighbors and others about it (John 9:8). Paul baptized the "household" of Stephanas (1 Cor.

1:16). Paul told Timothy to greet the "household" of Onesiphorus (2 Tim. 4:19).

Cultural Anthropology and Household Evangelism

The field of cultural anthropology also sheds light on this subject. David G. Mandelbaum, professor of anthropology at the University of California, states that every human is a part of three social groups: the family, the local community or neighborhood, and the clan or voluntary associations based on common interest (e.g., bridge clubs, trade unions, and parent-teacher associations).[3]

Spradley and McCurdy state and define these groups in the following way:

> Every social structure contains identities, roles, and groups outside of the kinship system. Anthropologists have classified these on the basis of some primary organizing principle. The most important groups identified by this means are kinship groups, territorial groups, associations. . . . A territorial group is one in which members inhabit a common locality over time and recognize that they share this locality.
>
> Associations are groups based on common interest, shared purpose, or some other attribute such as gender or age.[4]

These basic social groupings go under many headings: kinship-community-associations, webs of relationships, personal network, family-friends-associates, and others. In present-day society one's personal sphere of influence can be divided into four categories: family, neighbors, vocation-related contacts, and avocational-related contacts. Each of these areas has two spheres: a primary sphere (close family and friends) and a secondary sphere (acquaintances or more casual relationships), the major difference being how often the persons see each other.

The diagram on the following page illustrates these four categories or classifications in a person's personal sphere of influence.

In summary, a Christian's οἶκος or personal sphere of influence includes his family, friends, and associates in his neighborhood, work, and recreational activities. This personal sphere of influence is to be a primary target of a believer's personal evangelistic outreach.

Biblical Principles for Household Evangelism

The following factors seen in the Book of Acts are necessary for effective evangelism in one's sphere of influence.

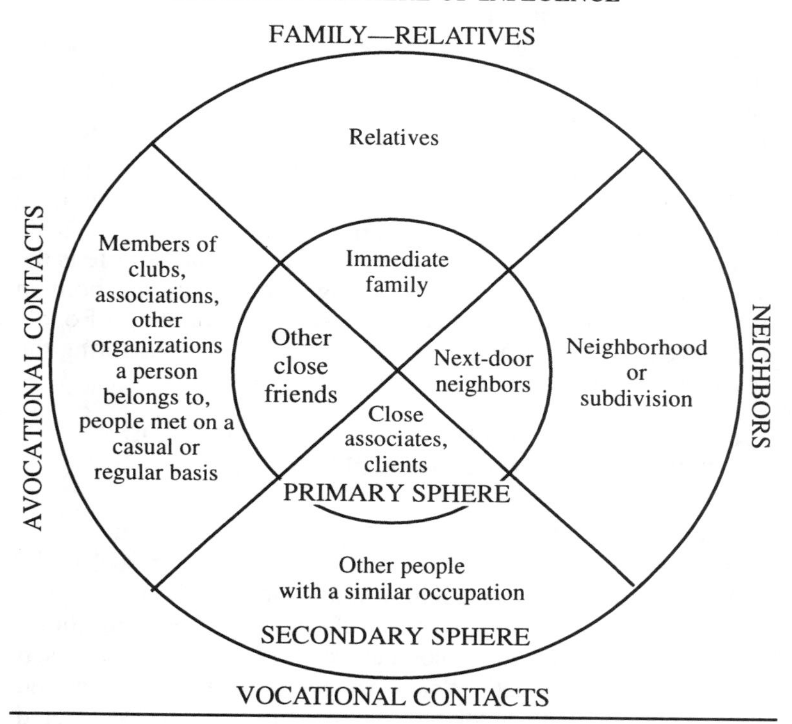

A TRANSFORMED LIFE

This is one of the more critical factors in seeing others come to know Christ. One of the reasons New Testament Christians were so bold is that their lives were radically impacted by the presence and power of the Holy Spirit. Having a personal relationship with Jesus Christ and experiencing the filling of the Holy Spirit with His supernatural power was a source of contagious excitement to the early Christians. With no training conferences or seminars, or any evangelistic tracts, they eagerly shared their faith with the people who were the closest to them relationally.[5]

The changes being wrought in the lives of Christians by the work of the Holy Spirit became attractive to the outside world. The beauty of the bride (of Christ) was something people admired, respected, and desired for themselves.[6] This transformed life also became an affirmation and validation of the reality of the gospel.[7]

People were open to hearing what these Christians had to say as a result of seeing changes take place in their lives.

One of the evidences of a changed life was the way Christians related to each other. The beauty of the love, unity, and meeting of each other's needs was a powerful witness to the reality of Christianity. Jesus prayed in John 17:21–23 that the oneness of believers would show the world that Jesus is the Son of God with the result that they would believe in Him. This indeed became a reality for many people, as seen in the Book of Acts.

A practical application of the power of a transformed life is the use of a personal testimony in evangelism situations, both in individual contacts and in group activities. The relating of one's personal experience is an excellent tool to use in augmenting the presentation of the gospel message.

A CLEAR PROCLAMATION OF THE WORD OF GOD IN ASSOCIATION WITH THE MINISTRY OF THE HOLY SPIRIT

In every case someone presented the gospel orally. Whether given by an apostle or a "layman," the presentation of the gospel in the Book of Acts always involved the Word of God and the Holy Spirit. The gospel was presented in a variety of settings: in public meetings, in the temple, in personal encounters such as Philip on the desert road, in small home meetings such as Peter in Cornelius' house and Paul in a public debate in Athens. The message was always centered on Jesus Christ but it was adapted to the audience it was spoken to.

PRAYER AS AN UNDERGIRDING FACTOR

When a Christian is involved in evangelism, he is also involved in a spiritual conflict. This creates the need for intercessory prayer. Prayer for boldness was an overriding theme in the early church. In the face of Jewish persecution the believers gathered together to pray (Acts 4:29–31). They did not pray that the persecution be removed, but that they would have greater boldness and confidence in proclaiming the gospel. Several times Paul asked Christians to pray for him so that he would have boldness to spread the gospel.

IDENTITY AND ANALYSIS OF THE PEOPLE IN ONE'S SPHERE OF INFLUENCE

In the New Testament, believers were definitely involved in reaching people in their sphere of influence. This is obvious from a study of Acts and the Epistles, but how many Christians today have ever taken the time to think about who is in their sphere of influence? By making a list of all the people in one's sphere of influence one can then begin to pray specifically for them. He can also begin to analyze the people, considering these questions: How well do I know them? What are their needs? What are their social patterns? From this a Christian can begin to determine what approaches and methods he should use to reach them.

USE OF A VARIETY OF METHODS TAILORED TO MEET THE NEEDS OF PEOPLE IN ONE'S SPHERE OF INFLUENCE

Peterson suggests that people may be thought of as being in one of two categories: people with a Judeo-Christian heritage, and people with no religious heritage.[8] People in the first group are those who have been exposed to the Bible and its teachings to at least some extent. Peterson calls these individuals "prepared people" because they at least have some understanding of who God is though they may not know much about Him. Paul went to this kind of people first when he visited a new town. His first stop was usually at the Jewish synagogue to speak to the Jews and the God-fearing Gentiles. As church-growth experts might put it, these were "receptive people."

For people in this "prepared" category, many times all that is needed is a simple presentation, in one form or another, of how to become a Christian. Many times the Lord has prepared them to receive the message and they trust Christ as their Savior on hearing the gospel the first time or perhaps after several times.

People without a religious heritage of any kind are those who have no general knowledge about who God is nor about Jesus Christ and the Bible. They may or may not have heard of Him but they have no real understanding of the Bible or of the God of the Bible. Peterson calls these individuals "secularized people."[9] He estimates that this group comprises approximately half the United States population. He believes that most of the evangelistic work being done today is among prepared people with little being done to reach secularized persons. To reach them Peterson recommends a more long-term approach to evangelism.[10] This involves several exposures to the gospel over a period of time. Church growth experts have deduced that people are often more receptive to the gospel when they are experiencing some kind of change in their lives. Tom Wolfe, a pastor in Los Angeles, has suggested that four of these major areas are "death, divorce (or other family troubles), illness, and status changes."[11] These changes tend to cause people to reflect more deeply on what is truly important in life. They force people away from superficial felt needs and desires to consider the fact that life consists of more than acquiring and enjoying material things. This growing awareness of the spiritual dimension of life causes people to be more open to the gospel.

RELATIONSHIPS WITH UNBELIEVERS

By its very definition, a person's sphere of influence consists of people with whom he has some type of relationship. But the question remains as to what quality or level of personal relationship believers have with these people. An overwhelmingly large number of people experience loneliness. Therefore the Christian distinctive of love and friendship should shine as a significant part of each believer's being a "light unto the world."

The ability to get beyond oneself, and initiate loving, friendship relationships should be the basis for evangelizing those people in one's sphere of influence. As a result two things may happen: they will be exposed to the reality of Christ's life-changing power (as evidenced in the Christian), and a Christian will get to know their spiritual backgrounds and spiritual needs thus enabling him to know how to relate the gospel effectively.

To develop meaningful relationships with nonbelievers, the Christian will need to go to non-Christians rather than waiting for them to come to him. This means that evangelism needs to be community-centered rather than church-centered. Meeting non-Christians where they are on "neutral turf" needs to be the central focus of one's strategy of outreach. This eliminates many unnecessary barriers for people who many times would never attend a church. This helps a Christian focus on Christ rather than making the nonbeliever feel he is being recruited to join a particular church.

Some church growth experts contend that evangelism ("disciple-making" is their term) is most effective when it is church-centered.

> The more distant evangelism is from the local church, the less "fruit" that remains; the closer evangelism is to the local church, the more "fruit" that remains. An effective strategy for disciple-making revolves around the local church. . . . The process of disciple-making has the church at the center of the evangelistic focus. . . .[12]

The author's disagreement with this philosophy is based on the examples of the Lord Jesus and the apostle Paul. Christians are to meet and engage people where they are (out in the world) and not wait for them to come to a church meeting. The first exposure and subsequent early exposures to Christ and the body of Christ often need to be in the confines of the οἶκος and not the church building itself. This is not a rigid rule, but it should be applied to individual situations based on a person's background and previous religious experience.

Another advantage to this concept is the ease with which a new believer can be assimilated into a local church. The vast majority who join a church do so because they know someone there. It follows that one led to Christ in one's sphere of influence will want to follow that person to the church where he attends.

USE OF ONE'S HOME AS A CENTER FOR EVANGELISM

Repeatedly in the New Testament, as already stated, the house was a center of evangelistic outreach. This was due partly to the culture of that time. No church buildings existed until many decades later. This was not because of the lack of money but because of the fact that Christianity was not generally held in high regard or favor. As a result, evangelism took place in homes and churches met in homes. Paul said he preached and taught the gospel from house to house (Acts 20:20). Acts 2:46 and 5:42 also speak of Christians meeting in homes as a place for preaching, teaching, and worship.

Wolfe makes the excellent point that "the front door of the home is the side door of the church."[13] The comfortableness of the warmth and friendship of a Christian's home is a powerful and attractive demonstration of the reality of the Christian faith.

Contemporary Methods of Household Evangelism

The following methods for evangelizing people in one's sphere of influence have been tested and shown to be effective. They are presented in two categories: one-on-one (or family-to-family) activities, and group "harvesting" activities.

ONE-ON-ONE (OR FAMILY-TO-FAMILY) ACTIVITIES

These are generally good pre-evangelism tools. They enable one to get to know the people he is trying to reach, to find out their religious thinking, and to discover any needs they may have. Most people who become Christians do so because of relationships built with Christians. McGavran calls these relationships "bridges to God."

These kinds of activities are good ways to utilize one's home. Hospitality is one of the best ways to demonstrate the love God empowers believers to have.[14] Some examples of these home-centered activities are these: (1) Have a family over for a meal and fun; (2) go to an event together, such as a ball game, concert, or cultural event; (3) do recreational things together, such as camping, fishing, hunting, bowling, exercising, or a cookout; (4) have a lunch together; (5) participate in neighborhood activities with friends, such as a baby-sitting co-op, food co-op, or Parent-Teachers Association. These activities help believers cultivate relationships and, as God gives the opportunity, they can also be occasions for sharing the gospel.

GROUP "HARVESTING" ACTIVITIES

Aldrich speaks of "harvesting vehicles" as activities used to present the gospel and give opportunity for people to respond.[15] The present author's research and personal experience confirm this. No matter what socioeconomic strata nonbelievers are in, these group activities expose people to the three critical factors in effective evangelism: a transformed life, the Word of God, and the body of Christ in action.

The following are some examples of proven group activities: (1) Evangelistic home Bible studies. This is one of the most commonly used group activities. (2) Evangelistic entertaining events. These can be in one's home or in a public eating place. They can be dinners, breakfasts (for businessmen), luncheons (for businessmen or women), or "coffees" or "teas" for women. Campus Crusade for Christ has excellent resources on how to put on such an event.[16] (3) Local evangelistic functions, such as concerts, Christian Businessmen's Committee luncheons, Christian Women's Club meetings, special outreach events, and a mayor's prayer breakfast. (4) Seasonal parties in one's home (on Christmas, Valentine's Day, etc.). (5) A Christian film shown in one's home. (6) A neighborhood block party. (7) A home open-discussion group.[17] (8) A craft class, marital enrichment class, child-raising class, or other classes. Many times these group activities can be planned and led effectively with some other Christian(s). These activities are effective because many people who are reluctant to attend a church are willing to go to an event in a person's home or some other "neutral" location.

Strategy

Christian laymen should develop a personal strategy to begin evangelizing the people in their spheres of influence. This strategy should employ the above-mentioned principles, Spirit-controlled creativity in choosing the right methods, and Spirit-empowered boldness and perseverance.

The following is a suggested approach to formulating such a strategy.

1. Read the appropriate Bible passages relating to this subject and commit to evangelizing the people in your sphere of influence.
2. Pray before, during, and after each step of the process.
3. Make a list of all the people in your sphere of influence and analyze their needs.
4. Select methods and activities suited to the people on the list. Use different methods, as necessary, to reach different people.
5. Find other Christians who have a similar sphere of influence and commitment to reach it, and form a team to work together.
6. Schedule and implement personal and group activities six months at a time.
7. Follow up all new Christians and interested people by personal and group fellowship studies and assimilate them into a local church as soon as possible.

This strategy is by no means a total and comprehensive plan. It is presented as a beginning point to enable Christians to launch into the exciting adventure of introducing people in their sphere of influence to Christ.

CHAPTER 19

Relationships: The Missing Link in Evangelistic Follow-Up

Gordon L. Everett

In his book, *Sharpening the Focus of the Church,* Getz remarks, "it is important to emphasize—and to emphasize emphatically—that outside of the context of the church and the experience of drawing upon other members of the body, a new babe in Christ will not grow into a mature responsible disciple of Jesus Christ."[1]

Arn echoes this idea when he states, "effective evangelism is not only making disciples, it is actively incorporating converts into the . . . church . . . where they function as responsible members."[2]

Mylander calls it the "follow-up gap."[3] Moore refers to it as the "baptism gap."[4] All are referring to the glaring difference between the number of decisions for Christ indicated through evangelistic efforts and the actual number of those converts who, a year or so later, are participating in the life of a local church.

Parachurch organizations have frequently been accused of neglecting or ignoring the local church in their zealous mass evangelistic campaigns. The local church, on the other hand, has been accused of laziness and of settling for an ineffective witness for Christ. Probably valid claims can be made on both sides. The contention of this article is that development of personal relationships between local church members and new believers who are not members is the key to incorporating new converts successfully into the church and closing the follow-up gap.

This proposition is not intended to discount the preaching and teaching of the Word of God, the role of the Holy Spirit, efficacious prayer, and bold evangelism. However, at least on the human level, the main thing that brings converts into the church and keeps them in is a relationship developed with an existing member. From the contemporary scene, consideration will be given to the nature of the follow-up gap and the crucial role played by personal relationships. Then an analysis of biblical examples will be offered as models for contemporary ministries.

Understanding the Gap

Too much "distance" exists between the member of a local church and those who are outside the church. Little or no intentional relationship-building and follow-up work is done by most churches.

As an example, the 1976 Billy Graham Crusade in Seattle was analyzed by a number of studies on the immediate and longer-lasting effects of the crusade on the local Christian community. One year after the crusade, Arn and the Institute for American Church Growth conducted a study that focused on new members assimilated into local churches and on pastors participating in the crusade.[5] Three and one-half years after the event, Glenn Firebaugh of Vanderbilt University conducted another study on area ministers, lay people, and crusade participants.[6] The results of the study are instructive.

According to Arn's figures, of the 18,136 "decisions" recorded during the crusade, 53.7 percent were rededications.[7] These were not considered in the study among new believers to be incorporated into churches, since they were presumed already to hold church memberships. Of the remaining 46.3 percent (8,400 individuals), only 15.3 percent or about 1,285 people were found to be incorporated into local churches one year after the crusade. Therefore 84.7 percent (about 7,100) were not so incorporated.[8] This is certainly cause for concern. In fact 82.7 percent of those responding to the survey said that the crusade's overall effect on the growth of their churches was little or none.[9]

However, Arn notes a crucial point. Of those individuals who *were* incorporated, 82.8 percent already had friends or relatives in that particular congregation.[10] The significance is clear: incorporation into a local church is most effective when a relationship is maintained between church members and those outside. A previous study by the Institute for American Church Growth (of eight thousand church members in thirty-five states and three countries) revealed that 75–90 percent of those responding entered their particular church as a result of a relationship link to either friends or relatives.[11]

Others have found similar results. For instance, Schaller found that when individuals were asked "Why are you a member of this particular congregation?" between two-thirds and nine-tenths indicated either friendship or kinship ties. Further, Schaller noted that in rapidly growing congregations, friendship ties were named predominately as the enfolding link to the congregation.[12] He also found that the people *least* likely to become inactive members were those who became part of a small group fellowship *before* entering into formal membership. They had been assimilated to some degree even before joining.[13] Therefore Schaller could say confidently, "The congregation which seeks to grow should look at how friendship ties can be increased between individual members and those persons who are not active members of any worshiping congregation."[14]

On the other hand Firebaugh's study of the Graham Crusade focused more on those who participated as assistants in the crusade. Firebaugh noted that only one out of nine of the local pastors and one out of five of the lay leaders felt that the crusade provided numerical growth for their churches.[15] It is interesting to note, however, that even though few churches experienced any numerical growth, seven out of eight lay leaders and two out of three pastors still said that the crusade had a positive effect on the community.[16] Firebaugh is undoubtedly correct in concluding that "the local church leaders considered more than numerical growth of their churches in evaluating the Crusade."[17] Apparently there was a perceived positive effect in terms of renewed personal commitment, heightened community awareness of Christianity, and so forth. However, if evaluated solely in light of new people added to local churches, an implication that can be drawn is "that Crusades are effective to the extent that they mobilize the individuals in an area. For this, the role of the church is paramount."[18] Other campaigns reveal similar results. Campus Crusade's "Here's Life, America" thrust demonstrated this same weakness as do many local church programs of various types of outreach.

Moore has said,

> There are heartbreaking gaps between the hundreds of professions of faith in the churches and the dozens of people who are actually baptized, effectively integrated in the life of the local church and growing in Christ a year later.
>
> Although there are many reasons why churches lose so many new converts, the major loss is the result of an inadequate understanding and philosophy of the follow-up principles in the New Testament.[19]

It can therefore be asserted that a gap exists between many contemporary outreach efforts and effective incorporation of new members into active fellowship in local churches. This author contends that the gap is primarily a relationship gap that can be bridged by development of relationships, member to nonmember.

> Friendship and love make it possible for non-Christians to hear the gospel with the inner ear of the soul. Some respond positively. Their personal relationship with a Christian friend then enables the new believer to bridge the gap from secular life to the church. Unfortunately, the lack of a personal relationship of genuine friendship is often the missing bridge of effective evangelism. Friendship bridges can span the "follow-up gap" between initial decision and responsible discipleship.[20]

The problem is that, as Schaller indicates, evangelism and receiving new members have become two separate actions.[21] Intentional relationship development, active assimilation, inclusionary thinking, making friends—whatever name is applied, the issue is the same: Discipleship requires relationships.

Biblical Perspective on Incorporation

What biblical examples of incorporation can be found in the early church? Do any of those examples suggest principles that are applicable for today? Is incorporation, indeed, a biblical concept?

First, it should be noted that numerical church growth with incorporation as one facet is an important concept in Scripture. Some would say at the outset, as does J. Randall Peterson, that Christian leaders should not focus so much on numerical growth. He says that, beyond the several thousand converts in the early chapters of Acts, the New Testament has little focus on numbers.[22] Churches should let numerical growth be the consequence,[23] presumably, of inner spiritual growth and the immeasurable growth in the Spirit. But the Bible, Peterson says, is not as concerned with numbers as the Church Growth movement seems to be. However, this writer concurs with McGavran[24] and Gerber[25] that numerical growth in Acts is mentioned throughout, either directly or by words expressing numerical ideas such as "multiplying," "added," "continued to increase," "considerable numbers," and others. Copland delineates this well in his article on growth in the early church.[26] Numbers do not conflict with qualitative or organic growth. In many cases they are indicative of such inner growth.

THE EXAMPLE OF THE EARLY CHURCH

The early church began with 120 awaiting the advent of the Spirit in Jerusalem, and on Pentecost, following Peter's sermon, about three thousand people were saved (Acts 2:41). One thing to notice was the natural course of things that followed. Those three thousand immediately began to fellowship together, worship together, mutually support each other, and eat together (v. 42). "And the Lord was adding to their number day by day" (v. 47). Acts 2:42–47 implies relationships among people, among friends sharing a common bond. The word "added" is important to consider from the standpoint of how believers were incorporated. In verse 41, the word is προσετέθησαν from προστίθημι, meaning "to add to, place beside, or increase." This word is used in Acts four times in the sense of incorporation into a society,[27] though neither verse 41 or verse 47 clearly states the object or group to which the three thousand people were added.[28]

> The word translated "added" literally means to place forward; that is, the placing of certain things next to things already in existence for the increase of that which is already in existence. Secondarily, these people were added to the one hundred and twenty; but primarily, they were added to the Lord.[29]

Calvin wrote, "They willingly embraced the Word of the apostles and were joined to the disciples of Christ, or ingrafted into the same Body, and continued in their doctrine."[30] Rackham also stated, "Baptism *added* or *joined* men—S. Luke does not say to whom but the next verse shews us—to the apostles as representing the church."[31]

Then the church grew to five thousand men (4:4), and "the congregation of those who believed were of one heart and soul" (v. 32). These people cared for one another. New believers were, as a matter of course, brought into the fellowship. There was no thought that they would not be included. It can be said, therefore, with Bruce in reference to 2:47 that, "It is the Lord whose prerogative it is to add new members to His own community; it is the joyful duty of the community to welcome to their ranks those whom Christ has accepted."[32] Not till later did the church begin to experience exclusionary thinking. When the Gentile wall was breached by Peter's encounter with Cornelius (Acts 10) it took James and the Jerusalem Council to be sure it was not erected again. Inclusionary thinking was part of God's plan for incorporating new believers.

THE EXAMPLE OF BARNABAS

From the time he was introduced as the "Son of Encouragement" (Acts 4:36) to his discipling of Paul and John Mark, Barnabas was an includer. Moore says, "Barnabas always looked past people's problems to the potential he saw by the work of God's grace."[33]

The first demonstration of this is found in Acts 9. After Saul was converted he began causing quite a stir in Damascus, and was ushered out of the city by his friends. When he eventually arrived in Jerusalem, the heart of the young church, his reception was understandably cold. No doubt his old reputation lingered and resentments may have gone deep. Incorporating Paul was undoubtedly the last thing on their minds. He was, for good reasons, suspect. However, Barnabas seemed to have had insight or perhaps knowledge beyond the reputation of the new convert. Barnabas literally "took hold of him" (v. 27) and brought Saul to the apostles when the majority of believers were prepared to reject him.

> It was Barnabas, who, true to his name, proved himself a "son of encouragement" and acted as Saul's sponsor . . . . When Saul desperately needed a true friend in Damascus, Ananias played that part to him; now when he stood in equal need of one in Jerusalem, he found a friend in Barnabas.[34]

The result was that Paul was accepted into the church fellowship. Self-incorporation certainly had not worked. He had tried to associate closely with the church but the people would not have it. Barnabas changed that. Had it not been for the sovereign work of God through a man who chose to advocate on Saul's behalf, who knows but that he might have been relegated to the ranks of those new believers in contemporary times who, on entering a church, experience cold rejection or lukewarm indifference. It took initiative and risk on the part of Barnabas to stand with Saul. It took initiative in that he was the only one willing to step forward and stand with an unpopular new believer. It took risk in that Barnabas could have been wrong. He could easily have precipitated the imprisonment or death of many in the church.

> It was Barnabas, Luke says, who was willing to risk accepting Saul as a genuine believer and who built a bridge of trust between himself and the Jerusalem apostles. Just why Barnabas alone showed such magnanimity, we are not told, though this is in character with what is said about him elsewhere in Acts . . . .[35]

Friendship that bridges the follow-up gap can be risky business. Reputation, time commitments, and other friendships may be placed on the line in order to stand with unpolished, sometimes offensive young believers. However, in this case, such friendship released Saul into the caring fellowship that he needed for his early growth.

Beyond his ministry to Saul, Barnabas again demonstrated his personal care to a young first-time ministry failure. Barnabas and Saul were accompanied by the young disciple John Mark on their first missionary journey, but he deserted them in Perga (13:13) and returned to Jerusalem. Whatever the reason for leaving, Paul felt that it was significant enough that Mark should not go with them on their second missionary journey (15:36–41). So strong were the feelings on both sides that Paul and Barnabas separated, Paul going on with Silas, and Barnabas joining John Mark. There has been considerable debate as to who, Paul or Barnabas, was at fault in this disagreement. Maclaren lays the blame squarely on Barnabas as a soft-hearted insubordinate.[36] Bruce[37] and Alexander[38] seem to take a middle ground, that both were at fault though the contention was sovereignly used to expand the ministry. Morgan, however, favors a more positive view of Barnabas. He said,

> Barnabas felt that Mark should have another chance. Perhaps there was a sense in which Paul and Barnabas were both right. Mark profited by the actions of both. The last thing we know about Mark, the "servant of Jesus," whom Paul for a time would not trust, but to whom Barnabas gave a second chance, is that it was he who wrote the Gospel of the perfect Servant.[39]

Again Barnabas' siding with Mark was a risk. Mark had failed once already and there was no guarantee he would not run out again. Barnabas could have discontinued the work with his young cousin and not have been criticized for doing so. Barnabas and Paul could have had a continued fruitful ministry together. However, Mark's martyrdom for the faith and his Gospel record stand as memorials, certainly to Mark, but also to Barnabas, the man who gave him a second chance. Barnabas in many ways portrays the kind of person that the church needed then and needs now to bridge to new believers and young, sometimes failing Christians.

THE EXAMPLE OF PAUL

It is not difficult to find the importance of relationships in the life of the apostle Paul. A cursory reading of his letters will indicate both breadth and depth of concern for individuals. In Romans 16 he mentioned thirty-five people by name and alluded to a number of households. Paul's circle of friends was enormous, and he built spiritual depth into those he befriended.

Paul's view of the functioning of the body of Christ clearly demonstrates a foundational mind set of "inclusion," that everyone is needed and important. One example is 1 Corinthians 12, with its lengthy discourse on the working of the body of Christ and the proper exercising of spiritual gifts. The theme of unity with diversity[40] is demonstrated particularly where Paul wrote, "But to each one is given the manifestation of the Spirit for the common good. . . . For even as the body is one and yet has many members, and all the members of the body, though they are many, are one body, so also is Christ" (1 Cor. 12:7, 12). The remainder of the passage illustrates this. For example, the foot cannot exclude itself simply because it is not a hand (v. 15). The eye cannot exclude the hand by saying, "I have no need of you" (v. 21). No one is excluded by self or by others. On the contrary, inclusionary action and inclusionary thinking are part and parcel of how the body of Christ is to function. "The body [of Christ] is an organism, it has many members but can only be what it is if it *possesses* all those members and if all those members are governed from one center; there is one life in all of them."[41]By failing to include new believers, the church is in danger of becoming like the aforementioned eye saying, "We have no need of you." This need not take the form of active exclusion. More commonly it may only be a lack of effort at inclusion.

A similar theme can be found in Ephesians 4. Again unity with diversity is central. Verses 15–16 speak of how the body grows: "But speaking the truth in love, we are to grow up in all aspects into Him, who is the head, even Christ, from whom the whole body, being fitted and held together by that which every joint supplies, according to the proper working of each individual part, causes the growth of the body for the building up of itself in love."

The words "fitted" and "held together" translate the Greek words συναρμολογούμενον and συμβιβαζόμενον, respectively. The first represents the shaping and forming of parts to fit exactly to each other. The second speaks of joining the pieces together, securing them, weaving them, compacting them together. Though the Lord places the parts, the growth is dependent on the proper working of each individual piece. Every part has a place, and every part is needed. To exclude or to fail to include some of those necessary pairs is unbiblical.

> Each member of this mystical body has a certain province assigned him to fill . . . . Thus should each tendon and sinew, ministrant in its own

> sphere however tiny, fulfill the task entrusted to it, each saint diffuse a savour of Christ in his environment to the well-being of his brethren whose good he seeks and also with a view to the incorporation of "those without" in the living temple of redeemed souls.[42]

Pattison and Moule wrote,

> The importance of the church as an association in which there is mutual dependence and aid, is here forcibly taught. Each individual's growth is made dependent on his connection with his fellow-disciples . . . . A selfish, isolated Christian is a moral absurdity.[43]

And, it may be added, church members are just as morally "absurd" for letting many young believers become isolated to the detriment both of them and the church of which they are a disassociated part.

Paul's concern for the care of young believers is clearly shown in 1 Thessalonians. In chapter 2, as Paul defended his motives for ministry, he wrote, "But we proved to be gentle among you, as a nursing mother tenderly cares for her own children. Having thus a fond affection for you, we were well-pleased to impart to you not only the gospel of God but also our own lives, because you had become very dear to us" (2:7–8).

There are in this passage two sides of the coin of evangelism. The gospel message is one and the imparting of Paul's life the other. The gospel of God is the evangelistic message, preached clearly yet not standing alone. Therefore Paul said, "not only the gospel of God but also our own lives."

> "Lives" *(psychas)* conveys more than just their physical lives; in the depths of their being they cared "because [the Thessalonians] had become so dear" to them. An even stronger relationship of love developed as the ministry continued—a relationship like that of a nursing mother with her child.[44]

Paul had on the one hand the message of faith and on the other hand the ministry of friendship—a deep relationship. He alluded to his care for them as a nursing mother and as an exhorting father (2:7, 11). They responded to his care by becoming imitators of Paul and of believers in churches in Judea (1:6; 2:14). It is this paternal and maternal care for people that is the missing element in incorporating new members today.

THE EXAMPLE OF JESUS

The greatest "assimilator" of all was Jesus Himself. For three years He dedicated Himself primarily to the Twelve. He built friendships, trust, and love with His men and expected them to do the same with others. His language was fraught with "inclusionary" terminology. His life was replete with "inclusionary" activity. "If any man is thirsty, let him come to Me and drink" (John 7:37). "Come to Me, all who are weary and heavy-laden" (Matt. 11:28). "Follow Me, and I will make you fishers of men" (4:19). "Permit the children to come to Me; do not hinder them" (Mark 10:14).

His commands were intended to embrace the whole of humanity. Thus He said, "Go therefore and make disciples of all the nations" (Matt. 28:19). "Go into all the world and preach the gospel to all creation" (Mark 16:15). "I in them, and Thou in Me . . . that the world may know" (John 17:23). "You shall be My witnesses . . . even to the remotest part of the earth" (Acts 1:8).

Jesus expected His church to embrace in oneness those who would believe worldwide. This was to be done not in a passive way, but boldly and actively. His concern for enfolding is probably most apparent in His shepherding commands to the apostle Peter in John 21:15–17. Three times He asked, "Simon, son of John, do you love Me?" And His command in the three cases was, "Tend My lambs . . . . Shepherd My sheep . . . . Tend My sheep." It is no wonder that Peter, in his first general epistle, exhorted the elders to "Shepherd the flock of God among you . . . nor yet as lording it over those allotted to your charge, but proving to be examples to the flock" (1 Peter 5:2–3). Peter passed on the inclusionary principle.

This, then, is incorporation. This is the biblical mind set of assimilation. It begins with evangelism but moves by means of relationships into full incorporation into the local church.

> To bridge the [follow-up) gap requires concerned Christians who will take personal interest in new believers. Their role can help those who make an initial decision for Christ develop into responsible members in the church and active disciples of the Lord Jesus. . . . God minted the coin of discipline with two sides. One is social, the other is theological. On the social side, new Christians must feel a part of the church's fabric of relationships. Otherwise they will become irregular in worship. . . and drift away into another church or drop out entirely. . . . On the theological side, disciplers help the new Christians develop disciplines that will spur them toward maturity.[45]

In conclusion, it has been shown that there is a gap in the church's contemporary ministry of outreach, and that gap is the initiation and building of personal relationships with those contacted by evangelism or other means. It has been shown that this separation between evangelism and incorporation is a concept outside the teaching of scriptural example. If churches were to understand this crucial missing link and respond by planning intentionally to incorporate the evangelized through development of relationships, those churches would experience accelerated numerical and organic growth. As Peters has written, "A church grows to the degree that it is able to move from a state of introversion to a state of extroversion."[46] This will take initiative and courage, but the results will be worth the effort.

CHAPTER 20

Go, Missions

J. Ronald Blue

World missions seems to spin around one little two-letter word—"Go!"

A bright banner stretches across the church auditorium with the catchy theme emblazoned in bold letters, "Don't take the 'go' out of the gospel!" It provides a good backdrop for the missionary speaker. He thrusts his arm into the air and, like some impassioned cheerleader in an overtime game, he dramatically cries "Go!"

At the ball game, of course, the whole crowd rises to their feet and carries the chant to deafening decibels, "Go! Go! Go!" Not so in the church. People yawn or dutifully stare at the pulpit. They quietly excuse themselves from this unreasonable command. "Go? Go where?"

It is not that the command is so unreasonable. It is just not applicable to the average listener. "I'm completely tied down with my work," reasons the businessman. "I'm not free to go anywhere." "I have responsibilities to my children and to my husband," ponders the housewife. "I'm in no position to go." "My major is chemical engineering," muses the university student. "I could hardly go as a missionary." "I'm too young to think about going anywhere yet," each high schooler says to himself, and every child looks at the frantic speaker in bewilderment, "What's he shouting about?" The "go" of missions seems to be addressed to someone else.

Could it be that "go" is only a part of the biblical missions equation? Perhaps the thoughts that pass through people's minds as the missionary speaker shouts "Go!" are not mere devilish deceptions but responsible conclusions. Are all these people simply looking for some cold, carnal "cop-out"?

Is "go" the unique and essential ingredient for effective world missions? Obviously mobility is necessary. If no one goes, there are no missionaries. Thousands of men and women have concluded that the command was theirs to obey and have gone to serve the Lord all over the globe.

But what about those who do not go? Is "go" the word for them? Could there be a mystery word for missions that has remained in some quiet corner while everyone is shouting "Go"? Is "go" really the "bottom line" for missions?

Surprisingly enough, the Bible seems to stress a word in the missions equation that is of greater significance than "go." "Go" is not the "bottom line" for world missions.

The Lord's Commission

"Surely you are not going to challenge the clear teachings of Christ in the Great Commission," a well-versed Bible teacher may argue. "Our Lord has commanded us to go and make disciples of all the nations [Matt. 28:19]. He has ordered us to go into all the world and preach the gospel to every creature [Mark 16:15]."

A closer look at these key passages reveals that while going is essential it is not the key element of Christ's assignment. Actually the word translated "go" is a participle in both of these Great Commission texts. In Matthew's gospel, the command is "make disciples" (μαθητεύσατε). In Mark, the central command is "preach the gospel" (κηρύξατε τὸ εὐαγγέλιον). These essentials of reaching people for Christ and teaching people in Christ are to be accomplished in "all the nations" (πάντα τὰ ἔθνη), "all the world" (τὸν κόσμον ἅπαντα), and "to every creature" (πάσῃ τῇ κτίσει). People need to come to know Christ and grow in Christ all over the globe. World missions demands some going.

The going is not some peripheral part of the equation as some have suggested by the translations, "As you are going" or "Since you are going," or "While going."[1] Both in Matthew and Mark, the participle (πορευθέντες) can best be considered a participle of attendant circumstance and therefore carries the force of the main verb.[2] It is not incidental. Going is imperatival. The translation as a command is a good one. "Go and make disciples." "Go and preach the gospel."

Matthew uses a similar grammatical construction in chapter 11 when Jesus said to John's disciples, "Go and report to John what you hear and see" (Matt. 11:4). The participle (πορευθέντες) would hardly be translated, "as you go," "since you're going," or "while you go." The force of the command (ἀπαγγείλατε) is transferred to the participle.

In the more immediate context of the Great Commission passage, Matthew uses a similar construction. The angel of the Lord who rolled away the stone of the tomb in which Jesus' body had been placed said to the women, "Do not be afraid, for I know that you are looking for Jesus who has been crucified. He is not here, for He has risen, just as He said. Come, see the place where He was lying. And go quickly and tell His disciples that He has risen from the dead" (Matt. 28:5–7).

The translation "go and tell" is a good one. The participle (πορευθεῖσαι) carries the force of the command (εἴπατε). The angel commanded the women to go and tell the disciples that Jesus had risen from the dead.

As appealing as it might be to render the Great Commission text, "Therefore as ye are going,"[3] a more complete exegetical study seems to mitigate against it.

The presence of the participles in Matthew's Great Commission text continues to lead to some intriguing conclusions. Wagner writes, "Notice that the passage contains four action verbs: *go, make disciples, baptize,* and *teach*. In the original Greek only one of them is imperative and three are participles. The imperative *make disciples* is the heart of the command. The participles *going, baptizing,* and *teaching* are helping verbs."[4] However, Wagner has failed to make the grammatical distinction between the aorist participle which precedes the aorist command and carries the force of that command and the present participles which follow.

In a comprehensive grammatical study of the Great Commission of Matthew, Rogers concludes that "the participle is vitally related to the command contained in the imperative." He explains, "The participle is not to be weakened to a secondary option which is not as important. The aorist aspect makes the command definite and urgent. It is not 'if you happen to be going' or 'whenever you might be' but rather 'go and perform an act.'"[5]

Nonetheless it can hardly be said that "go" is the foundational aspect of world missions. It may be imperatival but the "go" is clearly linked to making disciples and preaching the gospel. As Kane has so wisely expressed it, "the church has made the mistake of isolating one word—'go'—and building the entire missionary mandate on that."[6]

"Go" is essential to the Great Commission, but it is not the key ingredient. The major thrust of Christ's assignment is to proclaim the good news of His salvation and to prepare productive followers among all the peoples of the world. Obviously evangelization and edification will take place around the globe only if God's children go around the world to accomplish this assignment. To "preach" and "teach" effectively the church must first "reach" those who are scattered in people-groups from pole to pole and shore to shore.

Another element of missions, however, is even more basic than "reach," "preach," or "teach." It is foundational to the process of going, to the proclamation of the gospel, and to the production of growing disciples in every nation. What is the mystery ingredient on which world missions stands or falls? What is the "bottom line" of missions?

A Logical Conclusion

The apostle Paul in one of his most impressive "missionary letters" leads his readers to the basic, most essential element in world missions. Using the Socratic spade of deductive logic, the apostle digs down to the bedrock of all mission endeavor.

After disclosing the world's problem of sin (Romans 1–3), presenting God's provision of salvation (Romans 3–5), and outlining the believer's progress in sanctification (Romans 6–8), Paul turned his attention to his fellow Jews (Romans 9–11).[7] Chapters 9 through 11 are not a parenthesis or appendix as some commentators state.[8] Cranfield writes:

> A superficial reading of the epistle might easily leave one with the impression that chapters 9 to 11 are simply an excursus which Paul has included under the pressure of his own deep personal involvement in the matter of Israel's destiny but which is without any real inner relatedness to the main argument of Romans.[9]

Actually Romans 9–11 are an integral part of the book. They serve as the culmination of the preceding eight chapters showing God's sovereignty in His dealings with Israel in relation to their sin, salvation, and sanctification. Paul then turned to the theme of service in chapter 12. Chapters 9–11 serve as the mountaintop in the majestic range called Romans.

At the very peak of his discussion of God's sovereignty in chapter 10, Paul looked back to the valley from which he had climbed. He focused first on the world around him, a world that is religious but lost. His fellow citizens are indeed lost in sin, the point made so clearly in the first three chapters.

Paul then fixed his gaze on the Word, God's saving revelation to lost men everywhere, especially to his Jewish companions. This is the very salvation Paul outlined so clearly in chapters 3–5.

Finally, he saw again the vital role of witness each true believer shares in getting God's Word to people who have not yet discovered true salvation. The apostle emphasized again the fullness of a sanctified life that he so carefully presented in chapters 5–8. The believer is set apart by God for a purpose. He is a witness to the world. Paul's fellow Jews should have known this assignment. It had been theirs since the time of the Abrahamic Covenant. They were to be a blessing to all the families of the earth (Gen. 12:3). And long before Christ gave the assignment for the church to be a witness to "the uttermost part of the earth" (Acts 1:8), Israel had received the mandate to make known God's "salvation among all nations" (Ps. 67:2).

Paul's dramatic view from the summit of his book gives not only a clear focus on the three essential elements of missions but also the perfect site for excavating and uncovering the benchmark of missions, that vital ingredient on which all of world missions stands or falls.

Before uncovering that key element, however, Paul recorded his view of the world, God's Word, and man's witness.

The World

Paul focused on his fellow Jews. What he saw in that world around him is not unlike the world of today. He saw people who are very religious but desperately lost. They face three problems.

ACTIVITY WITHOUT ADVANCE (ROM. 10:2)

Paul's friends had plenty of zeal for God but they lacked the needed knowledge or experience (ἐπίγνωσιν). The Jewish citizens did not lack drive. They lacked direction. So it is in the world today among the majority of the world's inhabitants. It could be called the racetrack approach: Every participant is going at top speed—in circles!

RELIGION WITHOUT RIGHTEOUSNESS (ROM. 10:3)

The Jews had no lack of religion. Paul's friends were all wrapped up in the rules, regulations, and rituals of their Jewish heritage. Not knowing about God's righteousness, they sought to establish their own. The contemporary world is equally filled with a multiplicity of religions. The hocus-pocus approach is popular: follow a few rules, go through a few gyrations, burn a few candles, swing a few incense pots, mutter a few prayers, focus on a few images—do something religious.

GOODNESS WITHOUT GODLINESS (ROM. 10:4–5)

Actually there was no problem with God's rules. The problem was with those trying to fulfill the rules. Paul declared that those who were pretending to practice the righteousness based on the Law were then subject to that Law. Paul's friends were good people but not quite good enough. God demands perfection for salvation. Many wonderful people are in the world. There are no perfect people, however; only forgiven ones. The polished-apple approach is prevalent: "Do the best you can, live by the Golden Rule, love your neighbor as yourself, and don't kick any cats."

The challenge of Paul's day is that of the present. The world is filled with zealous, religious "do-good" people who are inoculated against the simple message of faith in the Savior. Of the twenty-six who die every ten seconds,[10] two are Buddhist, four are Hindu, five are Muslim, seven are "Christian," and eight are atheistic, agnostic, or animistic.[11] Of the seven who claim to be "Christian," four are Roman Catholic and three are Protestant. Only the Lord knows how many are truly redeemed. Religion abounds. The redeemed are rare.

The Word

From a world of great spiritual need, Paul turned his attention to the provision for that need—God's Word. The answer to the dilemma of so many self-righteous pagans is not found in the path of religious futility. It is found in the way of redeeming faith.

Paul contrasts the righteousness based on the Law with the righteousness based on faith. Actually law is the basis of religion. Faith is the basis for true righteousness. That is a major theme of Paul's letter. Justification is not achieved, it is received. Faith in Christ clothes the believer in His perfect righteousness. Paul speaks of these aspects of this exciting revelation.

AVAILABILITY OF THE WORD (ROM. 10:6–8)

Quoting Deuteronomy 30:12–14, Paul emphasized God's initiative in providing this message to receptive hearts. As Bruce points out,

> God has brought this salvation near to us, in Christ. We do not have to "climb the heavenly steeps" to procure it, for Christ has come down with it; we do not need to "plumb the lowest deeps" for it, for Christ has risen from the dead to make it secure to us. It is here, present and available . . . .[12]

"The word is near," wrote Paul, "in your mouth and in your heart—that is, the word of faith which we are preaching." Granted, there are masses of people on earth today who have never heard this word of faith.[13] Paul has already dealt with this problem in the first chapters of Romans. But to his readers, as to millions upon millions of people today, the Word has reached them. They have yet to respond.

SIMPLICITY OF THE WORD (ROM. 10:9–10)

The lack of response by those who have received God's good news is not because the message is overly complicated. On the contrary, many people seem to feel it is too simple. So simple is it that it becomes impossible for them to accept because they are not willing to admit they have a spiritual need, a major problem with religious people. They are not ready to take the medicine because they are convinced they suffer no illness.

The message is exceedingly clear. "If you confess with your mouth Jesus as Lord, and believe in your heart that God raised Him from the dead, you shall be saved" (v. 9). The word of salvation centers in the Lord Jesus Christ. God has provided salvation in Him and salvation is applied as man responds to Him. It simply involves an expressed act of the will. The verbal confession of a volitional commitment brings full salvation. He is Savior (Ἰῆσους) because He is the resurrected Lord (κύριος).[14] "Believe in the Lord Jesus, and you shall be saved," was Paul's message to the Philippian jailor (Acts 16:31).

"Believe" (πιστεύω) might be translated "trust." It is not mere mental assent. Paul wrote, "With the heart man believes, resulting in righteousness, and with the mouth he confesses, resulting in salvation" (v. 10). The righteousness people so earnestly seek is not attainable through zealous action, hocus-pocus religion, or some do-good lifestyle. It comes through a simple act of the will. Trust in the Lord Jesus Christ and this righteousness and full salvation are provided. The message is simple. The message is clear.

UNIVERSALITY OF THE WORD (ROM. 10:11–13)

God's saving message to man is readily available and amazingly simple—and it is uniquely universal. Quoting from Isaiah, Paul exclaimed, "Whoever believes in Him will not be disappointed" (v. 11). On the contrary, "Whoever will call upon the name of the Lord will be saved" (v. 13).

Lest his readers miss the point of the scope of the word "whoever" in these quotations from the Old Testament prophets, Paul explained, "For there is no distinction between Jew and Greek; for the same Lord is Lord of all, abounding in riches for all who call upon Him" (v. 12). His riches are available to all who call on Him. This marvelous message of life is not for a few isolated people nor for one select race. The message is for all.

The Witness

The view from the Romans mountain peak is not only breathtaking; it is also convicting. There is a vast world out there in desperate spiritual need. It may be an outwardly religious world, but it is an inwardly rebellious world. Like new-fallen snow in the Rockies, a clear word is voiced from heaven that can cover the dirty soil and sharp crevices of sin. God has a perfect provision for the world's problems. His Word is available; it is near. His Word is simple; it is clear. Above all, His Word is universal; it is for all. It is for everyone, everywhere.

The road to the mountain peak may seem long and somewhat toilsome, but it provides meaning to the search for the fundamental ingredient to world missions. With but four key questions, the apostle uncovers the missions benchmark.

"HOW THEN SHALL THEY CALL UPON HIM IN WHOM THEY HAVE NOT BELIEVED?" (ROM. 10:14a)

Paul made it clear that there is no conversion apart from an expression of faith in Christ. The "call" is simply evidence of a "commitment" in the heart. The grammatical construction here, ειϛ ὅν . . . ἐπίστευσαν, is somewhat unique for Paul. Although the construction is common in John's writings, the only other occurrences of πιστεύειν εἰϛ in Paul's epistles are in Galatians 2:16 and Philippians 1:29. It is used almost exclusively of faith in Christ, further evidence that "believe" is not to be taken as mental assent. Cranfield asserts that "πιστεύειν εἰϛ denotes a faith in Christ which includes faith that God has raised Him from the dead and the acceptance of Him as Lord."[15]

"AND HOW SHALL THEY BELIEVE IN HIM WHOM THEY HAVE NOT HEARD?" (ROM. 10:14b)

Just as the "call" with the mouth is but an audible evidence of what has taken place in the heart, so the heart is dependent on the mind. There is no saving confession of faith if there is no commitment in the heart. But the heart, or the will, does not work in a vacuum. Commitment depends on comprehension. Many are dark in the heart because they are dead in the head. They have not heard. That, of course, leads very clearly to the next question.

"AND HOW SHALL THEY HEAR WITHOUT A PREACHER?" (ROM. 10:14c)

There must be another person in the picture. In God's sovereignty, He has chosen "stick-em-and-they-bleed" people to proclaim His message of salvation. It is indeed incredible that He has not used the stars to spell out the message, or the wind to sound the message in every language of the world, or bright, shining angels to sweep down over mankind to proclaim the message, or a deafening shout directly from heaven, "Here I am. I'm God! Listen to Me!"

In His grace God gives the assignment of proclamation to His frail children, perhaps to show in a more vivid way His amazing power. The assignment, of course, is not to deliver some well-crafted homily with three points and a poem from a lavish lectern. "Preach" unfortunately conveys a pulpit image. The assignment is simply one of proclaiming, or heralding. Perhaps the best way to unveil the meaning of κηρύσσοντος would be to "chatter the gospel" to the whole world.

The apostle was about to uncover the key word for missions. With but one more penetrating question he revealed the benchmark and it was not "go."

"AND HOW SHALL THEY PREACH UNLESS THEY ARE SENT?" (ROM. 10:15)

The word is not "go." *The key word is "send."* World missions, and in a sense the entire ministry of accomplishing God's purpose in this age, revolves around the simple word "send."

There is no conversion, no confession, no commitment, no comprehension, and no communication without a commission of God's servant to reach the lost. The whole worldwide enterprise stands or falls on the word "send."

The old familiar word echoed in missions conferences across the country is likewise dependent on this more foundational ingredient as well. There is no "going" without "sending."

Paul's argument culminates in the key word "send." As

Käsemann writes, "The point of the whole lies in the last rather than the first member in the chain."[16] Using the analogy of the chain, Lenski comes to the same conclusion.

> Now faith is voiced in confession (calling upon the Lord) and comes from hearing the preaching of men sent or commissioned. An adequate presentation of the Word as the means of grace for producing faith must touch all the links in the chain. Paul lets them form a chain and fastens a golden Scripture pendant to the last link (v. 15).[17]

The pendant to which Lenski refers is the quotation from Isaiah 52:7, "How beautiful are the feet of those who bring glad tidings of good things!" Going is essential, of course. Whether "beautiful" or "timely" (ὡραῖοι), the feet, not the mouth, are the focus of attention. The touchstone of the proclamation of the gospel is to be found in sending. God's provision for the world's problem depends on His divinely devised process. As Hodge points out, "if God wills the end, He wills also the means."[18] God's good news (evident in both the verb and the object, εὐαγγελιζομένων ἀγαθά) is not going to reach the intended target without God's global newsmen sent out to publish the message of salvation.

A Linguistic Consideration

Actually the conclusion that "send" is the key for missions should not be so surprising since the word "mission" means "send." "Missions" is derived from the Latin *mitto,* a verb meaning "to send."[19]

The English word "missions" does not appear in the Bible. The omission hardly makes missions unbiblical, however. The word "Trinity" is not in the Bible either. The teaching of both the Trinity and world missions is evident throughout Scripture.

Obviously "missions" is not likely to be found in English translations of the Bible because the word is of Latin origin. The frequently used Greek verb ἀποστέλλω is rightly translated "send." The noun form ἀπόστελος is simply transliterated as "apostle" in English. The apostle was a "sent one" or a "missionary."

The questions of Romans 10 that missionary Paul used to arrive at the fundamental element in God's plan of world redemption culminated in the Greek word ἀποσταλῶχιν, "send."

The Greek verbs ἀποστέλλω or ἐξαποστέλλω occur 140 times in the New Testament. The more common Greek verbs for "send," πέμπω or ἐκπέμπω, appear only eighty-one times in the New Testament.[20] The verb ἀποστέλλω seems to focus more on the purpose and authority of the sending while πέμπω denotes the mere process or action involved. It is with good cause that ἀποστέλλω should be the more frequent verb used in the New Testament, just as ἀγαπάω rather than φιλέω is the more frequent New Testament verb for love. The apostle, or sent one, is thrust out with purpose and with authority. He is a missionary, an ambassador of the King, and a herald of the gospel. God's sending (ἀποστέλλω) and God's love (ἀγαπάω) are emphasized in the New Testament.

Conclusion

Contrary to the persistent emphasis on the word "go," mission leaders need to focus on the essential element of missions, "send." Churches need to consider the biblical challenge to cultivate proven workers in ministry and commission them for missionary service.

The shift in focus from "go" to "send" may produce some radical and much-needed changes in modern world missions. The problems sometimes inherent in volunteerism are solved by enlisting proven, qualified personnel to serve as missionaries sent out by their home churches. Dreaded deputation in which missionary candidates travel from coast to coast "raising support" is eliminated or at least largely curtailed. "Mystery missionaries" who receive limited finances but are totally unknown by the congregation are no longer added to the list of those who have gone but were not really sent. Mission boards spend more time with church boards to locate needed personnel and resources to reach areas of spiritual need or pockets of unreached people in the areas of the world in which the mission serves.

Bible college and seminary students detached from their home church are prompted to renew or establish a close contact with those responsible for sending out missionaries. The student does not decide he is going, join a mission board, and then "send a bill" to his local church. The people of his church are engaged with him in his decisions regarding missionary service. Ideally the student has already been sent by his church for the preparation he is receiving. He is being trained to be a missionary. He is being equipped as a "sent one."

Paying closer attention to God's "bottom line," send, could bring about changes in the whole balance sheet. With those changes, it is likely that the investment in God's world missions market will bring greater returns than ever. Who knows, one "send" might even be worth two "go's"!

Chapter Notes

Chapter 1

1. Robert E. Speer, *Christianity and the Nations* (New York: Revell, 1910), 17.
2. Ibid., 17–18.
3. J. E. Lesslie Newbigin, *Trinitarian Faith and Today's Mission* (Richmond, Va.: Knox, 1963), 31.
4. Georg F. Vicedom, *The Mission of God: An Introduction to a Theology of Mission* (St. Louis: Concordia, 1965), vii.
5. *Minutes of the Enlarged Meeting and the Committee of the International Missionary Council, Willingen, Germany, July 5th to 21st, 1952* (New York: International Missionary Council, 1952), Appendix A, 54.
6. Leslie Davison, *Sender and Sent* (London: Epworth, 1969), 20.
7. Douglas Webster, *Unchanging Mission* (Philadelphia: Fortress, 1965), 1.
8. Vicedom, *The Mission of God,* 5.
9. Davison, *Sender and Sent,* 20.

Chapter 2

1. Charles L. Chaney, *The Birth of Missions in America* (Pasadena, Calif.: William Carey Library, 1976), 68.

Chapter 3

1. New York: Harper & Brothers, 1951.
2. Bronislaw Malinowski, *The Dynamic of Culture Change,* ed. Phyllis M. Kaberry (New Haven, Conn.: Yale University Press, 1945), 48.
3. Peter Beyerhaus and Henry Lefever, *The Responsible Church and the Foreign Mission* (Grand Rapids: Eerdmans, 1964).
4. London: Lutterworth Press, 1966.
5. Norman A. Horner, *Cross and Crucifix in Mission* (Nashville: Abingdon, 1965), 180–81. The directory to which Horner refers is the *Directory of Christian Colleges in Asia, Africa, the Middle East, the Pacific, Latin America and the Caribbean,* comp. Clara E. Orr (New York: Missionary Research Library, 1961).
6. Joseph Houldsworth Oldham, *The World and the Gospel,* 3d ed. (London: United Council for Missionary Education, 1917), 141.
7. Ibid., 140–41.

Chapter 4

1. Lesslie Newbigin, *Trinitarian Faith and Today's Mission* (Richmond, Va.: Knox, 1964), 14.
2. Arno C. Gaebelein, *Christianity or Religion?* (New York: Our Hope, 1927).
3. Samuel G. Craig, *Christianity Rightly So Called* (Philadelphia: Presbyterian & Reformed, 1946).
4. W. H. Griffith Thomas, *Christianity Is Christ* (London: Longmans, Green, 1919).
5. J. H. Bavinck, *The Church between Temple and Mosque* (Grand Rapids: Eerdmans, 1966), 13.
6. Branislaw Malinowski, *Myth in Primitive Psychology* (Westport, Conn.: Negro Universities Press, 1926), 91.
7. George W. Peters, *A Biblical Theology of Missions* (Chicago: Moody, 1972), 320–21.
8. Hans-Werner Gensichen, "Dialogue with Non-Christian Religions," in *The Future of the Christian World Mission,* ed. William J. Danker and Wi Jo Kang (Grand Rapids: Eerdmans, 1971), 33–35.
9. Carl F. Braaten, *The Flaming Center* (Philadelphia: Fortress, 1977), 93–118.
10. Raymond Hammer, *Japan's Religious Ferment* (New York: Oxford University Press, 1962), 91.
11. Hendrick Kraemer, *The Christian Message in a Non-Christian World* (Grand Rapids: Kregel, 1956), 351.
12. William James, *The Varieties of Religious Experience* (New York: Longmans, Green, 1902).

Chapter 5

1. Jurgen Moltmann, *The Theology of Hope on the Grounds and Implications of a Christian Eschatology,* trans. James W. Leitch (New York: Harper & Row, 1965).
2. Rubem A. Alves, *A Theology of Human Hope* (Washington, D.C.: Corpus Books, 1969); Gustavo Gutiérrez, *Theology of Liberation, History, Politics, and Salvation,* trans. and ed. Caridad Inda and John Eagleson (Maryknoll, N.Y.: Orbis, 1972).
3. Charles C. Ryrie, *The Basis of the Premillennial Faith* (Neptune, N.J.: Loizeaux Brothers, 1953), 93.
4. Ibid., 98.
5. George Eldon Ladd, "The Gospel of the Kingdom," in *Perspectives on the World Christian Movement: A Reader* (Pasadena, Calif.: William Carey Library, 1981), 56–57.
6. Charles Feinberg, *Millennialism: The Two Major Views,* rev. ed. (Chicago: Moody, 1980), 313.
7. Henry Alford, *The Greek Testament,* 4 vols. (reprint, Chicago: Moody, n.d.), 4:726.
8. Ryrie, *The Basis of the Premillennial Faith,* 26.

9. Ibid., 19–26.
10. Ibid., 31. See also D. H. Kromminga, *The Millennium and the Church* (Grand Rapids: Eerdmans, 1945), 267–79.
11. Peter Beyerhaus (this author's recollection of his presentation at the Billy Graham Center, Wheaton, Ill., June 1981).
12. Edvard P. Torjesen, *Fredrik Franson: A Model for World Evangelism* (Pasadena, Calif.: William Carey Library, 1983).
13. Edvard P. Torjesen, "In Expectation of Christ's Return: A Study of Premillennialism in the Perspective of Church History and the Writings of Fredrik Franson" (Paper, Second Consultation of Missions with a Franson Heritage, Ewersbach, Germany, August 29–September 2, 1983).
14. David M. Howard, *Student Power in World Missions* (Downers Grove, Ill.: InterVarsity, 1979), 90ff.
15. William E. Cox, *Amillennialism Today* (Philadelphia: Presbyterian and Reformed , 1966), 8.
16. Moody Bible Institute alone has more than five thousand alumni active on mission fields around the world. Over one hundred graduates leave for mission fields annually.
17. Cox, *Amillennialism Today,* 10–12.
18. Fredrik Franson, "This Present Age," *Morgenstjernan,* January and February 1883, cited by Torjesen, "In Expectation of Christ's Return," 23–24.
19. Gutiérrez, *Theology of Liberation, History, Politics, and Salvation,* 90–91.
20. Moltmann, *The Theology of Hope,* 297. He says history is eschatological. It explains how God will act, thus preparing His people to count on His faithfulness.
21. Gutiérrez, *Theology of Liberation, History, Politics, and Salvation,* 162.
22. Ibid., 231.
23. Doug Wicks, "Will Bo Peep's Sheep Come Home?" *Wherever* 8 (winter 1984), 3.
24. "Report of Section 11: Salvation and Social Justice," World Conference on Salvation Today, Bangkok, 1972, cited by Orlando E. Costas, *The Church and Its Mission* (Wheaton, Ill.: Tyndale, 1974), 277. This quotation, incidentally, was authored by Jurgen Moltmann, who has been a leading influence in the cause of liberation theology.
25. Some evangelicals who attended the Vancouver Assembly reported very favorably on the difference between this and other WCC Assemblies. They cited an "overarching spiritual and biblical orientation." Richard Lovelace was one of the group who made this affirmation.
26. See Arthur P. Johnston, "Ecumenism: The Long Dark Shadow," *Horizons* (January–February 1984), 10–11. Johnston shows that the WCC understanding of the kingdom of God is exactly as described in this chapter. It "came to earth when Jesus the King was born. His Kingdom continues since Pentecost—not necessarily in the Church or in heaven

but in *morally evolving secular society,* all of which is the Lord's. . . . The transformation of society is more important than 'Band-Aid' solutions like education and medical handouts. . . . This theological posture of the WCC tends toward the elimination of evangelism in churches around the world!"

Chapter 6

1. All Scripture quotations are from the New International Version (NIV) unless specified otherwise.
2. John R. W. Stott, *The Spirit, the Church and the World* (Downers Grove, Ill.: InterVarsity, 1990), 235–37.
3. I. Howard Marshall, *Acts,* Tyndale New Testament Commentaries (Grand Rapids: Eerdmans, 1980), 240.
4. Some commentaries have more to say on verse 23 than on the previous verses. See, for example, F. F. Bruce, *The Acts of the Apostles: The Greek Text with Introduction and Commentary,* 3d ed. (Grand Rapids: Eerdmans, 1990), 325–27.
5. Both verbs are aorist participles, suggesting incidental action antecedent to the main verb in verse 21b, "they returned."
6. Michael J. Wilkins, *Following the Master: Discipleship in the Steps of Jesus* (Grand Rapids: Zondervan, 1992), 249 (italics his).
7. Ibid., 191.
8. A. Boyd Luter, "A New Testament Theology of Discipling" (Th.D. diss., Dallas Theological Seminary, 1985), 101–2; cf. idem, "Discipleship and the Church," *Bibliotheca Sacra* 137 (July–September 1980): 267–73.
9. A. Boyd Luter, "The Great Commission," in *Anchor Bible Dictionary,* 1992 ed., 2:1091.
10. Everett F. Harrison, *Interpreting Acts: The Expanding Church* (Grand Rapids: Zondervan, 1986), 237.
11. Richard N. Longenecker, "The Acts of the Apostles," in *The Expositor's Bible Commentary,* 12 vols. (Grand Rapids: Zondervan, 1981), 9:438.
12. Paul Bowers, "Fulfilling the Gospel: The Scope of the Pauline Mission," *Journal of the Evangelical Theological Society* 30 (June 1987): 189–90.
13. Wilkins, *Following the Master,* 268.
14. F. F. Bruce, *The Book of Acts,* rev. ed. (Grand Rapids: Eerdmans, 1988), 280. Cf. Paul R. House, "Suffering and the Purpose of Acts," *Journal of the Evangelical Theological Society* 33 (September 1990): 317–30.
15. "Suffering, defined as servanthood, is the essence of discipleship" (Jack Dean Kingsbury, *Matthew as Story,* 2d ed. [Minneapolis: Fortress, 1988], 140).
16. Bowers, "Fulfilling the Gospel: The Scope of the Pauline Mission," 198.
17. Wilkins, *Following the Master,* 273.

18. "It is commonly held that the mention of elders, and of their appointment, reflects the situation presupposed in the Pastoral Epistles rather than that of Paul's early ministry. It may be granted that *presbuteroi* was Luke's term for the people marked out as leaders" (Bruce, *The Acts of the Apostles,* 326).
19. Ibid., 280.
20. Stott, *The Spirit, the Church, and the World,* 236.
21. The significance of "prayer and fasting" merits further consideration, but for the purpose of the present study, it is enough to suggest that Paul and Barnabas were simply following the example of their home church which had sent them on their journey "after they had fasted and prayed" (Acts 13:3).
22. Walter Bauer, William F. Arndt, and F. Wilbur Gingrich, *A Greek-English Lexicon of the New Testament and Other Early Christian Literature,* 2d ed., rev. F. Wilbur Gingrich and Frederick W. Danker (Chicago: University of Chicago Press, 1979), 623.
23. Paul A. Beals, *A People for His Name: A Church-Based Missions Strategy* (Grand Rapids: Baker, 1988), 10.
24. Roland Allen, *Missionary Methods: St. Paul's or Ours?* (Grand Rapids: Eerdmans, 1962), 149.
25. James F. Engel, "Great Commission or Great Commotion?" *Christianity Today,* 20 April 1984, 52.
26. Cf. Arthur F. Glasser, "The Missionary Task: An Introduction," in *Perspectives on the World Christian Movement: A Reader,* ed. Ralph D. Winter and Steven C. Hawthorne (Pasadena: William Carey Library, 1981), 100–103.
27. Dallas Willard, *The Spirit of the Disciplines: Understanding How God Changes Lives* (San Francisco: Harper and Row, 1988), 258.
28. Wilkins, *Following the Master,* 271.

Chapter 7

1. Dan Bacon, "Should Mission Boards Send Teams as Well as Individuals?" *Evangelical Missions Quarterly* 14 (April 1978): 95–99.
2. Edward F. Murphy, "The Missionary Society as an Apostolic Team," *Missiology: An International Review* 4 (January 1976): 103–18; and Paul Thompson, "Synergism: A New Word and a New Way for Missions," *Harvest Today* 31 (July–September 1976): 11.
3. Jonathan Goforth, *Foreign Missions Conference Report* (Washington, D.C.: China Inland Mission, 1925), 77, quoted by Alexander Rattray Hay, *The New Testament Order for Church and Missionary* (Buenos Aires: SEMCA, 1947), 90. Also B. Broomhall wrote about a famous missionary team called "The Cambridge Seven" (*The Evangelization of the World: A Missionary Band* [London: Morgan and Scott, 1887]).
4. E. Earle Ellis, "Paul and His Co-Workers," *New Testament Studies* 17 (October–July 1970–71): 437. Also see D. Edmond Hiebert, *Personalities around Paul* (Chicago: Moody, 1973), 5–6, for a list of

Paul's most prominent friends and coworkers. Also see Roy B. Zuck, *Teaching as Paul Taught* (Grand Rapids: Baker, 1998), 133–42.

5. Ellis, "Paul and His Co-Workers," 439.
6. F. F. Bruce, *Paul: Apostle of the Heart Set Free* (Grand Rapids: Eerdmans, 1977), 458.
7. Of interest is the observation that even before his conversion and call, Saul of Tarsus worked with others (see Acts 9:7).
8. It is not known exactly how long Paul was in Jerusalem (cf. Gal. 2:1), nor what he did during that time, nor whether he was alone or with others. This period may have included trials mentioned in 2 Corinthians 11:23–27, the experience recorded in 2 Corinthians 12:1–4, and most certainly a ministry to Gentiles in that region (cf. Acts 22:17–21). See Richard N. Longenecker, "Paul the Apostle," in *Zondervan Pictorial Encyclopedia of the Bible,* ed. Merrill Tenney (Grand Rapids: Zondervan, 1975), 4:632.
9. For a discussion on the authenticity of the "we" sections of the Book of Acts, see Donald Guthrie, *New Testament Introduction* (Downers Grove, Ill.: InterVarsity, 1970), 367–68.
10. See Ronald F. Hock, "The Workshop as a Social Setting for Paul's Missionary Preaching," *Catholic Biblical Quarterly* 41 (July–September 1979): 438–50, on how Paul's tentmaking activity may have been not only for meeting his material needs but also a natural setting in which to share the gospel.
11. First Thessalonians 3:1–8 seems to indicate that Silas and Timothy joined Paul in Athens and then were sent by him on missions elsewhere before they met him again in Corinth (F. F. Bruce, *Commentary on the Book of Acts,* New International Commentary on the New Testament [Grand Rapids: Eerdmans, 1954], 347–48).
12. See F. F. Bruce, "II Thessalonians," in *The New Bible Commentary Revised,* ed. Donald Guthrie, J. A. Motyer, A. M. Stibbs, and D. J. Wiseman (Grand Rapids: Eerdmans, 1970), 1161; and Longenecker, "Paul the Apostle," 4:644.
13. Longenecker conjectures that "the missionary party came to Ephesus" ("Paul the Apostle," 4:645), probably basing his assumption on the fact of Paul's previous practice of traveling with others. W. J. Coneybeare and J. S. Howson make a plausible case for the inclusion of Timothy on this trip, and perhaps even Titus (*The Life and Epistles of St. Paul* [Grand Rapids: Eerdmans, 1950], 362–63). Frequent mention is made of Timothy in Acts and Paul's letters in connection with Paul's stay at Ephesus (cf. Acts 19:22; 1 Cor. 4:17; 16:10; 2 Cor. 1:1; Rom. 16:21; Acts 20:4). And Paul often mentioned Titus in 2 Corinthians (2:13; 7:6, 13–14; 8:6, 16, 23; 12:18 [twice]).
14. There was a church in Caesarea (18:22; 21:16) and Philip the evangelist lived there and had previously entertained Paul in his house (21:8).
15. Longenecker suggests that Timothy was also present, probably because of the inclusion of Timothy's name at the opening of Paul's epistles to the Philippians, the Colossians, and Philemon ("Paul the Apostle," 4:651).

16. Nine people continued in rather close association with Paul, though not without interruptions, to the end of his life. They were Mark, Titus, Timothy, Priscilla, Aquila, Luke, Erastus, Trophimus, and Tychicus (Ellis, "Paul and His Co-Workers," 439). With the exception of Erastus, Trophimus, and Tychicus, all of these were called "co-workers."
17. James Stalker mentioned "castles of robbers, who watched for passing travelers to pounce upon" in Asia Minor (*Life of St. Paul* [New York: Revell, 1912], 68).
18. Bruce believes the seven men who accompanied Paul (20:4) were representatives of the churches in Macedonia, Galatia, and Asia, delegated to take relief to the Jerusalem Christians (*Commentary on the Book of Acts,* 405–6).
19. Adolf Deissmann discusses Paul's tentmaking activities (*Paul: A Study in Social and Religious History* [New York: Hodder and Stoughton, 1926], 48–51).
20. Some of the same references have been included under both the ministry of edification and the ministry of evangelism. As Gene A. Getz says, "In some instances *evangelistic activity* and *edification activity* are so interrelated in Luke's records they are indistinguishable" (*Sharpening the Focus of the Church* [Chicago: Moody, 1974], 23 [italics his]).
21. This study is not seeking to show that Paul never worked or evangelized alone, but rather that he often evangelized together with others. Passages that report Paul's working alone are these: *9:19–25:* Paul apparently preached alone in the Damascus synagogue (yet he was "with the disciples," v. 19, and "his followers," v. 25 [NIV], helped him escape); *17:16–34:* Paul was preaching alone in Athens, yet while he was "waiting for" Silas and Timothy (17:15–16); *18:19:* he preached in the synagogue in Ephesus alone; *18:23:* he traveled in Galatia and Phrygia, strengthening the disciples; and *20:2–3:* he traveled in Macedonia and Greece, encouraging the believers.
22. Not only did Paul evangelize corporately, but he also engaged in a team ministry of edification: with Barnabas in Antioch (11:25–26); with Barnabas in Lystra, Iconium, and Antioch (14:21–23); with Barnabas again in Antioch (15:35); with Silas in Syria and Cilicia (15:41); with Silas and Timothy in Lystra and Iconium (16:4–5), and with Luke and seven others in Troas and Miletus (20:6–38).
23. Timothy was probably present as well (17:10, 14).
24. From Berea Paul went to Athens without Silas and Timothy (17:15). He valued their presence, for he urged them "to come to him as soon as possible."
25. The verb προσκέκλημαι is in the perfect tense, indicating that this call from God had already come to them before this word came from the Holy Spirit.
26. Bruce suggests that Mark's role as "helper" may had been in imparting to Paul and Barnabas his special knowledge of certain important phases of the story of Jesus, in particular the passion narrative (*Commentary on the Book of Acts,* 263). This word for "helper" (ὑπηρέτην) is the same

word used in Luke 1:2 ("servants of the word"). Luke may have had Mark in mind as one of his sources. B. T. Holmes confirms this by explaining that ὑπηρέτην signified, in the language of the time, a person whose function involved looking after documents ("Luke's Description of John Mark," *Journal of Biblical Literature* 54 [1935]: 63–72). Later Paul said of John Mark, "He is helpful to me in my ministry" (2 Tim. 4:11 NIV).

27. Albert Barnes comments that "the work" means "preaching the gospel" (*Barnes' Notes on the New Testament* [reprint, Grand Rapids: Kregel], 315). Ernst Haenchen says "the work" is "the work of mission" as in 13:2 and 14:26 (*The Acts of the Apostles,* trans. Bernard Noble and Gerald Shinn [Philadelphia: Westminster, 1971], 474).
28. The phrase "Paul and his companions" is literally, "those with Paul" (οἱ περὶ παῦλον, 13:13). This denotes "persons who are standing, sitting, working, or staying close to someone" (Walter Bauer, William F. Arndt, and F. Wilbur Gingrich, *A Greek-English Lexicon of the New Testament and Other Early Christian Literature,* 2d ed., rev. F. Wilbur Gingrich and Frederick W. Danker [Chicago: University of Chicago Press, 1979], 651).
29. John Calvin suggested that the talking and urging were done by the people, not by Paul and Barnabas (*Acts of the Apostles,* trans. W. J. G. McDonald, *Calvin's Commentaries,* ed. David W. Torrance and Thomas F. Torrance [Grand Rapids: Eerdmans, 1965], 1:387–88).
30. Alford observes that "διδάσκοντες [was] to those who had received [the Word, and] εὐαγγελιζόμενοι [was] to those who had not" (*The Greek Testament,* 2:172).
31. The Greek word order is of interest: διδάσκοντες καὶ εὐαγγελιζόμενοι μετὰ καὶ ἑτέρων πολλῶν τὸν λόγον τοῦ κυρίου ("teaching and preaching *with many others* the word of the Lord").
32. The verb "called" (προσκαλέω) is also used in 13:2 in reference to God's call to Barnabas and Saul. In both instances the verb is in the perfect tense.
33. Bruce suggests the women met there because there were not enough male Jews in Philippi to establish a synagogue (*Commentary on the Book of Acts,* 331).
34. Their reference to Paul and Silas's proclaiming unlawful customs probably referred to their gospel preaching, since there were laws prohibiting foreign religious propaganda among Roman citizens (ibid., 335–36). Pliny the Younger, writing about Christians in Pontus, referred to the banning of foreign cults (*Epistolae* 10.96.2; cited in A. N. Sherwin-White, *Roman Society and Roman Law in the New Testament* [Grand Rapids: Baker, 1978], 79–80).
35. Dominic Grassi notes that Paul believed in corporate evangelism because "he felt it necessary to present a visible picture of the Church in action" (*A World to Win,* 74). Hay states that "a single believer cannot function as the Church" (*The New Testament Order for Church and Missionary,* 132).

36. Darrell Fledderjohann, "North American Missions in Italy Today" (M.A. thesis, Trinity Evangelical Divinity School, 1979), 143.
37. Arnold Dittberner, "Who Is Apollos and Who Is Paul?" *Bible Today* 71 (1974): 1549–52.
38. "Missionary Loneliness . . . It's Only Human," *Team Horizons* 54 (July–August 1980): 11.
39. Paul Thompson, *The Challenge of the City* (Coral Gables, Fla.: Worldteam, 1978), 23.
40. Waldron Scott, "Teams and Teamwork," *Evangelical Missions Quarterly* 7 (winter 1971): 112–13.
41. See I. Howard Marshall, *Luke: Historian and Theologian* (Grand Rapids: Zondervan, 1970).

Chapter 8

1. Ralph P. Martin, *The Epistle of Paul to the Philippians* (Grand Rapids: Eerdmans, 1959), 46.
2. Ibid.
3. All Scripture quotations are from the New International Version, unless noted otherwise.
4. It is not wrong to equate Christ with the gospel. "If we were to sum up the content of the Gospel in a single word, it would be *Jesus the Christ"* (Gerhard Friedrich, "εὐαγγελίζομαι κτλ.," *Theological Dictionary of the New Testament,* ed. Gerhard Kittel and Gerhard Friedrich, trans. and ed. Geoffrey W. Bromiley [Grand Rapids: Eerdmans, 1964], 2:731 [italics his]).
5. Francis Foulkes, "Philippians," in *The New Bible Commentary,* ed. Donald Guthrie et al. (Grand Rapids: Eerdmans, 1970), 1126.
6. Robert P. Lightner, "Philippians," in *The Bible Knowledge Commentary, New Testament,* ed. John F. Walvoord and Roy B. Zuck (Wheaton, Ill.: Victor, 1983), 653.
7. Jacobus J. Müller, *The Epistles of Paul to the Philippians and to Philemon,* New International Commentary on the New Testament (Grand Rapids: Eerdmans, 1980), 40.
8. It also occurs in Acts 2:42; Hebrews 13:16; and 1 John 1:3 (twice), 6–7.
9. J. Schattenmann, "κοινωνία," in *New International Dictionary of New Testament Theology,* ed. Colin Brown (Grand Rapids: Zondervan, 1975), 1:640.
10. Friedrick Hauck, "κοινός κτλ.," in *Theological Dictionary of the New Testament* (1965), 3:801.
11. Schattenmann, "κοινωνία," 1:643.
12. J. Y. Campbell, "Κοινωνία and Its Cognates in the New Testament, *Journal of Biblical Literature* 51(1932): 353.
13. Friedrich, "εὐαγγελίζομαι κτλ.," 2:732.
14. J. B. Lightfoot, *St. Paul's Epistle to the Philippians* (1913; reprint, Grand Rapids: Zondervan, 1953), 83. Peter T. O'Brian points out that

the Philippians shared in Paul's sufferings because they were engaged in gospel witness ("The Fellowship Theme in Philippians," *Reformed Theological Review* 37 [1978]: 13).

15. John Eadie, *A Commentary on the Greek Text of the Epistle of Paul to the Philippians* (1859; reprint, Minneapolis: James and Klock, 1977), 9.
16. Ibid.
17. Müller, *The Epistles of Paul to the Philippians and Philemon,* 40.
18. William Hendricksen, *Exposition of Philippians,* New Testament Commentary (Grand Rapids: Baker, 1962), 52.
19. Lightfoot, *St. Paul's Epistle to the Philippians,* 83; and Müller, *The Epistles of Paul to the Philippians and Philemon,* 39.
20. Lightfoot, *St. Paul's Epistle to the Philippians,* 84.
21. For example Martin, *The Epistle of Paul to the Philippians,* 63; and Müller, *The Epistles of Paul to the Philippians and Philemon,* 43.
22. Eadie, *A Commentary on the Greek Text of the Epistle of Paul to the Philippians,* 14.
23. Lightfoot, *St. Paul's Epistle to the Philippians,* 85.
24. Eadie, *A Commentary on the Greek Text of the Epistle of Paul to the Philippians,* 14.
25. Their suffering resulted directly from evangelism. Paul wrote, "I am in chains for Christ" (1:13) and "I am put here [prison] for the defense of the gospel" (v. 16).
26. Hendricksen, *Exposition of Philippians,* 86–87.
27. Eadie, *A Commentary on the Greek Text of the Epistle of Paul to the Philippians,* 74.
28. Raymond R. Brewer, "The Meaning of *Politeuesthe* in Philippians 1:27," *Journal of Biblical Literature* 73(1954): 83.
29. Francis W. Beare, *A Commentary on the Epistle to the Philippians,* 2d ed. (London: Adam and Black, 1969), 66.
30. Lightfoot, *St. Paul's Epistle to the Philippians,* 105.
31. In Philippians 3:20 Paul reinforced this idea by pointing out that "our citizenship" [πολίτευμα] is in heaven.
32. John Calvin, *The Epistle of Paul the Apostle to the Galatians, Ephesians, Philippians and Colossians,* trans. T. H. L. Parker, vol. 11 of *Calvin's Commentaries* (Grand Rapids: Eerdmans, 1965), 242; and Heinrich August Wilhelm Meyer, *Critical and Exegetical Handbook to the Epistles to the Philippians and Colossians, and to Philemon,* trans. John C. Moore, vol. 9 of *Critical and Exegetical Commentary on the New Testament* (Winona Lake, Ind.: Alpha, 1884), 44.
33. Lightfoot, *St. Paul's Epistle to the Philippians,* 106.
34. Homer A. Kent Jr., "Philippians," in *The Expositor's Bible Commentary* (Grand Rapids: Zondervan, 1978), 119; and Hendricksen, *Edition of Philippians,* 90.
35. H. A. A. Kennedy, "Philippians," in *The Expositor's Greek Testament,* ed. W. Robertson Nicoll (Grand Rapids: Eerdmans, 1970), 3:440.
36. Beare, *A Commentary on the Epistle to the Philippians,* 92.

37. Ἐπέχοντες can also be translated "hold fast" as in the *New American Standard Bible*. However, the force of the prefix ἐπι-, the use of the word in nonbiblical literature (Homer, *Iliad* 9.489; 22.494), and the immediate context (in which it is linked with the shining stars) make "hold out" (in the sense of "to offer") preferable. See Lightfoot, *St. Paul's Epistle to the Philippians,* 118; Eadie, *A Commentary on the Greek Text of the Epistle of Paul to the Philippians,* 143–44; and Müller, *The Epistles of Paul to the Philippians and Philemon,* 94.
38. Timothy was a member of Paul's evangelistic team in the apostle's second and third missionary journeys (Acts 16:3; 19:22). Apart from Philip (Acts 21:8), Timothy is the only person called an "evangelist" in the New Testament (2 Tim. 4:5).
39. The word συνεργός appears thirteen times in the New Testament; twelve of these occurrences are in Paul's writings (Rom. 16:3, 9, 21; 1 Cor. 3:9; 2 Cor. 1:24; 8:23; Phil. 2:25; 4:3; Col. 4:11; 1 Thess. 3:2; Philem. 1, 24), and the other is in 3 John 8. The word means "helper or fellow workers" and often referred to those who helped in spreading the gospel. The word συστρατιώτης appears only twice in the New Testament (Phil. 2:25; Philem. 2). It means "comrade in arms," and is used figuratively "of those who devote themselves to the service of the gospel" (Walter Bauer, William F. Arndt, and F. Wilbur Gingrich, *A Greek-English Lexicon of the New Testament and Other Early Christian Literature,* 2d ed., rev. F. Wilbur Gingrich and Frederick W. Danker [Chicago: University of Chicago Press, 1979], 795).
40. Georg Bertram, "συνεργός κτλ.," in *Theological Dictionary of the New Testament* 7 (1971): 872, 875.
41. Lightfoot, *St. Paul's Epistle to the Philippians,* 123.
42. The word used here is λειτουργία, "service as a priest." Paul equated such service with the preaching of the gospel when he said that God gave him grace "to be a minister [λειτουργὸν] of Jesus Christ to the Gentiles with the priestly duty of proclaiming the gospel of God" (Rom. 15:16).
43. W. E. Vine, *Vine's Complete Expository Dictionary of Old and New Testament Words* (Nashville: Nelson, 1996), 692, 246.
44. Hendricksen, *Exposition of Philippians,* 191. Bruce believes Paul was addressing Luke, who seems to have stayed in Philippi for the seven years separating the first "we" passage of Acts (16:17) from the second (20:5). If so, Paul used the word "yokefellow" to describe one with whom he had engaged in evangelistic activity (16:13). See F. F. Bruce, "Synzygus," in *The New Bible Dictionary,* ed. J. D. Douglas (Grand Rapids: Eerdmans, 1962), 1229.
45. The word συλλαμβάνω in the active voice occurs often in the Gospels and Acts and means "to seize." However, in the middle voice with the dative of a person it means "to take hold of together, to support, aid, help" (Bauer, Arndt, and Gingrich, *A Greek-English Lexicon of the New Testament and Other Early Christian Literature,* 784).
46. G. T. Griffen and W. W. Tarn, *Hellenistic Civilisation,* 3d ed. (1958), 98–99, cited in Martin, *The Epistle of Paul to the Philippians,* 165.

47. E. Earle Ellis, "Paul and His Co-Workers," *New Testament Studies* 17 (July 1971): 445–48.
48. Ibid.

Chapter 9

1. Among contemporary authors who deny the exclusive condition are Paul F. Knitter, *No Other Name? A Critical Survey of Christian Attitudes Toward World Religions* (Maryknoll, N.Y.: Orbis, 1985); and John Hick, *God and the Universe of Faiths* (London: Macmillan, 1973). For a substantive evangelical response to their arguments, see Harold A. Netland, *Dissonant Voices: Religious Pluralism and the Question of Truth* (Grand Rapids: Eerdmans, 1991).
2. Clark H. Pinnock, *A Wideness in God's Mercy: The Finality of Jesus Christ in a World of Religions* (Grand Rapids: Zondervan, 1992); and John Sanders, *No Other Name: An Investigation into the Destiny of the Unevangelized* (Grand Rapids: Eerdmans, 1992). Pinnock claims to be an "orthodox theologian" (40); and Sanders lists his "agreement with traditional evangelical theology" (32).
3. Dispensationalism has often been caricatured. Two recent dispensational efforts show the genius, tensions, and change within the movement: John S. Feinberg, ed., *Continuity and Discontinuity: Perspectives on the Relationship between the Old and New Testaments* (Wheaton, Ill.: Crossway, 1988); and Craig A. Blaising and Darrell L. Bock, eds., *Dispensationalism, Israel and the Church* (Grand Rapids: Zondervan, 1992).
4. This writer uses "wider hope" as synonymous with "inclusivism." Sanders uses "wider hope" as a third category outside restrictivism (i.e., a traditional Calvinistic, limited atonement, double predestinarian view) and universalism. Inclusivism refers to "universally accessible salvation apart from evangelization" (*No Other Name,* x). Many evangelicals are not restrictivists in the traditional Calvinistic sense but still insist "that there is no hope whatsoever for salvation apart from their [the unevangelized] hearing the message about the person and work of Christ and exercising faith in Christ before they die" (ibid., 37). These evangelicals are theologically wider than five-point Calvinism (for instance, they hold to unlimited atonement) but are narrower than an "inclusivist wider-hope" view.
5. While there is no monolith of a dispensational *system,* there are dispensational perspectives and emphases. Blaising and Bock identify some of these dispensational emphases, though they do not agree with the concept of *sine qua non* distinctives of dispensationalism (*Dispensationalism, Israel and the Church,* 379).
6. Pinnock, *A Wideness in God's Mercy,* 163. The examples of Abraham and David are easy ones to deal with. As a result of God's covenants (Gen. 12; 17; 2 Sam. 7; Ps. 16:9–11; John 8:56) these two had more theological knowledge and spiritual insight than the common Israelite.

Yet these "giants" were not the only redeemed in the Old Testament. Pinnock could make his case stronger by appealing to the fact that lesser-known Israelites could have been saved without actually confessing Jesus.

7. Ibid., 162. Sanders defines the issue this way: "Furthermore, if worshippers of Yahweh such as Cornelius were not saved until they heard about Christ, then what of all the other worshippers of God in the Old Testament, such as Moses and David? Were they all damned to hell?" (*No Other Name,* 65).
8. Other arguments for the "wider hope" include the universal salvific will of God as seen in 1 Peter 3:9; 1 Timothy 2:4; 4:10; the universal orientation of early Genesis; God as Creator of *all* men; the "faith principle" of Hebrews 11:6; the mediation of salvation by general revelation; preincarnate appearances of Christ; the work of the Holy Spirit in the world before and outside of Christ; and the existence of positive features in non-Christian religions.
9. Pinnock, *A Wideness in God's Mercy,* 161.
10. In highlighting this difference between covenant theology and dispensationalism the present writer does not care to derail or minimize attempts at theological rapprochement between these rival perspectives. Both systems are going through development and modification (see Blaising and Bock, eds., *Dispensationalism, Israel and the Church;* and Vern Poythress, *Understanding Dispensationalists* [Grand Rapids: Zondervan, 1987]). Real differences do exist, for both systems have hermeneutical, theological, and world view principles by which claims are made for comprehensiveness and internal consistency. The degree of parity between the two systems as found in recent discussions is somewhat amazing after decades of theological feuding. In these intramural discussions, larger doctrinal issues and missiological applications such as the one addressed here should not be forgotten.
11. One could also add a "correspondence" criterion in comparative religious observations: What Old Testament saints confessed does not correspond with what the unreached masses all over the world believe today. The "how" of the sincere seeker—religious devotion, penitence, and humility (Pinnock's and Sanders's characteristics of faith)—are not questioned. Indeed the "what" is challenged.
12. "Continuity" is a self-appellation in covenant theology writings. For example VanGemeren writes, "Reformed Theology is an expression of a *continuity* system" (Willem A. VanGemeren, "Systems of Continuity," in *Continuity and Discontinuity,* 61). Also see Fred H. Klooster, "The Biblical Method of Salvation: A Case for Continuity," in ibid., 131–60. In contrast to the "Christocentric continuity" of covenant theology, dispensationalism can be said to hold to an "epoch-related discontinuity" in reference to the content of salvation. Actually there are entire ranges of continuity and discontinuity in how theologians from both spectrums see salvation in the Old and New Testaments. This article addresses the basic meanings of continuity and discontinuity.

13. Roger Nicole, "One Door and Only One?" *Wherever* 4 (1979): 3.
14. Charles Hodge, *Systematic Theology,* 3 vols. (London: Nelson, 1872), 2:366.
15. John Calvin, *Institutes of the Christian Religion,* cited by VanGemeren, "Systems of Continuity," 56. VanGemeren notes, "Though some have questioned whether Calvin was a covenant theologian, no one disputes his position as a theologian with a christological focus" (ibid.).
16. Pinnock constantly refers to what may be termed a "faith principle" unrelated to specific, salvific content as connecting the saved of the Old and New Testaments (*A Wideness in God's Mercy,* 157–63).
17. Ibid., 157.
18. Sanders, *No Other Name,* 223.
19. Both Pinnock and Sanders approvingly use dispensationalist Charles Ryrie to affirm the fact of Old Testament salvation without great knowledge of Christ. Pinnock quotes Ryrie twice (*A Wideness in God's Mercy,* 106, 162), and Sanders cites him once (*No Other Name,* 44) for this manifest criticism of covenant theology. All three citations include Ryrie's well-known answer to the "two ways of salvation" objection to dispensationalism: "The *basis* of salvation in every age is the death of Christ; the *requirement* of salvation in every age is faith; the *object* of faith in every age is God; the *content* of faith changes in the various dispensations" (Charles C. Ryrie, *Dispensationalism Today* [Chicago: Moody, 1965], 123 [italics his]).
20. Ibid., 122–23.
21. Allen P. Ross, "The Biblical Method of Salvation: A Case for Discontinuity," in *Continuity and Discontinuity,* 170. "We cannot grant to the OT believer more understanding than the Scripture indicates he had" (ibid., 171).
22. Also see John Feinberg, "Salvation in the Old Testament," in *Tradition and Testament: Essays in Honor of Charles Lee Feinberg,* ed. John S. Feinberg and Paul D. Feinberg (Chicago: Moody, 1981), 39–77, for problems with covenant views of salvation, interaction with critiques of dispensationalism, and the explication of a dispensational theology of salvation. Dispensationalism as a system does not demand two ways of salvation; Old and New Testament saints were saved by faith. However, in anxiety to dispel charges that dispensationalism teaches two ways of salvation (ibid., 48–49), dispensationalists have not emphasized the uniqueness of the content of faith in the dispensations. The inclusivist issue presently compels this emphasis to be brought forward.
23. In the covenant-dispensational discussion, see Klooster, "The Biblical Method of Salvation: A Case for Continuity," 131–60. Though advocating continuity, he admits the following adjustment to the older position on the amount of knowledge and understanding of Old Testament saints: "The details of their [Adam and Eve's understanding of the promise of Gen. 3:15] personal knowledge are not revealed to us. Unless Scripture provides specific clues, we can never know how

much understanding a particular believer of any period had. Perhaps, we tend to underestimate what OT believers understood. . . . What we have to concentrate on is the intent and content of the revelation presented without being able to discern the precise measure of a contemporary's understanding of that revelation" (ibid., 141–42).

24. On "the unity of the Covenant of grace" approach to Scripture in covenant theology see Nicole, "One Door and Only One," and Willem A. VanGemeren, *The Progress of Redemption: The Story of Salvation from Creation to the New Jerusalem* (Grand Rapids: Zondervan, 1988). In any case, covenant theology is highly and rightly exclusive. It does not permit a generic, contentless epistemology in the Old Testament, let alone in the New Testament. The New Testament is even more defined or advanced in its exclusivity than the Old Testament, since it points to a Savior who has come.
25. Ryrie, *Dispensationalism Today,* 123. Reformed scholar Bruce K. Waltke argues this difference in "Evangelical Spirituality: A Biblical Scholar's Perspective," in *Journal of the Evangelical Theological Society,* 31 (March 1988): 9–24. He writes, "Evan-gelicals disagree, however, in their understanding of the object of faith. Dispensationalists contend that OT saints believed the Word of God relative to their dispensation, without specific reference to Jesus Christ. Reformed theologians believe that the elect in all dispensations, have always had Christ as the object of their faith" (12).
26. Ross, "The Biblical Method of Salvation: A Case for Discontinuity," 172.
27. John Feinberg records a similar comment: "I am not denying that God could have revealed the truth about Jesus to Old Testament saints. But I doubt that He did on any widespread basis" ("Salvation in the Old Testament," 51). Dispensational insistence on "literal" interpretation could be associated with this issue as well. In some ways the Old Testament was "allegorized" by covenant theologians on this issue. For if Christ is the center of the Christian faith, He must be found everywhere in the Old Testament in relation to all who were saved. This observation was suggested from Ernest Best's criticism of those who find the Trinity in the Old Testament: "The Old Testament is allegorized in order to discover within it the doctrine of the Trinity. The syllogism runs: the Old Testament must be used; Christ is the center of Christian faith; therefore Christ must be found everywhere in the Old Testament in his relation to the Father and the Spirit. The conclusion does not follow" (Ernest Best, *From Text to Sermon: Responsible Use of the New Testament in Preaching* [Edinburgh: Clark, 1988], 59).
28. Judging by mere numbers, the entire world, except for eight believers, was destroyed in the Flood. (Here one could also include God's intent for Israel to destroy the Canaanites.) If one needs to argue for a general rule, it must not be based on too small a sample. Against inclusivism, the general rule actually yields widespread judgment rather than salvation in the Old Testament.

29. On inductive procedures from simple enumeration in relation to generalization, see Max Black, *Critical Thinking: An Introduction to Logic and Scientific Method* (Englewood Cliffs, N.J.: Prentice-Hall, 1952), chap. 15.
30. Regarding progressive revelation, it seems that in covenant theology there is a progressive unfolding of the core redemptive content—a quantitative issue. In dispensational theology there is newness to the additions—qualitative increments through the epochs. Both theologies affirm that Jesus is the universal and exclusive epistemological issue for this age, and both share similar notions of progressive or incremental revelation.
31. Pinnock, *A Wideness in God's Mercy,* 158.
32. Inclusivism is also not theologically or emotionally that resourceful. The problem of the high numbers of human masses is still not solved. Inclusivism still has a manner of exclusivity, though not related to Jesus. One simply has to echo Pinnock's problem with Aquinas's theory of the special human messenger, "the theory is not adequate for the size of the problem" (Pinnock, *A Wideness in God's Mercy,* 166), or his problem with Warfield, "it still leaves large numbers eternally lost in absolute terms, even though the overall percentage is lowered" (ibid., 42).
33. A dispensational framework requires at least a "historical" distinction between Israel and the church, attended by a future for ethnic Israel. Elsewhere the present writer addressed the relationship between the people(s) of God as one of redemptive continuity (i.e., salvifically related and therefore not ontologically divided) and administrative discontinuity (i.e., historically differentiated in national, sociopolitical, covenantal constituents). There are also underlying transdispensational constants in human history (e.g., the nature of God, man, Satan, sin, salvation, marriage). See Ramesh P. Richard, "Selected Issues in Theoretical Hermeneutics, Part 4: Application Theory in Relation to the Old Testament," *Bibliotheca Sacra* 143 (October–December 1986): 307–10.
34. The number of dispensations is always a matter of interest in any discussion of dispensationalism. Dallas Seminary faculty annually sign a doctrinal statement that highlights only *three* dispensations—Israel, the church, and the millennial kingdom—a statement that could be signed by most premillennialists. Several covenant theologians also recognize the progressive character of God's redemption in history, "emphasizing much more the discontinuities and advances not only between Old Testament and New Testament, but between successive epochs within the Old Testament" (Poythress, *Understanding Dispensationalists,* 40).
35. Again the term "dispensationalism" is used here to refer to the moderate, minimalist branch of evangelicalism that maintains distinctions between Israel and the church in the administration of God's program in history. An "integrative" relationship between Israel and the church would

include these features: (1) *ontological unity* of God's kingdom program based on God's eternal nature and unchanging plans, (2) *redemptive continuity* of the saved throughout history premised on God's unique salvation in Jesus Christ, (3) *administrative discontinuity* in the supervision and execution of the divine program in history, emerging from the consistent use of a valid hermeneutical method, and (4) a *functional analogy* between the people(s) of God in all ages in their spiritual competence and earthly calling. All correlations to the "inclusivist" view in this article arise from implications and extrapolations relative to points three and four.

36. Bruce Demarest, *General Revelation* (Grand Rapids: Zondervan, 1982), 253.
37. The distinction between soteriology and ecclesiology is a consequence of the distinction between Israel and the church. The theological distinction generates a particular doctrine of salvation in the church. In contrast to inclusivists, this view claims that salvation is exclusive (available only through Christ) and it is the primary story of Scripture. In contrast to covenant theology, dispensationalism claims that the church is not a sociopolitical theocracy and that salvation is not the only story in Scripture.

    The nonsoteriological dimensions of God's activity provide dispensational resources for "positive features" of non-Christian religions outside special grace. Interestingly dispensationalist Lewis Sperry Chafer's definition of systematic theology included "truth about God and His universe from any and every source" (*Systematic Theology,* 8 vols. [Dallas, Tex.: Dallas Seminary Press, 1948; reprint (8 vols. in 4), Grand Rapids: Kregel, 1992], 1:5). Dispensationalists are open to the truth of God's common grace as an explanation for positive features in non-Christian religions. But, as with covenant theologians, they are not open to "salvific truth" about God outside the Bible and Jesus Christ.
38. This "qualitative inferiority" because of less knowledge is one of the reasons the phrase "progressive revelation" should be replaced with a more appropriate one. This writer suggests "incremental revelation" (Ramesh P. Richard, "Selected Issues in Theoretical Hermeneutics, Part 1: Methodological Proposals for Scripture Relevance," *Bibliotheca Sacra* 143 [January–March 1986]: 14–25).
39. Sanders, *No Other Name,* 52. Pinnock also refers to Porphyry (from Augustine in a letter to Deogratias; Philip Schaff, ed., *Nicene and Post-Nicene Fathers* [1886; reprint, Grand Rapids: Eerdmans, 1974], 1:416: "If Christ declares himself to be the way of salvation, the grace and truth, and affirms that in him alone, and only to souls believing in him, is the way of return to God, what has become of the men who lived in the many centuries before Christ came?" [Pinnock, *A Wideness in God's Mercy,* 149]).
40. Gavin D'Costa's argument retains force if one does not follow the contributions of the discontinuity position (*Theology and Religious*

Pluralism [New York: Basil Blackwell, 1986], 66). D'Costa argues that "if this exclusivist contention is taken seriously, then it must imply that the revelation of God in Israel's history was either (a) not revelation after all, or (b) a revelation, but somehow inadequate for salvation" (ibid., 65, n. 63).

41. Pinnock, *A Wideness in God's Mercy,* 26.
42. While Pinnock mentions Abimelech's encounter with Abraham (Genesis 20), he does not mention a similar encounter of Abraham with another pagan, Pharaoh (Gen. 12:10–20). The implications for inclusivism from this episode in Genesis 12 are not promising.
43. From the perspective of a biblical theology of missions such a position concerning Israel, God, and the Law is faulty. For example in Genesis 1–11 God offered salvation long before Israel was established (cf. Ex. 19:6; Deut. 4:6–8).
44. The distinction between soteriology and ecclesiology as major segments of systematic theology allows dispensationalism to be separated from the soteriological systems (Calvinism, Arminianism, etc.). As a hermeneutical principle dispensationalism is employed by many soteriological traditions. A response to John Gerstner's vitriolic dismissal of Calvinistic dispensationalism as an oxymoron (*Wrongly Dividing the World of Truth: A Critique of Dispen-sationalism* [Brentwood, Tenn.: Wolgemuth & Hyatt, 1991]) is that these two systems have distinct, theological "drivers" to their respective structures. Calvinism is soteriologically driven, and dispensationalism is ecclesiologically driven. For dispensationalism, the church is an independently valid historical entity, even though it is not an ontologically distinct entity. Though the present writer does not hold to the parenthetical (an interruption in the flow of God's overall plan and purpose—an "after-thought" view) identity to the church, as held in some circles of dispensationalism, neither does he hold to a parasitic view (the "footnote or endnote" view) of the church in God's redemptive plans.
45. Sanders, *No Other Name,* 224–32. "Inclusivists contend that all Christians are believers but not all believers are Christians" (ibid., 225).
46. Ibid., 224–25.
47. Ibid., 225.
48. "Responding positively to premessianic revelation can make them [premessianic believers] right with God, but it cannot make them messianic believers" (Pinnock, *A Wideness in God's Mercy,* 105).
49. Ibid., 178. Sanders cites J. N. D. Anderson (*Christianity and Comparative Religion* [Downers Grove, Ill.: InterVarsity, 1977], 99) in the same vein. "Does ignorance disqualify for grace? If so, where in Scripture do we have the exact amount of knowledge required set out? For *assurance,* no doubt, knowledge is required, but for grace it is not so much knowledge as a right attitude towards God that matters" (Sanders, *No Other Name,* 225 [italics his]).
50. Pinnock, *A Wideness in God's Mercy,* 79, 91.

51. On an evangelical critique of this and other "conciliar" views of mission, see Arthur F. Glasser and Donald A. McGavran, *Contemporary Theologies of Missions* (Grand Rapids: Baker, 1983), chaps. 3–5.
52. Pinnock, *A Wideness in God's Mercy,* 117.
53. Ryrie sees the time element as being built into the meaning of the church. The body of Christ is "that spiritual organism of which Christ is the Head, and is composed of all regenerated people from Pentecost to the rapture" (Charles C. Ryrie, *The Ryrie Study Bible* [Chicago: Moody, 1978], 1951).
54. For example both are called "royal priesthood" and carry a missiological vocation (Ex. 19:6; Isa. 61:6; 1 Peter 2:9). But one of the reasons they are analogous and not identical is found in 1 Peter 2:10: "for you once were not a people."
55. For a recent treatment of the levels of meaning in the term "Israel" see J. Lanier Burns, "The Future of Ethnic Israel in Romans 11," in *Dispensationalism, Israel and the Church,* 188–229.
56. Ross, "The Biblical Method of Salvation: A Case for Discontinuity," 174.
57. Charles H. Kraft, *Christianity in Culture: A Study in Dynamic Biblical Theologizing in Cross-Cultural Perspective* (Maryknoll, N.Y.: Orbis, 1979), 253.
58. In note 11 the "correspondence" test for comparative religious studies was mentioned. For instance the three great monotheistic religions have vital differences in theistic doctrine (Pinnock recognizes this), even though they can use similar theistic arguments for the existence of God. And when one compares the "ideas" of God among the populous belief blocs of the world, there are hardly theological parallels to make Kraft's point stick. A helpful comparison of world views is given in Ninian Smart, *World Views: Cross Cultural Exploration of Human Beliefs* (New York: Scribner's, 1983).
59. While making this major point built on "ignorance," Kraft also wants to emphasize that information itself is not a distinctive of Christian salvation witness (Sanders uses Kraft for this point too [*No Other Name,* 267]). Kraft writes that this view "focuses our attention on the proper function of witnessing—stimulation to faith—rather than on the lesser end to which our western predilections would likely lead us—to inundate our hearers with new information" (*Christianity in Culture,* ibid.). This is an ironic statement since lack of information was the main reason for the inclusivist view in the first place.
60. Kraft preceded Pinnock and Sanders in the "holy pagan" argument. "Can people who are chronologically A.D. but knowledgewise B.C. (i.e., have not heard of Christ), or those who are indoctrinated with a wrong understanding of Christ, be saved by committing themselves to faith in God as Abraham and the rest of those who were chronologically B.C. did (Heb. 11)?" (ibid., 254). Kraft not only refers to those with insufficient knowledge of Christ (cf. Old Testament saints), but also to those who positively hold to a wrong understanding of Christ.

61. Romans 1 notes that all people have knowledge of God (vv. 18–21) and "the ordinance of God" in terms of moral accountability (v. 32).
62. Here one may ask inclusivists why a later dispensation cannot provide the archetypal paradigm of salvation? This is covenant theology's alternative and a valid one if their hermeneutical premises and theological principlization are granted. That is, covenant theology classifies Old Testament believers in the chronologically B.C. but informationally A.D. (to some degree, at least) category.
63. See covenant theologian VanGemeren's response to the progressive dispensationalism expounded by Blaising and Bock: "These words may seem harsh, but I must wonder whether, after all the qualifications, the *sine qua non* of the dispensational hermeneutic is a distinct view of history" ("A Response," in *Dispensationalism, Israel and the Church,* 345–46).
64. Or to connect this statement even more to a philosophical position, a Neoplatonic archetypal occurrence in the cosmic or Divine Mind would be all that it takes to accomplish the ontological fact independent of or regardless of the crucifixion.
65. A recent book on this topic is Scot McKnight's, *A Light among the Gentiles: Jewish Missionary Activity in the Second Temple Period* (Minneapolis: Fortress, 1991).
66. Dispensationalists differ on whether the church was a completely or relatively unknown "mystery" in the Old Testament. "Essentialist" dispensationalists generally pursue the former interpretation while "progressive" dispensationalists hold the latter. For an attempted resolution, see Robert L. Saucy, "The Church as the Mystery of God," in *Dispensationalism, Israel and the Church,* 127–55.
67. This interpretation allows for the ὡς ("as") clause of Ephesians 3:5 to refer to a comparatively significant newness or a chronologically pivotal newness to the church in God's program. See Harold W. Hoehner, "Ephesians," in *The Bible Knowledge Commentary, New Testament,* ed. John F. Walvoord and Roy B. Zuck (Wheaton, Ill.: Victor, 1983), 629, for a concise, exegetical case in support of the latter, preferred view (cf. Col. 1:26).
68. Kraft, *Christianity in Culture,* 255.
69. Pinnock desires to show that "many varieties of unevangelized will attain salvation" (*A Wideness in God's Mercy,* 168).
70. Many thoughtful writers on eschatology have come from dispensational circles. J. Dwight Pentecost's *Things to Come: A Study in Biblical Eschatology* (Grand Rapids: Zondervan, 1964) and John F. Walvoord's writings (e.g., *Major Bible Prophecies* [Grand Rapids: Zondervan, 1991]), are well known. Unfortunately some trivialized and imaginative eschatological presentations for popular and immediate application form a perception of modern American dispensationalism (e.g., Hal Lindsey, *The Late Great Planet Earth* [Grand Rapids: Zondervan, 1970]). Blaising notes, "On the matter of sensational apocalypticism, many point to Hal Lindsey as if he typifies the meaning of dispensationalism. It might be

said that Lindseyism is to dispensationalism as Reconstructionism is to Reformed Theology. . . . In the case of Lindseyism, besides many hermeneutical problems, there is the matter of compromising the futurism that has always been central to dispensational eschatology" (Blaising, "Dispensationalism: The Search for Definition," in *Dispensationalism, Israel and the Church,* 14–15).

71. Ross, "The Biblical Method of Salvation: A Case for Discontinuity," 178.
72. Such figurative or metaphorical adjustments were not unknown to the Reformed hermeneutical tradition (see, for instance, Louis Berkhof, *Principles of Biblical Hermeneutics* [Grand Rapids: Baker, 1950], esp. chap. 7).
73. A framework of dispensational hermeneutical principles that they desire to use *consistently* would be to find (and limit) meaning (a) in the text, (b) within the context, (c) according to the authors' (plural) intention, and (d) in continuity with audience's initial understanding. The last point may show a dispensationalist penchant and distinctive. That is, subsequent revelation does not amend, alter, or break the initial link between authorial intention and audience understanding. For an illustration of this hermeneutical method, see Elliott E. Johnson, "Hermeneutical Principles and the Interpretation of Psalm 110," *Bibliotheca Sacra* 149 (October–December 1992): 428–37.
74. Pinnock, *A Wideness in God's Mercy,* 100.
75. Ibid., 97.
76. This article has intentionally not interacted with Pinnock's bibliology because his book does not directly express bibliology. On this, see Ray C. W. Roenfeldt, *Clark H. Pinnock on Biblical Authority: An Evolving Position* (Berren Springs, Mich.: Andrews University Press, 1993). It does, however, reveal bibliological positions. While holding to Scripture as authority (he quotes the Bible extensively), Pinnock says that God's salvific revelation in ordinary and special events is uncovered by the "faith principle," as he calls it. However, if salvation is possible outside the Bible, why is the Bible treated as if it were special at all? These points are raised concerning Pannenberg in Roger E. Olson, "Review of *Systematic Theology,* by Wolfhart Pannenberg," *Christianity Today,* June 22, 1992, 44.
77. In discussing the future of religions Pinnock says, "John Hick was right to speak of eschatological verification" (*A Wideness in God's Mercy,* 146). See John Hick, *An Interpretation of Religion: Human Responses to the Transcendent* (London: Macmillan, 1989). Pinnock also holds that the middle position between relativism and dogmatism in truth-seeking dialogue is epistemologically modest since "truth will be resolved eschatologically. This means that we will never fully resolve the conversation but patiently await the arrival of full knowledge from God" (*A Wideness in God's Mercy,* 146).
78. Another area of discussion between dispensationalists is the present

kingship of Christ in relation to the Davidic throne (see Darrell Bock, "The Reign of the Lord Christ," in *Dispensationalism, Israel and the Church,* 37–67), and the article by Johnson mentioned above in note 73.

79. Braaten has a fine discussion on the quarantining of Christianity from history that yields a "relativity of all things historical" (C. Braaten, *No Other Gospel!: Christianity Among the World's Religions* [Minneapolis: Fortress, 1992], 32). Troeltsch left a legacy on both ends of the spectrum. "Troeltsch said that even though there are no absolutes in history, still there are norms pulsating through the religions that become part of one's personal value system" (ibid., 37). According to Troeltsch, Christianity became "the highest religion as long as we admit that it is only a matter of personal conviction and not of anything inherently absolute" (ibid.). Pluralists have brought Christianity back into a relativistic history-of-religions framework, shifting from a "Christ-centered model to a God-centered model giving all religions equal footing" (ibid., 38). This is an interesting indictment of a position similar to Pinnock and Sanders from a theologian not particularly concerned with evangelical theologies of salvation.
80. This exclusivity too is suggested by Braaten about Pannenberg who sees an integral connection of the eschatological absolute to Jesus' own Person so that one can have a distinctively Christian criterion for evaluating religions. This kind of a position "does not collapse the unique revelation of God in Christ into the general experience of divine revelation in the non-Christian religions" (ibid., 46).
81. Pinnock also appeals to the exceptions evangelicals make for babies and the mentally incompetent as reason for including those who have not heard the gospel for no fault of their own (*A Wideness in God's Mercy,* 158, 166, 177). The issue of babies and the mentally incompetent is not an exclusive dispensational problem. It is not discussed here since it is not an argument based on Old Testament salvation patterns. In any case, just as evangelicals make these exceptions, it seems that the inclusivists also have to make exceptions for babies and the mentally incompetent from the "faith principle." There may be an additional exception for the "faith principle" for religious people who have "heard," do not trust in Christ, and continue with the internal and external evidences of the so-called "faith principle." An increasing number of the unevangelized are coming under this category in this time of extensive missionary presence through various media in global evangelism.
82. On a related note, the history and geography of one's birth are not necessarily commendable to present occupants of the globe. They provide some advantages to the *hearing* of the gospel, but not necessarily to *accepting* it. There are other factors in the sequence of salvation than merely information.

Chapter 10

1. Colin Chapman, "The Riddle of Religions," *Christianity Today,* May 14, 1990, 20.
2. John Hick and Paul Knitter, *The Myth of Christian Uniqueness: Toward a Theology of Plurality of Religions* (Maryknoll, N.Y.: Orbis, 1987).
3. Lesslie Newbigin, "Religious Pluralism and the Uniqueness of Jesus Christ," in *International Bulletin of Missionary Research* 13 (April 1989): 51. Gavin D'Costa also raises this concern in "The Pluralist Paradigm in the Christian Theology of Religions," *Scottish Journal of Theology* 39 (1986): 220–21.
4. For example Tom F. Driver, *Christ in a Changing World: Toward an Ethical Christology* (New York: Crossroad, 1981), 66–74.
5. Don Richardson, *Eternity in Their Hearts* (Ventura, Calif.: Regal, 1984), 34, 61. For helpful critiques of Richardson's view see Tite Tienou, "Eternity in Their Hearts?" in *Through No Fault of Their Own?* ed. William V. Crockett and James G. Sigountos (Grand Rapids: Baker, 1991), 209–27; and Bruce A. Demarest and Richard J. Harpel, "Don Richardson's 'Redemptive Analogies' and the Biblical Idea of Revelation," *Bibliotheca Sacra* 146 (July–September 1989): 330–40.
6. Norman Anderson, *Christianity and World Religions: The Challenge of Pluralism* (Downers Grove, Ill.: InterVarsity, 1984), 175 (italics his).
7. J. I. Packer, "'Good Pagans' and God's Kingdom," *Christianity Today,* January 17, 1986, 22–25 (italics his).
8. Newbigin, "Religious Pluralism and the Uniqueness of Jesus Christ," 50.
9. This view is defended by Carl F. H. Henry, *God, Revelation, and Authority* (Waco, Tex.: Word, 1983), 6:360–69; J. Ronald Blue, "Untold Billions: Are They Really Lost?" *Bibliotheca Sacra* 138 (July–September 1991): 338–49; J. Oswald Sanders, *How Lost Are the Heathen?* (Chicago: Moody, 1972); J. Robertson McQuilkin, "The Narrow Way," in *Perspectives on the World Christian Movement: A Reader,* ed. Ralph D. Winter and Steven C. Hawthorne (Pasadena, Calif.: William Carey Library, 1981), 127–34; Robert H. Gundry, "Salvation according to Scripture: No Middle Ground," *Christianity Today,* December 9, 1977, 16; Harry M. Orlinsky, "Nationalism, Universalism and Internationalism in Ancient Israel," in *Translating and Understanding the Old Testament: Essays in Honor of Herbert Gordon May,* ed. H. T. Frank and W. L. Reed (Nashville: Abingdon, 1970), 206–36; Harold A. Netland, *Dissonant Voices: Religious Pluralism and the Question of Truth* (Grand Rapids: Zondervan, 1994); D. A. Carson, *The Gagging of God: Christianity Confronts Pluralism* (Grand Rapids: Zondervan, 1995); and D. L. Okholm and T. R. Phillips, eds., *Religious Pluralism: Four Views* (Grand Rapids: Zondervan, 1995).
10. This term is used by inclusivist John Sanders, *No Other Name: An Investigation into the Destiny of the Unevangelized* (Grand Rapids: Eerdmans, 1992), 37–79.

11. See for example Millard J. Erickson, "The State of the Question," in *Through No Fault of Their Own?* 29, and idem, "Hope for Those Who Haven't Heard? Yes, But . . . ," *Evangelical Missions Quarterly* 11 (April 1975): 122–26.
12. Karl Rahner, *Theological Investigations* (Baltimore: Helicon, 1969), 4:390–98. Advocates of inclusivism include Anderson, *Christianity and World Religions;* Clark Pinnock, *A Wideness in God's Mercy* (Grand Rapids: Zondervan, 1992); idem, "Toward an Evangelical Theology of Religions," *Journal of the Evangelical Theological Society* 33 (1990): 359–68; and Sanders, *No Other Name.* Among North American evangelicals Clark Pinnock has been the most vocal advocate of inclusivism.
13. "Unitive pluralism," a term coined by J. A. T. Robinson (*Truth Is Two-Eyed* [Philadelphia: Westminster, 1979], 39), argues that each religion is unique, yet each is similar in that it fosters a unified vision of God. This model is expressed by Paul F. Knitter, *No Other Name? A Critical Survey of Christian Attitudes toward the World Religions* (Maryknoll, N.Y.: Orbis, 1985); John B. Cobb Jr., *Christ in a Pluralistic Age* (Philadelphia: Westminster, 1975); Alan Race, *Christians and Religious Pluralism* (London: SCM, 1983); and Bernard J. Lee, *The Galilean Jewishness of Jesus: Retrieving the Jewish Origins of Christianity* (New York: Paulist, 1988). For a constructive critique of Knitter, see Timothy D. Westergren, "Do All Roads Lead to Heaven? An Examination of Unitive Pluralism," in *Through No Fault of Their Own?* 169–82. The pluralist model is also rejected by D'Costa, "The Pluralist Paradigm in the Christian Theology of Religions," 211–24.
14. John Hick offered the description of the shift from a "Ptolemaic" perspective to a Copernican revolution in *God and the Universe of Faiths* (New York: St. Martins, 1973), 121. The Ptolemaic understanding would emphasize the centrality and exclusiveness of salvation through Christian faith.
15. See Wayne G. Strickland, "The Inauguration of the Law of Christ with the Gospel of Christ: A Dispensational View," in *The Law, the Gospel, and the Modern Christian,* ed. Wayne G. Strickland (Grand Rapids: Zondervan, 1993), 243.
16. Erickson, "Hope for Those Who Haven't Heard? Yes, But . . . ," 125.
17. Ibid.
18. Willis J. Beecher, *The Prophets and the Promise* (Grand Rapids: Baker, 1977); Alphonsus Benson, "From the Mouth of the Lion: Messianism of Amos," *Catholic Biblical Quarterly* 19 (1957): 199–212; E. W. Hengstenberg, *Christology of the Old Testament and a Commentary on the Messianic Predictions* (Grand Rapids: Kregel, 1970); Brian McKenzie, "Messianism of Deuteronomy," *Catholic Biblical Quarterly* 19 (1957): 299–305; R. A. Martin, "Earliest Messianic Interpretation of Gen. 3:15," *Journal of Biblical Literature* 84 (1965): 425–27; C. R. North, *The Suffering Servant in Deutero-Isaiah* (Oxford: Clarendon, 1956); and W. Vischer, *The Witness of the Old Testament to Christ*

(London: Lutterworth, 1949). See G. van Groningen, *Messianic Revelation in the Old Testament* (Grand Rapids: Baker, 1990) for a survey of Old Testament revelation of the Messiah.

19. This trend began with Moses and his miracles as polemics against the gods of Egypt and surfaced repeatedly as demonstrated by Elijah and his encounter with the prophets of Baal. For a discussion of the polemic of Moses, see John J. Davis, *Moses and the Gods of Egypt: Studies in Exodus* (Grand Rapids: Baker, 1986), 94–104. Also see the discussion of "prophetic satire" in C. J. H. Wright, "The Christian and Other Religions: The Biblical Evidence," *Themelios* 9 (January 1984): 9.
20. Pinnock, *A Wideness in God's Mercy,* 27–28.
21. Isaiah 11:9; 19:24; 25:6–7; 56:7; 60:1–3; 64:2; 66:19–23; Jeremiah 3:17; 33:9; Ezekiel 36:23, 35–36; 37:28; Hosea 14:6–7; Joel 2:28; Amos 9:11–12; Jonah; Micah 4:1–5; Zephaniah 3:9; Zechariah 2:11; 8:13, 20–23; 14:16–19.
22. Ibid., 15.
23. J. J. M. Roberts, "Isaiah in Old Testament Theology," in *Interpreting the Prophets,* ed. J. Mays and Paul Achtemeier (Philadelphia: Fortress, 1987), 64–66.
24. This contradicts the view of inclusivist Pinnock who advocates a second chance at redemption for the unsaved after death.
25. For a helpful discussion on the contrast between Yahweh and false gods in Isaiah, see A. Gelston, "The Missionary Message of Second Isaiah," *Scottish Journal of Theology* 18 (1965): 311–14.
26. John N. Oswalt, "The Mission of Israel to the Nations," in *Through No Fault of Their Own?* 94.
27. E. Kautzsch, *Gesenius' Hebrew Grammar,* 2d English ed., trans. A. E. Cowley (London: Oxford University Press, 1910), 126d; Francis Brown, S. R. Driver, and Charles A. Briggs, *A Hebrew and English Lexicon of the Old Testament* (Oxford: Clarendon Press, 1907), 42. For other examples of הָאֵל, see Jeremiah 32:18 and Daniel 9:4.
28. August Pieper, *Isaiah II: An Exposition of Isaiah 40–66* (Milwaukee: Northwestern, 1979), 184.
29. Abraham J. Heschel, *The Prophets: An Introduction* (New York: Harper and Row, 1969), 1:155–58.
30. Also see Isaiah 49:6 and 51:4–5. Scholars differ on whether these verses on the servant refer to Israel or the Messiah. Gelston argues in favor of the servant as an individual as distinct from the nation ("The Missionary Message of Second Isaiah," 314–17). For other discussions on the issue see S. Mowinckel, *He That Cometh* (Nashville: Abingdon, 1954) and H. H. Rowley, *The Servant of the Lord,* 2d ed. (Oxford: Blackwell, 1965).
31. Robert Davidson, "Universalism in Second Isaiah," *Scottish Journal of Theology* 16 (1963): 168–72.
32. Further, the prophet explicitly refers to God's salvific activity in Isaiah 45:8 (John Scullion, *Isaiah 40–66,* Old Testament Message: A Biblical-Theological Commentary [Wilmington, Del.: Glazier, 1982], 69).

33. Gerhard von Rad, *The Message of the Prophets* (New York: Harper and Row, 1965), 206–28.
34. D. W. Van Winkle, "The Relationship of the Nations to Yahweh and to Israel in Isaiah XL–LV," *Vetus Testamentum* 35 (1985): 448. This article presents a helpful survey of the various options regarding the relationship of Israel to the nations.
35. Heschel, *The Prophets,* 94–95.
36. As early as Genesis 4:26, salvation came when people began "to call upon the name of the Lord." The Old Testament clearly states that salvation comes by calling on the name of Yahweh (Jer. 33:2–3; Joel 2:32; Zeph. 3:9).
37. Scullion, *Isaiah 40–66,* 51.
38. For a helpful discussion on references to Yahweh in Jonah 1, see Hans Walter Wolff, *Obadiah and Jonah: A Commentary* (Minneapolis: Augsburg, 1986), 114–16.
39. For a discussion of this phrase as descriptive of faith, see ibid., 121. This phrase is used in the sense of a dynamic relationship of trust and obedience in many passages including Genesis 22:12; Exodus 20:20; Psalm 111:10; and Proverbs 1:7. Also see James Limburg, *Jonah: A Commentary,* Old Testament Library (Louisville: Westminster/John Knox, 1993), 57–58.
40. Limburg writes, "It is clear that for the author of Jonah, the Lord is more than a local or tribal god. The worldwide, ecumenical focus of the book is evident from the first sentence. The story begins with a declaration of the Lord's concern for far-off Nineveh, indicating that the Lord is a God who cares about the great cities and nations of the earth" (*Jonah: A Commentary,* 45–47).
41. Wolff, *Obadiah and Jonah,* 150.
42. For a critique of the argument that God may change His mind regarding the unsaved, based on the example of the Ninevites, see Jerry L. Walls, "Will God Change His Mind? Eternal Hell and the Ninevites," in *Through No Fault of Their Own?* 61–69.
43. For a discussion of אָמַן see James Barr, *The Semantics of Biblical Language* (Oxford: Clarendon, 1961), 161–205; A. Jepson, "*'aman,*" in *Theological Dictionary of the Old Testament,* 1:298–309; and Allen P. Ross, *Creation and Blessing: A Guide to the Study and Exposition of the Book of Genesis* (Grand Rapids: Baker, 1988), 309–10.
44. Allen P. Ross, "The Biblical Method of Salvation: A Case for Discontinuity," in *Continuity and Discontinuity: Perspectives on the Relationship between the Old and New Testaments, Essays in Honor of S. Lewis Johnson Jr.,* ed. John S. Feinberg (Westchester, Ill.: Crossway Books, 1988), 168.
45. H. C. Leupold, *Exposition of Genesis* (Grand Rapids: Baker, 1976), 476–77; and O. P. Robertson, "Genesis 15:6: New Covenant Expositions of an Old Covenant Text," *Westminster Theological Journal* 42 (1980): 264–65.
46. Brevard S. Childs, *Biblical Theology of the Old and New Testaments* (Minneapolis: Fortress, 1992), 597.

47. Some other verses that include this Hebrew phrase are Exodus 14:31; Numbers 14:11; 20:12; Deuteronomy 1:32; 2 Kings 17:14; 2 Chronicles 20:20; and Psalm 106:12. Another key occurrence of this absolute faith motif is in Habakkuk 2:4, where faith is described as trust in God. In summary, faith is basic to the message of the Old Testament (cf. Pss. 7:1; 11:1; 107:2–28; Isa. 7:9; Joel 2:32; Hab. 2:4).

Chapter 11

1. George Barna, *The Barna Report 1992–93: America Renews Its Search for God* (Ventura, Calif.: Regal, 1992), 76–78, 294–95.
2. John Hick, *God Has Many Names* (Philadelphia: Westminster, 1982), 19.
3. Raimundo Panikkar, *The Trinity and the Religious Experience of Man* (New York: Orbis, 1973).
4. Hick, *God Has Many Names,* 62–66.
5. Panikkar, *The Trinity and the Religious Experience of Man.*
6. Russell Chandler, *Racing Toward 2001: The Forces Shaping America's Religious Future* (Grand Rapids: Zondervan, 1992), 183–85.
7. James Leo Garrett Jr., "'Evangelicals' and Baptists—Is There a Difference?" in *Are Southern Baptists "Evangelicals"?* ed. James Leo Garrett Jr., E. Glenn Hinson, and James E. Tull (Macon, Ga.: Mercer University Press, 1983), 81.
8. James F. Engel and Jerry D. Jones, *Baby Boomers and the Future of World Missions* (Orange, Calif.: Management Development Associates, 1989), 20–27.
9. John Hick, "The Non-Absoluteness of Christianity," in *The Myth of Christian Uniqueness: Toward a Pluralistic Theology of Religions*, ed. John Hick and Paul F. Knitter (Maryknoll, N.Y.: Orbis, 1987), 20.
10. For example *Through No Fault of Their Own?* ed. William V. Crockett and James G. Sigountos (Grand Rapids: Baker, 1991), and Larry Dixon, *The Other Side of the Good News* (Wheaton, Ill.: Victor, 1992).
11. *Christianity Today*, June 16, 1989, 62–63.
12. This may appear to be a circular argument, so that if the traditional position is correct, it is correct. Rather, annihilationists contend that the traditional position is correct in saying that God has threatened eternal suffering but that that position is wrong in that God does not carry through on that threat. Instead, He exercises "grace," thereby simply obliterating those who do not believe.

Chapter 12

1. Donald G. Bloesch, *Essentials of Evangelical Theology,* 2 vols. (San Francisco: Harper & Row, 1978), 2:225.
2. Ibid., 228.
3. Ibid., 226–27.
4. Ibid., 227–28 (italics his).

5. Ibid., 228.
6. John Peter Lange, *The First Epistle General of Peter* (New York: Scribner, 1868), 75.
7. John Sanders, *No Other Name: An Investigation into the Destiny of the Unevangelized* (Grand Rapids: Eerdmans, 1992), 283.
8. Ibid., 191.
9. Ibid., 191, n. 32.
10. Ibid., 209.
11. Clark H. Pinnock, *A Wideness in God's Mercy: The Finality of Jesus Christ in a World of Religions* (Grand Rapids: Zondervan, 1992), 171.
12. Ibid.
13. Clark H. Pinnock, "God Limits His Knowledge," in *Predestination and Free Will*, ed. David Basinger and Randall Basinger (Downers Grove, Ill.: InterVarsity, 1986), 146, 157.
14. Donald G. Bloesch, "Descent into Hell (Hades)," in *Evangelical Dictionary of Theology*, ed. Walter A. Elwell (Grand Rapids: Baker, 1984), 314.
15. Edward G. Selwyn, *The First Epistle of St. Peter* (Grand Rapids: Baker, 1981), 340.
16. Friedrich Loofs, "Descent to Hades (Christ's)," *Encyclopedia of Religion and Ethics*, ed. James Hastings (New York: Scribners, 1955), 4:648–63.
17. J. Rendel Harris, "The History of a Conjectural Emendation," *Expositor* 6 (1902): 378–90. Cf. Edgar J. Goodspeed, *An Introduction to the New Testament* (Chicago: University of Chicago Press, 1937), 353; idem, "Enoch in 1 Peter 3:19," *Journal of Biblical Literature* 73 (1954): 91–92.
18. Augustine, *Letter 164,* chaps. 15–17.
19. Selwyn, *The First Epistle of Peter.*
20. Bo Reicke, *The Epistles of James, Peter, and Jude* (Garden City, N.Y.: Doubleday, 1964), 109.
21. See William Joseph Dalton, *Christ's Proclamation to the Spirits: A Study of 1 Peter 3:18–4:6* (Rome: Pontifical Biblical Institute, 1965), 29–30.
22. A. B. Hunter, "1 Peter," in *The Interpreter's Bible,* ed. George A. Buttrick, 12 vols. (Nashville: Abingdon, 1955), 12:132–33.
23. R. C. H. Lenski, *The Interpretation of the Epistles of St. Peter, St. John and St. Jude* (Minneapolis: Augsburg, 1966), 160–69.
24. Thomas Aquinas, *Summa Theologica,* part 3, question 52, article 2, reply to objection 3.
25. T. Schott, *Der erste Petrusbrief erklärt* (Erlangen: 1861).
26. Dalton, *Christ's Proclamation to the Spirits,* 185.
27. Wolfhart Pannenberg, *The Apostles' Creed in the Light of Today's Questions* (Philadelphia: Westminster, 1972), 94.
28. Ibid.
29. Wolfhart Pannenberg, *Jesus: God and Man* (Philadelphia: Westminster, 1968), 272.

30. Ibid.
31. Selwyn, *The First Epistle of Peter*, 199.
32. Wayne Grudem, "Christ Preaching through Noah: 1 Peter 3:19–20 in the Light of Dominant Themes in Jewish Literature," *Trinity Journal* NS 7 (fall 1986): 6–7.
33. Ibid., 3–31; and John S. Feinberg, "1 Peter 3:18–20, Ancient Mythology, and the Intermediate State," *Westminster Theological Journal* 48 (fall 1986): 303–35.
34. Sanders, *No Other Name*, 191, n. 32.
35. Donald Bloesch, "Descent into Hell," 314.
36. George R. Beasley-Murray, *Baptism in the New Testament* (London: Macmillan, 1962), 258–59 (italics his).
37. Pinnock, *A Wideness in God's Mercy,* 169.
38. Ibid.
39. Robert Mounce, *A Living Hope: A Commentary on 1 and 2 Peter* (Grand Rapids: Eerdmans, 1982), 54.

Chapter 13

1. These descriptions are largely drawn from the overview given by Benjamin B. Warfield, "Annihilationism," in *Studies in Theology* (New York: Oxford University Press, 1932), 447–57.
2. *Christianity Today,* June 16, 1989, 62–63.
3. Edward William Fudge, *The Fire That Consumes: A Biblical and Historical Study of Final Punishment* (Houston: Providential, 1982), 51.
4. Edward Bouverie Pusey, *What Is of Faith as to Everlasting Punishment? In Reply to Dr. Farrar's Challenge in His "Eternal Hope," 1879* (Oxford: James Parker, 1880), 27.
5. Harry Buis, *The Doctrine of Eternal Punishment* (Philadelphia: Presbyterian and Reformed, 1957), 8.
6. Fudge, *The Fire That Consumes*, 54.
7. Ibid., 67.
8. Ibid., 59–60.
9. Ibid., 60–62.
10. Ibid., 64.
11. John Stott, in *Evangelical Essentials: A Liberal-Evangelical Dialogue,* ed. David L. Edwards (Downers Grove, Ill.: InterVarsity, 1988), 315–16.
12. Ibid., 316.
13. Ibid. (italics his).
14. Clark H. Pinnock, "The Destruction of the Finally Impenitent," *Criswell Theological Review* 4 (spring 1990): 256.
15. Stott, *Evangelical Essentials*, 318–19.
16. Pinnock, "The Destruction of the Finally Impenitent," 254–55.
17. Stott, *Evangelical Essentials*, 319.
18. Pinnock, "The Destruction of the Finally Impenitent," 253–54.

19. Ibid., 255.
20. Millard J. Erickson, *Christian Theology* (Grand Rapids: Baker, 1986), 361.
21. C. S. Lewis, *The Problem of Pain* (New York: Macmillan, 1962), 122–23.
22. Nels F. S. Ferré, *The Christian Understanding of God* (New York: Harper & Brothers, 1951), 242–43.
23. John A. Broadus, *Commentary on the Gospel of Matthew* (Philadelphia: American Baptist, 1886), 512.
24. John A. T. Robinson, *In the End, God* (New York: Harper and Row, 1968), 131, n. 8.

Chapter 14

1. Michael Green, *Evangelism through the Local Church* (Nashville: Nelson, 1992), 72.
2. Philip Edgcumbe Hughes, *The True Image: The Origin and Destiny of Man in Christ* (Grand Rapids: Eerdmans, 1989), 405–6.
3. David L. Edwards and John Stott, *Evangelical Essentials: A Liberal-Evangelical Dialogue* (Downers Grove, Ill.: InterVarsity, 1988), 320.
4. John Wenham, "The Case for Conditional Immortality," in *Universalism and the Doctrine of Hell,* ed. Nigel M. de S. Cameron (Grand Rapids: Baker, 1992), 190.
5. Ibid., 170.
6. Ibid., 171.
7. Ibid.
8. In the parable of the net Jesus also described hell as "the furnace of fire," where "there shall be weeping and gnashing of teeth" (Matt. 13:49–50). Here too hellfire imagery signifies terrible pain.
9. Ibid., 171–72.
10. Ibid., 172.
11. Ibid.
12. Ibid.
13. Edward Fudge, *The Fire That Consumes: The Biblical Case for Conditional Immortality,* rev. ed. (Carlisle, Penn.: Paternoster, 1994), 155, n. 31.
14. Wenham, "The Case for Conditional Immortality," 173.
15. Ibid., 180–81.
16. Green, *Evangelism through the Local Church,* 70.
17. Ibid., 70–74.
18. Ibid., 70.
19. Ibid., 72.
20. Ibid., 72–73.
21. J. A. T. Robinson, *In the End God* (New York: Harper & Row, 1968), 133.
22. Twenty-seven times in Revelation, John used "the lamb" as a symbol of Christ. The only other use is in a simile in Revelation 13:11, where John wrote that he saw a "beast" who had "two horns like a lamb."

23. Also see Revelation 11:17–18 and 14:10.
24. Hughes, *The True Image,* 398–407.
25. Ibid., 405.
26. John Stott, *Evangelical Essentials,* 318–19.
27. Thomas Aquinas wrote, "The magnitude of the punishment matches the magnitude of the sin. . . . Now a sin that is against God is infinite; the higher the person against whom it is committed, the graver the sin . . . and God is of infinite greatness. Therefore an infinite punishment is deserved for a sin committed against him" (*Summa Theologiae* [New York: McGraw-Hill, 1974], 25).
28. Hughes, *The True Image,* 405–6.
29. John Piper, *Let the Nations Be Glad! The Supremacy of God in Missions* (Grand Rapids: Baker, 1993), 128 (italics his).
30. Hughes, *The True Image,* 406–7.
31. Jonathan Edwards, quoted in John H. Gerstner, *Jonathan Edwards on Heaven and Hell* (Grand Rapids: Baker, 1980), 75.
32. D. A. Carson, *The Gagging of God* (Grand Rapids: Zondervan, 1996), 536.

Chapter 15

1. Richard Schaull, *Encounter with Revolution* (New York: Association Press, 1955).
2. See Robert McAfee Brown, *Theology in a New Key: Responding to Liberation Themes* (Philadelphia: Westminster, 1978).
3. Carlos Fuentes, in *Latin America: Yesterday and Today,* ed. John Rothchild (New York: Bantam, 1973), 370.
4. W. Stanley Mooneyham, *What Do You Say to a Hungry World?* (Waco, Tex.: Word, 1975), 45.
5. Richard Gott, *The Guardian* (London: Nelson, 1977), 8.
6. Mooneyham, *What Do You Say to a Hungry World?* 117–18.
7. Alan B. Mountjoy, ed., *The Third World: Problems and Perspectives* (New York: St. Martin's Press, 1978), 81.
8. Arthur F. McGovern, *Marxism: An American Christian Perspective* (Maryknoll, N.Y.: Orbis, 1980), 173.
9. Richard J. Barnet and Ronald E. Muller, *Global Reach: The Power of Multinational Corporations* (New York: Simon and Schuster, 1974), 179.
10. "1988 World Population Data Sheet" (Washington, D.C.: Population Reference Bureau, 1988).
11. Ibid.
12. Lester R. Brown, *World Population Trends: Signs of Hope, Signs of Stress* (Washington, D.C.: Worldwatch Institute, 1976), 10.
13. Gustavo Gutiérrez, *A Theology of Liberation,* trans. Caridad Inda and John Eagleson (Maryknoll, N.Y.: Orbis, 1973), 88.
14. Emilio A. Núñez, *Liberation Theology* (Chicago: Moody, 1986), 47.
15. Lester DeKoster, "Is Liberation Theology Christian?" *The Outlook* 10 (May 1984): 11.

16. Walter M. Abbott, ed., *The Documents of Vatican II,* trans. Joseph Gallagher (New York: American Press, 1966), 226.
17. Thomas G. Sanders, "The Theology of Liberation: Christian Utopianism," *Christianity and Crisis,* September 17, 1973, 168.
18. Gutiérrez, *A Theology of Liberation,* 46. See also Juan Luís Segundo, *Función de la iglesia en la realidad rioplantense* (Montevideo: Barrerro y Ramos, 1962), 41.
19. Ibid., 190–91.
20. Julio de Santa Ana, "Notas para una ética de la liberación: A partir de la Biblia," *Cristianismo y Sociedad* 8 (1970): 55.
21. Abbott, *The Documents of Vatican II,* 303.
22. Gutiérrez, *A Theology of Liberation,* 88.
23. Gustavo Gutiérrez, *The Power of the Poor in History* (Maryknoll, N.Y.: Orbis, 1983), 18.
24. Reinhold Niebuhr, *Faith and Politics* (New York: Braziller, 1968), 143.
25. Gordon Chutter, "Riches and Poverty in the Book of Proverbs," *Together* 3 (April–June 1984): 31.
26. Gutiérrez, A Theology of Liberation, 216.
27. Ibid.
28. Thomas More, *Utopia* (London: D. Van Nostrand, 1947).
29. Gutiérrez, *A Theology of Liberation,* 109. Gutiérrez here quotes a statement of 300 Brazilian priests, "Brazilian Realities and the Church."
30. José P. Miranda, *Marx and the Bible: A Critique of the Philosophy of Oppression,* trans. John Eagleson (Maryknoll, N.Y.: Orbis, 1974), 182.
31. Waldron Scott, *Bring Forth Justice* (Grand Rapids: Eerdmans, 1980), 263.
32. Edward Schillebeeckx, *World and Church,* trans. N. D. Smith (New York: Sheed and Ward, 1971), 115–39.
33. Gutiérrez, *A Theology of Liberation,* 308.

Chapter 16

1. Wilbur Smith, *Therefore, Stand: A Plea for a Vigorous Apologetic in the Present Crisis of Evangelical Christianity* (Boston: Wilde, 1945).
2. Heinrich Dumoulin, *Christianity Meets Buddhism* (LaSalle, Ill.: Open Court, 1974), 35.
3. Masao Abe, "Kenotic God and Dynamic Sunyata," in *The Emptying God: A Buddhist-Jewish-Christian Conversation,* ed. John B. Cobb Jr. and Christopher Ives, Faith Meets Faith Series, ed. Paul F. Knitter (Maryknoll, N.Y.: Orbis, 1990), 3 (italics his).
4. Hans Waldenfels, *Absolute Nothingness: Foundations for a Buddhist-Christian Dialogue,* trans. J. W. Heisig (New York: Paulist, 1980), 191.
5. Keiji Nishitani, *Religion and Nothingness,* trans. with an introduction by Jan Van Bragt, Nanzan Studies in Religion and Culture, ed. James W. Heisig (Berkeley, Calif.: University of California Press, 1982).

6. Thomas J. J. Altizer, "Emptiness and God," in *The Religious Philosophy of Nishitani Keiji: Encounter with Emptiness,* ed. Taitetsu Unno, Nanzan Studies in Religion and Culture, ed. James W. Heisig (Berkeley, Calif.: Asian Humanities Press, 1989), 70.
7. Langdon Gilkey, "Nishitani Keiji's Religion and Nothingness," in *The Religious Philosophy of Nishitani Keiji,* 49.
8. Steve Odin, "*Kenōsis* as a Foundation for Buddhist-Christian Dialogue: The Kenotic Buddhology of Nishida and Nishitani of the Kyoto School in Relation to the Kenotic Christology of Thomas J. J. Altizer," *Eastern Buddhist,* n.s. 20 (spring 1987): 34–61.
9. Jan Van Bragt, "Translating *Shūkyō to wa nani ka* into *Religion and Nothingness,*" in *The Religious Philosophy of Nishitani Keiji,* 11.
10. Nishida Kitarō is cited as saying, "I think that we can distinguish the West to have considered being as the ground of reality, the East to have taken nothingness as its ground" (Robert E. Carter, "The Nothingness beyond God," *Dialogue and Alliance* 1 [fall 1987]: 70).
11. Garma C. C. Chang, *The Buddhist Teaching of Totality: The Philosophy of Hwa Yen Buddhism* (University Park, Pa.: Pennsylvania State University Press, 1971), 60.
12. Ibid.
13. Jan Van Bragt, translator's introduction to *Religion and Nothingness,* xxv.
14. *Religion and Nothingness,* 25.
15. Ibid., 26 (italics his).
16. Paul O. Ingram, *The Modern Buddhist-Christian Dialogue—Two Universalistic Religions in Transformation,* vol. 2 of *Studies in Comparative Religion* (Lewiston, N.Y.: Mellen, 1988), 92 (italics his).
17. Ninian Smart, *Buddhism and Christianity: Rivals and Allies* (Honolulu: University of Hawaii Press, 1993), 19.
18. Ibid., 35.
19. Howard Coward, *Pluralism: Challenge to World Religions* (Maryknoll, N.Y.: Orbis, 1985), 87.
20. *Religion and Nothingness,* 99.
21. Ibid., 36–37.
22. And since all parts of the one *śūnyatā*-centered system have come into being through the interaction of previous entities, and since they themselves change as they interact and produce new entities, it is easy to see how Buddhism and Nishitani find a close kinship with process theology.
23. *Religion and Nothingness,* 215.
24. Ibid., 48.
25. Ibid., 49.
26. Robert P. Lightner, *The First Fundamental: God* (Nashville: Nelson, 1973), 5.
27. L[ouis] Berkhof, *Systematic Theology,* 4th ed. (Grand Rapids: Eerdmans, 1941), 64.
28. Ibid., 65.

29. Masao Abe, "Kenotic God and Dynamic Sunyata," in *The Emptying God: A Buddhist-Jewish-Christian Conversation,* 10 (italics his).
30. Karl Barth, *Church Dogmatics,* ed. George W. Bromiley and Thomas F. Torrance (Edinburgh: Clark, 1975), vol. 1, part 1: *The Doctrine of the Word of God,* 2d ed., trans. George W. Bromiley, 140.
31. Millard J. Erickson, *Christian Theology* (Grand Rapids: Baker, 1985), 352.
32. John Jefferson Davis, *Foundations of Evangelical Theology* (Grand Rapids: Baker, 1984), 273, n. 42.
33. Donald Wiebe, *Religion and Truth: Towards an Alternative Paradigm for the Study of Religion,* Religion and Reason 23: Method and Theory in the Study and Interpretation of Religion, ed. Jacques Waardenburg (New York: Mouton, 1981), 104.
34. Ibid., 145.
35. Anne Bancroft, *Zen—Direct Pointing to Reality* (New York: Thames and Hudson, 1979), 21.
36. David K. Clark and Norman L. Geisler, *Apologetics in the New Age: A Christian Critique of Pantheism* (Grand Rapids: Baker, 1990), 30.
37. Nishitani, *Religion and Nothingness,* 170–72.
38. Ibid., 140.
39. Ibid., 70.
40. Arthur L. Johnson, *Faith Misguided: Exposing the Dangers of Mysticism* (Chicago: Moody, 1988), 38.
41. Ibid., 39.
42. Ronald H. Nash, *Worldviews in Conflict: Choosing Christianity in a World of Ideas* (Grand Rapids: Zondervan, 1992), 74.
43. Thomas P. Kasulis, "Whence and Whither: Philosophical Reflections on Nishitani's View of History," in *The Religious Philosophy of Nishitani Keiji,* 272.
44. Alister E. McGrath, "The Christian Church's Response to Pluralism," *Journal of the Evangelical Theological Society* 35 (December 1992): 500.
45. David Tracy, *Dialogue with the Other: The Inter-Religious Dialogue,* Louvain Theological and Pastoral Monographs (Grand Rapids: Eerdmans, 1990), 68.
46. Stephen H. Phillips, "Nishitani's Buddhist Response to 'Nihilism,'" *Journal of the American Academy of Religion* 55 (spring 1987): 84, n. 10.
47. Nishitani, *Religion and Nothingness,* 128.
48. Ibid., 191.
49. Ibid., 194.
50. Winston King, ed., "Buddhist-Christian Dialogue: Past, Present and Future. Masao Abe and John Cobb Interviewed by Bruce Long," *Buddhist-Christian Studies* 1 (1981): 24.
51. *Religion and Nothingness,* 188–89, 197, 215, 252, 257.
52. Ibid., 189.
53. Ibid., 285.

54. David Little, "The Problem of Ethics in Nishitani's *Religion and Nothingness,*" in *The Religious Philosophy of Nishitani Keiji,* 181–82.
55. Ibid., 185 (italics his).
56. Stephen H. Phillips, "Nishitani's Buddhist Response to 'Nihilism,'" 94–95.
57. Ibid., 97.
58. Steven Heine, "'The Buddha or the Bomb': Ethical Implications in Nishitani Keiji's Zen View of Science," in *Buddhist Ethics and Modern Society: An International Symposium,* ed. Charles Wei-hsun Fu and Sandra A. Wawrytko, Contributions to the Study of Religion, no. 31, ed. Henry Warner Bowden (New York: Greenwood, 1991), 288.
59. This does not refer to deeds done by merely professing Christians or rulers, or deeds done in the name of Christ but which contradict biblical principles. But when such principles as the value of each individual as made in the image of God, the honor of work, concern for the weak and downtrodden, or a sense of stewardship rather than ownership of creation have been the driving force of policy, good has resulted. Such a pragmatic test, of course, in no way proves Christianity. Also there is much in Western society that is degenerate and much in Eastern society that can be admired. But a dispassionate study of the history of nations illustrates the biblical principle that "righteousness exalts a nation, but sin is a disgrace to any people" (Prov. 14:34 NIV).
60. For a fuller treatment of Nishitani and Christian-Buddhist dialogue see the author's *Someone or Nothing? Nishitani's* Religion and Nothingness *as a Foundation for Christian-Buddhist Dialogue,* Asian Thoughts and Culture, no. 27, ed. Charles Wei-hsun Fu (New York: Lang, 1995).

Chapter 17

1. Stephen R. Covey, *The Seven Habits of Highly Effective People* (New York: Simon and Schuster, 1989), 72.
2. Muhammed is known as a prophet and as an apostle. The creed calls him an apostle.
3. Hans Wehr, *A Dictionary of Modern Written Arabic,* ed. J. Milton Cowan (London: Macdonald and Evans, 1974), 917.
4. A. J. Wensinck, "Ka'ba," in *Shorter Encyclopedia of Islam,* ed. H. A. R. Gibb and J. H. Kramers (Leiden: Brill, 1953), 197.
5. Bill A. Musk, Touching the Soul of Islam: Sharing the Gospel in Muslim Cultures (Crowborough, U.K.: MAR, 1995), 167.

Chapter 18

1. Michael Green, *Evangelism in the Early Church* (Grand Rapids: Eerdmans, 1970), 194–228.
2. *New International Dictionary of New Testament Theology,* ed. Calvin Brown (Grand Rapids: Zondervan, 1976), 247–50.

3. David G. Mandelbaum, *Social Groups: Cultural and Social Anthropology*, ed. Peter Hammond (New York: Macmillan, 1964), 146–63.
4. James P. Spradley and David W. McCurdy, *Anthropology: The Cultural Perspective* (New York: Wiley & Sons, 1975), 216.
5. Michael Green, *Evangelism, Now and Then* (Downers Grove, Ill.: InterVarsity, 1982), 14–15.
6. Joseph C. Aldrich, *Lifestyle Evangelism: Crossing Traditional Boundaries to Reach the Unbelieving World* (Portland, Oreg.: Multnomah, 1981), 64–82.
7. Jim Peterson, *Evangelism as a Lifestyle* (Colorado Springs: NavPress, 1980), 64–82.
8. Ibid., 46–48.
9. Ibid., 17.
10. Ibid., 106–11.
11. Stephen VanHorn, "Oikos Evangelism and Church Growth" (M.A.B.S. thesis, International Christian Graduate University, School of Theology, Arrowhead Springs, Calif., 1981), addendum.
12. Win Arn and Charles Arn, *The Master's Plan for Making Disciples* (Pasadena, Calif.: Church Growth, 1982), 69.
13. VanHorn, "Oikos Evangelism and Church Growth," addendum.
14. Bruce Rowlson, *Creative Hospitality as a Means of Evangelism* (Campbell, Calif.: Green Leaf Press, 1981), 5.
15. Aldrich, *Lifestyle Evangelism.*
16. *How to Develop an Effective Executive Ministry through Evangelistic Dinner Parties* (Atlanta: Executive Ministries [CCC], 1982); and Here's Life America Ministry of CCC, *Evangelistic Entertaining* (San Bernardino, Calif.: Campus Crusade for Christ, 1981).
17. Search Ministries uses this kind of evangelistic outreach successfully.

Chapter 19

1. Gene A. Getz, *Sharpening the Focus of the Church* (Chicago: Moody, 1974), 47.
2. Win Arn, ed., *The Pastor's Church Growth Handbook* (Pasadena, Calif.: Church Growth Press, 1979), 98.
3. Charles Mylander, *Secrets for Growing Churches* (San Francisco: Harper and Row, 1979), 39.
4. Waylon B. Moore, *Multiplying Disciples: The New Testament Method of Church Growth* (Colorado Springs, Colo.: NavPress, 1981), 42.
5. Win Arn, "Church Growth Leader, Win Arn, Responds to Firebaugh's Conclusions," *Christianity Today,* March 27, 1981, 26–27.
6. Ibid., 26.
7. Arn, *The Pastor's Church Growth Handbook,* 100.
8. Ibid., 101.
9. Ibid., 103.
10. Ibid., 102.

11. Ibid.
12. Lyle E. Schaller, *Assimilating New Members* (Nashville: Abingdon, 1978), 74.
13. Ibid., 76.
14. Ibid., 75.
15. Glenn Firebaugh, "How Effective Are City-Wide Crusades?" *Christianity Today,* March 27, 1981, 25.
16. Ibid., 28.
17. Ibid.
18. Ibid.
19. Moore, *Multiplying Disciples,* 42.
20. Mylander, *Secrets for Growing Churches,* 39.
21. Schaller, *Assimilating New Members,* 16.
22. J. Randall Peterson, "Church Growth: A Limitation of Numbers?" *Christianity Today,* March 27, 1981, 19.
23. Ibid., 23.
24. Donald A. McGavran, "Countering the Criticism," *Christianity Today,* March 27, 1981, 21.
25. Virgil Gerber, "What Happens at Church Growth Workshops Overseas," *Christianity Today,* March 27, 1981, 20.
26. E. Luther Copland, "Church Growth in Acts," *Missiology* 4 (January 1976): 13–26.
27. Christian Maurer, προστίθημι, in *Theological Dictionary of the New Testament,* 8:167–68.
28. There is some debate over certain Greek terms in Acts 2:47. J. A. Alexander states that ἐκκλησίᾳ is part of the text (*Commentary on the Acts of the Apostles* [Grand Rapids: Zondervan, 1956], 89, 96). Therefore the English should include "unto the church." Consequently, addition to the church fellowship is in mind. G. Campbell Morgan states that ἐκκλησίᾳ is not part of the original and therefore both 2:47 and 2:41 have more in view the increase in the numbers of believers in the Lord rather than the local church (*The Acts of the Apostles* [Old Tappan, N.J.: Revell, 1924], 89).
29. Morgan, *The Acts of the Apostles,* 89.
30. John Calvin, *The Acts of the Apostles,* trans. W. J. G. McDonald and John W. Fraser, *Calvin's New Testament Commentaries,* 12 vols. (1965: reprint, Grand Rapids: Eerdmans, 1979), 6:84.
31. R. B. Rackham, *The Acts of the Apostles* (1901; reprint, Grand Rapids: Baker, 1964), 33.
32. F. F. Bruce, *The Book of Acts,* New International Commentary on the New Testament (Grand Rapids: Eerdmans, 1954), 81.
33. Moore, *Multiplying Disciples,* 37.
34. Bruce, *The Book of Acts,* 205–6.
35. Richard N. Longenecker, "The Book of Acts," in *The Expositor's Bible Commentary,* vol. 9 (Grand Rapids: Eerdmans, 1981), 378.
36. Alexander Maclaren, *Expositions of Holy Scripture* (Grand Rapids: Baker, 1974), 12:91–97.

37. Bruce, *The Book of Acts,* 318–19.
38. Alexander, *Commentary on the Acts of the Apostles,* 560–61.
39. Morgan, *The Acts of the Apostles,* 370.
40. F. W. Grosheide, *Commentary on the First Epistle to the Corinthians* (Grand Rapids: Eerdmans, 1953), 291.
41. Ibid., 291 (emphasis added).
42. E. K. Simpson and F. F. Bruce, *Commentary on the Epistle to the Ephesians* (Grand Rapids: Eerdmans, 1957), 101.
43. R. E. Pattison and H. C. G. Moule, *Exposition of Ephesians* (Boston: Gould and Lincoln, 1859; reprint, Minneapolis: Klock & Klock), 145.
44. Robert L. Thomas, "1 Thessalonians," in *The Expositor's Bible Commentary,* vol. 11 (Grand Rapids: Zondervan, 1978), 254.
45. Mylander, *Secrets for Growing Churches,* 71.
46. George W. Peters, *A Theology of Church Growth* (Chicago: Moody, 1977), 209.

Chapter 20

1. Roland O. Leavell, *Evangelism: Christ's Imperative Commission* (Nashville: Broadman, 1951), 3, and Robert D. Culver, "What Is the Church's Commission?" *Bibliotheca Sacra* 125 (July–September 1968):253.
2. James Hope Moulton, *A Grammar of New Testament Greek,* vol. 1: Prolegomena, 3d ed. (Edinburgh: T & T Clark, 1908), 230–31.
3. Roy B. Zuck, "Greek Words for Teach," *Bibliotheca Sacra* 122 (April–June 1965):163.
4. C. Peter Wagner, *On the Crest of the Wave* (Ventura, Calif.: Regal, 1983), 108.
5. Cleon Rogers, "The Great Commission," *Bibliotheca Sacra* 130 (July–September 1973): 262.
6. J. Herbert Kane, *Understanding Christian Missions,* rev. ed. (Grand Rapids: Baker, 1978), 119.
7. It is easy to think through the Book of Romans in five sections: Sin, chapters 1–3; Salvation, 3–5; Sanctification, 6–8; Sovereignty. 9–11; Service, 12–16. Actually the first section ends with Romans 3:20 and the second section begins with 3:21. This accounts for the repetition of chapter 3 in this simplified outline.
8. R. C. H. Lenski, *The Interpretation of St. Paul's Epistle to the Romans* (Minneapolis: Augsburg, 1966), 579, and F. F. Bruce, *The Epistle of Paul to the Romans* (Grand Rapids: Eerdmans, 1963). 181.
9. C. E. B. Cranfield, *A Critical and Exegetical Commentary on the Epistle to the Romans* (Edinburgh: T & T Clark, 1979), 2:445.
10. *The World Almanac* (New York: Newspaper Enterprise, 1981), 434.
11. P. J. Johnstone, *Operation World,* rev. ed. (Bromley, England: STL Publications, 1980), 33–34. The percentages of world religions are applied to the twenty-six who die every ten seconds.
12. Bruce, *The Epistle of Paul to the Romans,* 202.

13. J. Ronald Blue, "Untold Billions: Are They Really Lost?" *Bibliotheca Sacra* 138 (October–December 1981):338–50.
14. To say that Christ is Savior because He is Lord is not "lordship salvation." It is simply recognizing who He is. Were He not the Son of God He could not have conquered death and could not save. To insist that a person recognize Jesus as Lord is not the same as requiring him to respond to His lordship in every area of life. Salvation is instantaneous; practical sanctification is a lifelong process.
15. Cranfield, *A Critical and Exegetical Commentary on the Epistle to the Romans,* 534.
16. Ernst Käsemann, *Commentary on Romans,* trans. and ed. Geoffrey W. Bromiley (Grand Rapids: Eerdmans, 1980), 285.
17. Lenski, *The Interpretation of St. Paul's Epistle to the Romans,* 660.
18. Charles Hodge, *Commentary on the Epistle to the Romans* (Grand Rapids: Eerdmans, 1886), 346.
19. D. P. Simpson, *Cassell's Latin Dictionary* (New York: Macmillan, 1977), 375.
20. *Englishman's Greek Concordance of the New Testament* (Grand Rapids: Zondervan, 1970), 76–77, 611.